NAKED ON THE HIGHWAY

STORIES OF A LIFE WELL LIVED

Naked on the Highway

A Memoir

THOMAS M. WELLS

COPYRIGHT © 2025 THOMAS M. WELLS
All rights reserved.

NAKED ON THE HIGHWAY
A Memoir

FIRST EDITION

ISBN 978-1-5445-4688-9 *Hardcover*
  978-1-5445-4687-2 *Paperback*
  978-1-5445-4689-6 *Ebook*

Dedicating this book is easy. There is no one who has been more my inspiration and my support than the love of my life, my wife, Carol. I dedicate this book most especially and devotedly to her, but also to the folks she has helped me create or otherwise add to my life: my three spectacular daughters, their wonderful husbands, and my five oh-so-special grandchildren. For a memoir that is about a life well lived, these folks are the ultimate evidence that mine has been.

Contents

Preface 9

SECTION I: BACKSTORY

Short and Sweet 15
The Rest of My Origin Story... 17
My Family, the Original One 21
Child of the Sixties.. 33
Sex Education 39
Day Jobs 43
Public Speaking... 49
On Being a Writer? 53
My Gorgeous Blonde 57
It's the Law 65
Nonspecific D 79
Living Your Dream 83
BIG GOD... 97

SECTION II: GIVING BACK

God's Gifts.. 109
White Guy in Africa 113
In This Truck…a Haiti Perspective 117
Dream, Plan, Do!.. 129

SECTION III: JUST LIVING

Alone at Sea 147
The Fire 153
My Russian Friends 157

Perfect Me 163
Organize the Pictures 165
House Full of Women... 167
Cute Dollars... 171
You Can't Prove It! 173
The Eyes 177
Miracles 179
Sailing Through Life 185
On Being a Guy 189
December 1959 193
Evelina 197

SECTION IV: ON THE SOAPBOX

Just Do It! 209
We All Have Something... 217
Lessons Learned.. 225
Middle of the Road 233
Fifties Values... 237
Death and Dying.. 241
Coincidents 243
Real Americans 247
Separation of Church and State 251
Evangelicals... 255
9/11.. 259
Damn Good Country 271
The First Amendment.. 275
Who Will Buy the Yearbook Ads? 279
Going Green 281
Me and the Donald 285

SECTION V: END GAME

Bucket List.. 309
My Family, the Girls.. 313
Gorgeous Blonde Gets Even Better 325
Making Memories 331
Camp Carol 337
What Makes Me Happy 347

Epilogue... 355
Acknowledgments 359
About the Author 361

Preface

Naked on the Highway. Okay, I admit it. I was definitely trying to suck you in with the title. Nudity and sex sell. *Naked* at least implies there will be some of one of these. Actually, this title comes from a recurring dream I had for a number of years, but more on that in a minute.

Later, you will learn that a part of my story is about books and bookstores. I owned a bookstore called Deerleap Books in Bristol, Vermont, for ten years, and along the way, I learned a couple things. One was that covers and titles do matter, and face-outs of good covers with catchy titles make you want to read the book. There is a reasonable chance you are reading this book right now based on seeing the same. Of course, it could just be because the writer, me, was somebody you met or even more likely is your grandfather.

Back to *naked*. I dream a lot, and one dream that seemed to pop up with some regularity for many years had me in a school where I could not remember my locker combination, or for that matter, my course schedule, nor the rooms I was supposed to go to or anything much else relevant. The cause seemed to be that I had cut so many classes that these seemingly critical facts had become lost to me. And, oh yes, I was naked and walking around somehow trying to make both my confusion and my unclothed state not noticeable. As you can imagine, it did not work well.

In real life, it has been many years, as in more than fifty, since I had a locker in school. I remember forgetting my locker combination once, but I rarely, if ever, cut class. Reading this book may help you figure out why the hell I dreamt this stupid dream; then you can clue me in.

The *highway* part? I just threw that in because I like the metaphor. Life itself feels to me like a highway, one with much to see and do and also lots of possible turns off the road. Stoplights and accidents too. Mine has had all of these and more.

This book is a memoir, of sorts. I say *of sorts* because it is not organized in an extremely logical fashion, nor is it strictly chronological, nor all that autobiographical. One could actually say it is no more than written-down notes, stories, and opinions from a busy life. However, since my day job was a lawyer, it is a little more disciplined than that. When I first started writing stuff for this book, I called the place in the computer where I stored the stuff "Life Lessons." Stripped of the need for the catchy title that got you this far, that is probably what describes this book most accurately. There are also several amusing stories with no particular lesson I just could not leave out.

While I was busy, actually very busy, living my life, I occasionally took time out, frequently on vacations, to write what you are now reading. I redoubled my efforts and wrote a lot more in the past several years, in a sense filling in the gaps. It now seemed time to tell the entire story. Much of what I wrote down in this second effort were the harder lessons learned and the passionately held opinions. More than once I attempted to wax philosophical. Once or twice, I let loose and became profound. I am nothing if not diverse in my interests, so if you hit a chapter and you don't like it, skip it. Maybe you will want to revisit it later. If not, I won't mind a bit.

I said this book was a memoir "of sorts." As you can see, there are more than fifty chapters. Well, my life has been kind of long. To make all this at least somewhat understandable, I divided the book into five sections. Section I, "Backstory," and Section V, "End Game," include the most biographical sections of this book. Here is when I talked about the family I grew up in, the one I raised, my spectacular wife, and—by all accounts—my very blessed life. I also lift the curtain and share stuff about me I have never shared easily. It seemed like the time to do this.

Section II, "Giving Back," homes in on my abiding and strongly felt commitment to the importance of just that, giving back. This philosophy pops up all over in my stories and opinion pieces, but here is where I tell where it came from, and how I share it in action.

Section III, "Just Living," is where I go full storyteller and share significant moments in my life, but even more often just regular everyday stuff that seemed worth writing down. I also use humor. After all, much of it seemed funny, at least to me.

Finally, there is Section IV, which I call "On the Soapbox." This is when I let loose with my oh-so-many opinions. Many of these will be well known to those who know me. My passionately middle-of-the-road "compromise is good" philosophy has dictated many of my actions. My religious views, strongly spiritual and very focused on living by the Golden Rule, but with real reticence and concern about much of organized religion, may surprise many, in particular, my fellow Christians.

Mixed in with the stories and opinions are some lists, at least a half dozen of them. So, what is with all the lists, you might want to ask? The answer is simple enough. I am a list guy. I make them for myself. When I finish a crazy day, I update my list, or more often just create a new one. This list never gets finished and is way too long. Usually it has a number one column and a number two column. Number one is for all the "do it now" stuff, or at least as soon as I can. Number two is the column for all the rest. Number one is always much longer than number two.

The lists in this book have basically nothing to do with these everyday lists I just described, other than to introduce you to why and how I think lists help organize a busy life. My other type of list comes from when I get deep into a subject and start to learn a lot by reading and studying what others have to say, but also from my own experience. When I feel a sense of mastery, I turn what I have learned into a list. I do this for me, because the beginning of teaching for me is writing it down in an organized form. As I organize and put ideas into words, I combine those related or redundant. I think of new stuff. Usually, the list gets better with editing. Since I love to teach and share knowledge, making a list is often an important step in the sharing process.

As I began writing this book, I knew I wanted to share knowledge, but I also wanted to write a memoir. My editors told me both forms could be great books, but not necessarily together. Bluntly put, I was told if you put both in one book you break an unstated promise to the reader. People do not read books to make the author feel gratified; they read to advance their goals.

Now, of course, the reader could have the goal to hear your story, in which case they will tolerate and maybe even enjoy some meandering. However, the reader could also be on board to hear the knowledge you have to share. In this latter case, the whole book should be tied to the purpose of the knowledge being shared. Stories are fine, I was told, but only if they are clearly tied to the overall message or knowledge-share goal of the book.

My editors were really smart, so I struggled with this some. If you keep reading this book after this warning, it will be because you want to read the book even after learning I largely ignored the advice. I decided my book could be the exception to the rule.

I think knowledge sharing is a big part of my root story. If this book, and for that matter my life, has a theme, it is my strong belief in giving back and helping others. My message is a life well-lived, and it's built around this principle. Since my well-lived life is all about sharing knowledge and often stating my considered opinions, it is to me, my story. Thus, sharing knowledge cannot be ignored in telling it. So I left all the knowledge share in; sometimes I even organized it into a list!

I had fun writing this book. I learned a lot along the way. One is when you are naked…stay off the highway…or find some clothes, quickly.

SECTION I

Backstory

The first section of this book, which I have called "Backstory," is just that my backstory, although it is organized more by topic than chronological. Here I share all the basics of my early years: the good (most of it), the bad, and the ugly (not so much, but all real enough to me). Not until I get to the last section, "End Game," will I get so autobiographical again.

Short and Sweet

"Short and sweet," I am neither. Actually, I am rather tall and lots of things, but not generally described as sweet. However, since it is my plan to ply you with my stories and opinions, you deserve a little "short and sweet" context, as in just who the hell is giving you these opinions and telling you his stories.

I am white, male, and as I write this, I'm on the lower edge of old age. I just turned seventy-three. I was born in 1952. Nixon and Vietnam, I believe, made me a Democrat, although the rest of my family are Republicans—a few even of the MAGA variety.

I like pragmatism more than ideology. I went to school for a bunch of years and graduated as a lawyer, which was my main day job, although I have done a lot of other things too. I have owned eight businesses, most, but not all, successful. I am the oldest of six kids and the father of three, all daughters. I have been married to the same woman for fifty-one years and love her more now than at any time in the fifty-three years I have known her—it's been an upward progression during the whole time.

If I have a life philosophy, it has two principal parts: "just do it," and "give back." Much more on both ahead. I live in Vermont, a state that has more writers per capita than any other state and better scenery than most places. We also have a lot of cows. I lived in New Jersey, which has some scenery and a lot more people and the nation's longest list of Superfund cleanup sites. It also has the Jersey shore! I like both of my home states very much. I have visited forty-two of the fifty states. In an interesting coincidence, I also spent time in forty-two other countries.

I am patriotic, but realistic. I have very deep faith in God but am often unimpressed, sometimes really annoyed, with what men and women do in His name and with the churches, sects, denominations, and the folks who run them. I read. I sail. I downhill ski, or at least I did until the last couple years. I drink alcohol, pretty much every day if I have my preference, but not in excess. I eat, often badly and more than I should. With advancing neuropathy these days and at the "suggestion" of the neurologist, I don't drink or eat nearly so much anymore. I smoke an occasional cigar. I love cookies. I do community service as my hobby, almost more than I worked as the years went by.

I started a foundation twenty years ago to do good things in developing nations. This foundation helps young people become change agents in their communities, and I am deeply proud of these kids.

I have broken eight bones: my collarbone twice, my hand, both wrists (yup, simultaneously), my leg once (tibia, fibula, and ankle) and a second time just the fibula, and my sternum.

I work at it—my life, that is—every day and am a perfectionist at heart. Most days I like my life; more often than not, I like it a lot. This said, I am in every way a work in progress, with some ways to go, and lately I know my time may be running out, so I need to keep moving forward, even if more slowly.

The Rest of My Origin Story

I GREW UP IN PARAMUS, NEW JERSEY, THE FIRSTBORN OF DAD, Raymond, and Mom, Betty. Paramus was not the county seat but was in many ways the cultural center of a sprawling million-person Bergen County, immediately west across the river from Manhattan. Dad was an architect. Mom was a homemaker, which in short meant she never worked outside the home after she was married.

I was the oldest of six children, although, of course, I would not know that until some years later. My youngest sister, Juliann, was born in 1965, thirteen years after me. My mother, an only child, was determined to have six children, but my youngest sister was not that magic sixth child. The sixth child did not arrive until 1972, when my sister, Kerry, was plugged in to fill in the seven-year gap between Juliann and the next youngest sibling. Kerry was eight when she arrived from Korea and two years older than number six. Three more siblings—a sister, Holly, two years younger than me, and brothers, Peter and Jeff, four and six years my junior—filled out the brood. My parents were a bit more orderly about producing the first four of the required half dozen. We were not Catholic, as everyone seemed to assume when a family had six kids in 1950s and 1960s America.

My parents grew up Presbyterians—in fact, both were "children of the church," both regular attendees, my dad with his parents, my mother all by herself, when they married. Our parents raised us, six kids, as members of the Dutch Reformed Church—now simply called Reformed, likely because so many families at the church were not Dutch. Our mixed but unmistakably Waspy ancestry was a bit of Irish—a quarter, I recollect—equal part German, and the rest English. The first ancestor on the American shore came over from Colchester, England, in 1635 and interestingly enough, bore my name, Thomas Wells. This Thomas Wells, called Deacon by everyone, lived his life in Ipswich, Massachusetts, where he fathered ten children. He is my ninth great-grandfather.

They did not name me after this ancestor. My namesake was much more recent and short lived. My mother named me after her brother, whom she never knew. She lost him before she was even born. My maternal grandmother, who worked as a house servant for a wealthy family in New Britain, Connecticut, after moving from Canada, had landed a young squire and found herself married at age sixteen. Soon after, still sixteen years old, she welcomed a son, Thomas Martin, in his case, Thomas Brooks Martin. The first Thomas Martin only lived three months and died in 1928 of what later my sister, a nurse, diagnosed as spina bifida.

My mother, who never knew her brother, missed this young man dearly, all of her childhood. As a result, when her first son was born, she reused the name, this time as Thomas Martin Wells.

Thomas Martin Wells spent the first year and a half of his life with two women: Mom, Betty, then twenty-two, and Grandmother, Dora, who by then had just turned forty. My dad was away in the post–World War II army, stationed in Austria. I am told these two women took incredible care of me. My grandmother, who I always called "Mamie" as a variant on *mommy*, had perhaps found her long-lost son in this boy of the same name. We lived in my grandmother's house in Lyndhurst, New Jersey.

My dad rejoined the scene after his two-year army enlistment ended in April 1953. His arrival evened the odds of men to women in the house, which made everyone happy, even my grandmother, who adored her son-in-law as he did her.

By 1954, their version of the American dream had kicked into full swing. That year my sister Holly arrived in February and my parents moved into their own house in a development of new ranch houses in what was then "the country," Paramus, New Jersey. The house had two bedrooms, a living room, a dining room and kitchen, and a full, unfinished basement. Early pictures show no landscaping.

The house cost $9,000. My dad tells a story of going to his boss and telling him he had to lie on the mortgage application and say he made $100 a week. My dad was hoping for a raise to that number. His boss smiled and told my dad not to worry, he would lie if anyone asked him to verify the salary.

My dad, who at this time worked in New York City at a large architectural firm, started moonlighting to earn extra money. He did little house addition plans. He would work on big institutions, mainly hospitals, during the day, and extra bedrooms, garages, and breezeways at night. He had an office in the house and continued moonlighting, mostly on garden apartments, until he opened his own practice in 1965.

To this day I picture my father as he was most nights: hunched over his drafting board working away. I would go there to say good night or just chat as a child. A neighbor accused him of burning the "eternal light" in the window where my dad worked—the neighbor claimed to have never gone to bed without seeing it burning.

The best stories about my early childhood—when I was five or six—aren't my memories but are things others told me or were sparked by seeing a picture. A good example of this is when I pulled over "my Christmas tree" to get it to my bedroom, or perhaps when I gave a truck to my infant brother Peter by throwing it over the crib rail to him.

Those early years were all good. Except perhaps that I managed to break my collarbone three times by age six. The first time I was hit by a bike, the second falling off the couch during the move to the new house, and the third time falling off a bike myself. All probably a good predictor of a young man with little or no athletic prowess.

I had a great childhood. No dark tales. No abuse of any kind. I admittedly had a penchant for eating an inordinate amount of fattening sweet stuff, so I was a little chubby. I was smart in school but, as alluded to above, not very athletic, so I was not popular, but I had friends and got along fine, mostly on my wits and always active mouth.

My distinguishing feature from early on was my height. I was tall, five foot seven by fifth grade, six foot one by ninth grade, and finally six foot four by the time I graduated from high school in 1970. I had my father to thank for this. He was six foot three, and my mom was only five foot four. Lest you think being tall is not a good thing for a boy, ask a short guy. It's just too bad I couldn't jump better or get a ball through a hoop.

My family went to church from my earliest memories. As a result, I consider myself a lifelong believer. I will discuss this in more detail later, but I can't remember a time when I did not feel God's influence in my life and His protection and grace.

School, church, my siblings, summers at the shore, my friends, and girlfriends all came and went in a very pleasant mix that made me who I am. Some stuff stands out, so I write about it here, but more just blends in.

My Family, the Original One

As I previously mentioned, when I think of my father, I see him at his drafting board. When I was really small, this was in his little office over the garage. Later, this was in the office he built as an addition onto the Glen Avenue house. I can't conjure up a picture of my dad with legs up in front of the television, although I am sure he did this once in a while. He was always at his drafting board working. If I wanted to discuss something with him, this is where I would find him.

My dad was not without a sense of humor, but he was generally very serious. His passions were his service clubs, first Jaycees, then Rotary. Through his love and endless activity in Rotary, he became known to us as Rotary Ray. He liked that my brothers and I became active Rotarians, and Dad was particularly proud when Peter followed him as a district governor.

My father was also a lifelong Yankees fan. He liked the Giants too, but with less passion for the latter team. He enjoyed a bunch of Wells men (my dad and his three sons) Yankees games that I took us to each spring in his sixties and seventies.

I never heard my father expound on it, but he must have loved convertibles too, as he had three of them: a Pontiac Firebird, a Rambler, and a Chrysler coupe. In the last twenty years of his life, his vehicle of choice switched to minivans. He loved to play tennis and was good at it, and also golf, but with this sport much more occasionally and mostly socially. My dad was no auto mechanic, nor a DIY building project person, although he tried a couple times in the early years.

One of my special memories of my dad was playing golf with him at a chamber of commerce outing when I was in high school, and I was invited back to the dinner after winning the low gross award. My dad was proud of me, and this made me happy.

My father had a definite German reserve that kept him from expressing himself emotionally. I knew my dad loved me, although I never heard him say so, likewise that he was proud of me, but I knew this from what he said to others.

I thought my father's retirement passions for writing novels and painting were fun to watch him execute. Neither effort had very good results; actually, the novels were rather terrible, but his enthusiasm for them and his painting was special. My efforts to get him to consider book doctors and other writing courses or tutorials, or even to read books of the type he sought to write, went completely ignored.

Unlike my mom, my dad was not a natural storyteller, not even of his own stories. The novels, on careful reading, revealed more about my dad than he ever revealed to me. In one of them, a movie star visiting post–World War II Europe develops a relationship with a young second lieutenant who is an architect and years later reconnects with him in Vermont. Besides the heroic description of the transparently autobiographical architect and second lieutenant, and the over-the-top movie star who somehow cannot disconnect herself from the same, there are eight murders that take place in the Vermont part of this story. Honestly, my dad's books were far and away the worst fiction I have ever read.

When my mom passed away recently, it fell upon her kids to clean out her house. My mom had lived on seven more years after losing my dad. Years earlier, when he passed, I had cleaned out his office. I threw away unnecessary papers and reams of Rotary stuff. With so much to throw away, I carefully lined up his ten "novels" on the shelf behind his desk. My mom had suggested they be thrown away too. Now with my mom also gone, I was back in the same spot. I decided to move these "family literary heirlooms" to a basement shelf in the lodge at Camp Carol in Vermont. *Who knows*, I thought, *some future heir might want to explore them.*

When I was loading up the three-ring binders, I discovered among the fiction epics a book with a strange title on the binder. It was labeled "Natural Childbirth." I was confused. Inside, the title turned out to be *Born Again, Why?* The tome was not fiction at all, but rather a collection of autobiographical stories, mostly from my dad's teenage years and later life in which my dad lays out his opinions on living a Christian life. Without a theological rationalization or analysis, he just tells stories of himself and others doing the right thing...walking the walk. He over and over again queries what, if anything, this Christian-like walk has to do with what he calls the "born again mission." His question was by no means mean-spirited, just very questioning.

My mother was a homemaker when we kids were growing up, and actually after that as well. Her working career was all over by the time I came on the scene. It began with a high school part-time job at a swanky department store in Newark, New Jersey, a half-hour bus ride from her home. She worked in the young ladies' department. Her job began as a stock girl and her boss promoted her to salesgirl after she graduated high school and went to work full time. She was on the verge of being promoted to assistant buyer when she got married and decided to quit her job and end her fledgling career because she didn't want to work on Saturdays.

We all know experience is the best teacher. Nonetheless, I find it amazing that for the rest of my mom's life, some seventy more years, she freely diagnosed any business situation or management issue from her four years in the trenches at Hahne's department store. "When I was at Hahne's, we were told..."

My mom was like this with most of the rest of her opinions as well. Although she developed some tolerance of doing things another way, my mother pretty much solidified all her personal opinions based on what she knew early in her life. Marriage was the goal for all young women; work, or career, not so much. Once married, the husband comes first. Women belong at home. Sons were a step above, or at least more to be deferred to than daughters. You get the picture. You could call my mom "set in her ways," and some might say "old-fashioned."

As I shared above, my only-child mom wanted six kids, so she had them. Despite the multitude of children, my mother was never a doting parent. She raised us to be independent. I liked this a lot growing up, and it was not until I got out of the home by going to college that I figured out this was unusual, at least in the 1950s and '60s. Although, in school, I noticed other mothers made breakfast and school lunches rather than sleeping in with dad, and took their kids shopping rather than giving them a clothing allowance. It was not until I got to college and was the only one who declared the plentiful cafeteria food "absolutely fantastic" that I figured out my mom was not the typical homemaker I thought she was.

All this said, my mom was always my buddy. She and my dad were careful not to have favorites among their kids, but being the firstborn and a son of an oh-so-traditional mom seems to have given me extra status. I could always talk to my mom.

My mother had some form of this close relationship with each of her six kids, although it differed with each of us. One on one, she would focus hard and find a connection. On contemplation, my mom often tailored her opinions to get along with whoever she was talking to. This, if anything, has become more the case in recent years. As a progressive stalwart in political matters, I know I heard a very different perspective than my almost uniformly pretty far-right siblings. This ability to meet all, not just her kids, our spouses, and later grandkids, with a ready smile and genuine joy was my mom's greatest trait. It made her unique.

I will confess, as a kid, I perhaps abused my mom's willingness to match perspectives and to feel sympathetic. I learned that if I seemed "oppressed by guilt" and to move quickly to affect this state, I would find understanding with anything I had done. A sad face, often very much my creation, and an explanation, "I always seem to be the one who gets caught," merited a hug and would just as frequently shut down any desire my mom might otherwise have for discipline.

My mom had a bit of a mixed childhood. Born in the Depression to young parents, her grandparents raised her until she was five. Her parents, who were already working multiple jobs to keep up in New Jersey, would visit her in Connecticut. She says she thought of them as a visiting older brother and sister. Her grandfather, Sylvester, was an apartment superintendent, and she describes her early years as being the Eloise of the Mansion, as the princess of an apartment building occupied by fairly comfortable older people.

After she moved to New Jersey and eventually moved to the working-class town of Lyndhurst, tragedy struck her little family. When she was just twelve years old, her much loved, always genial, prankster father died in a plant explosion at the DuPont Chemical plant where he worked. My mom's mother, who was decidedly not a prankster, was left reeling, and life got tough. DuPont gave my grandmother $1,000, which she split with her mother-in-law, and promised the widow a job for life; she considered matters settled.

Fortunately, at this DuPont job, my grandmother met an older man, Jack, who became a friend and then a protector of her and her daughter, my mom. Jack paid for things, shared ration cards, fixed things, and had contractors fix what he could not. He was around all the time but only slept over occasionally. When my mom got married to my dad at twenty-one, Jack gave her away.

Jack died a couple years later, just before I was born. My mother could not go to the funeral, her mother only to the back row. As my mother had learned just a few years earlier, but as my grandmother and apparently everyone else knew, Jack had a whole other life with a wife and family. When we discussed this many years later, my mom expressed a sense of shock at how unbelievably naive she had been during the years her mom was the "other woman" in this long affair.

The mom I remember growing up was a whirlwind of activity, mainly focused on my younger siblings. She was a Girl Scout leader for my next oldest sister, was in the garden club and the Junior Women's Club, sang in the church choir, and volunteered at the hospital. Our house was always clean and orderly, and clothes always freshly laundered. We kids had chores and very much had to care for our own rooms, but it was all good.

My parents' passion was eating out, and they did this a lot. From when I was about ten until my grandmother moved in when I was sixteen, this meant I would babysit for my younger siblings. When my dad informed me at thirteen that I was about to have yet another sister, I recall telling him, "I am not babysitting this one!" It turned out I did not have to once my mother's mother moved in.

By the time I was seventeen, my mom and dad traveled, and it became a second passion for them. The first trip, I think, was to Ireland. After that they crisscrossed the country and the world, often with Rotary-sponsored trips. This active travel continued for about thirty-five years from my parents' forties until they entered their eighties. My younger siblings participated in some of this, but they were often left behind.

The big trips when I was a kid were driving to Florida, the first time when I was in fifth grade, the second when I was a senior in high school. The fifth-grade adventure was pre–Juliann and Kerry, so six of us then, when my dad drove us to Miami, Florida. We stayed at the Driftwood Hotel when my dad, without reservations, found it by chance. My mom and dad went back to this hotel several times, and the whole family went back to this same hotel on another road trip to Florida, which included Christmas of my senior year in high school.

I confess the two trips, one at eleven and the second one at seventeen, now blend a little in my mind. A nice but kind of shabby chic motel—yup, doors to the outside and the parking lot. The Driftwood was on the beach and also had a pool where we spent more time than in the ocean. Both times to get to Florida, then back home, we drove and stopped along the way. I recall the famous South of the Border

Mexican-style resort south of the North Carolina border. What made it particularly cool and more memorable than the place itself was the hundreds of signs counting down the distance on the road before you got there.

My dad died in August 2017. He was eighty-nine, and he had reluctantly given up driving. He and my mom had also decided to end their annual, much loved, Florida winter-months pilgrimage. Neither decision set very well with my dad. He was not vocal about it, but he seemed to start checking out. By midsummer that year, he had lost interest in watching Yankees baseball games. That's when we knew he was getting ready. He suddenly passed away, which was especially tough on my mom, and we treated him to a very special and loving send-off. We all took comfort in the fact he had avoided the suffering of any debilitating illness.

As I write this, my mom has just left us at age ninety-three. If my dad was checking out, my mom was, as she asked me to report to all who might otherwise be sad at the funeral, absolutely ready to "go home." In her words, tell them, "Betty was ready."

Having grown up as an only child, through her six kids, then grandchildren, great-grandchildren, and this year even a great-great-grandchild, and all the spouses, this extraordinary lady who married her church friend had created with him a family of seventy-eight souls. With her unique gift of making everyone feel very special, saying goodbye was both sad and glorious. My mom had shouldered the job of family matriarch magnificently, all by herself for the last seven years; cards, letters, visits, phone calls, texts, parties, spreading cheer and love always to all in her gigantic family. Mom had traveled to Vermont, despite a walker and often a wheelchair, for our daughter Jordyn's wedding just two weeks before she died.

When we posted the special pictures for a slideshow by the funeral home, we literally broke the software. Never having posted more than 250, it gave out at 850 pictures after we submitted more than 1,200.

The thought of my mom back together with my dad, her boyfriend and husband of more than seventy years, who even after he passed she had joined every night for a five o'clock drink over the last seven years so she could share a few quiet words with his cremated ashes, is just so special. I can hear my dad's casual greeting, "What took you so long, Bet?"

I had three living grandparents and one step-grandfather when I was growing up. My dad's parents, Harold and Julia Wells, were Pop Pop and Tootsie to me. Actually, Tootsie was Tootsie to everyone. This couple was very much Archie and Edith Bunker. My grandfather was a cigar-smoking (in the house—everything smelled of it), tough-talking, yet sentimental man. For him, Italians were "wops," Catholics were "cross-backs," and, although I never remember hearing him say it, I understand the n-word was operative as well. He made his living as a commercial printer, but my earliest memories of him are as retired, when he actively had a large vegetable garden and was a woodworker with a neat workshop.

Tootsie was as quiet and sweet as Pop Pop was larger than life. She died of brain cancer in 1964 when I was just twelve, so memories of her are not as many. She loved to cook and sew. I remember her making clothes and dolly clothes for my sister Holly.

Just before Tootsie died, I vividly recollect I was allowed to visit her at home in a hospital bed at the side of the bedroom she had shared with my grandfather. She was home to die, was very feeble, and had lost all her hair. This memory is searing even now. When she died, my father cried. It was the only time I ever saw him cry.

After Tootsie died, I would take my bike across the highway and hang out with Pop Pop. He would let me help him in his workshop. We worked together on a section of a miniature golf course for the Paramus Boys' Club and got our picture in the paper doing it.

My grandfather was not all that good at taking care of himself, and he stayed single for a little over a year. During that time, he had a refrigerator full of casseroles (from his sisters, I think).

I learned a valuable lesson by sharing dinner with him one night. He was serving tongue. Gagging to get it down, I declared it delicious. Kids did not tell their elders what they really thought in those days.

After that, every time I came over, he pulled out the tongue for me. "Your favorite," he'd say. He seemed to have an endless supply! Having told the initial fib, I was stuck. Ever since that experience when I was twelve years old, I've never told anyone I liked a food that I really didn't like. Carol can testify to this.

My maternal grandmother, Mamie, was my second mother. Until I was two, my mom lived with her mom, while my dad was in the army. The three of us had a special connection from then on.

Later, in the 1960s, after my step-grandfather, Red, died, she moved in with us and helped with the five kids. I was still her favorite, and unlike my parents who tried never to have favorites, she was transparent in her feelings. She also connected well with the new baby, Juliann.

Grandma Mamie died in 1968. It was a blow, like losing a parent. I visited her grave at the cemetery not far from our house often and felt her presence in prayer. I inherited her car, a very grandmotherly Chevrolet Biscayne, but they were wheels for a new driver. Grandma Mamie died at fifty-six years old, an age which as I have grown older never ceases to stun me. I thought she was old when she died. I now know she was no such thing.

My next oldest sibling was my sister Holly. She was born two years and one month after me. Despite a few gorgeous little kid pictures together, we were never terribly close. I don't think it was just a gender thing. I know plenty of brothers and sisters with close bonds. We were just cut out of different cloth, to use the cliche. I was always a curious mix of shyness and gregariousness. I liked people, but I was embarrassed easily. Holly was and still is outspoken and, at least superficially, confident. In a word, she was "bossy."

Holly married a great guy, also named Tom, and became an evangelical Christian early on. Her life's work was to create and run a for-profit day-care center, Little Lambs. She has every reason to be very proud of this school, and all the kids it has helped along the way, as well as her three and all their progeny.

Holly and I get along well, based on a promise I extracted from her years ago that she could pray for me and my salvation as much as she wanted. (Prayer is great, but not so much evangelical fervor, as I will explain elsewhere), but she needed to stop talking to me about it.

My brother Peter is four and half years younger than me, and brother Jeff was born two years after him, is six and a half years younger than me. Divided by just one year in school, my brothers were part of a set always referred to in the family as "the boys."

Peter was the first of the architect sons thus blessing my dad later on with an easy-exit strategy for early retirement. He was a serious, almost grouchy kid, but did well in school and made and kept genuine friends. He eventually grew out of the grouchiness. As Peter has grown older, I love to hear him speak to a group. He truly teaches when he talks. Peter is a salt-of-the-earth good guy, a great husband and father. If we ever had an issue, it was because he sometimes coveted that mysterious status of being the oldest son. This has never been a problem for me. He is welcome to it.

My brother Jeff has always been the family "joy boy." He is friendly, generous, and loyal, if just a bit happy-go-lucky. Jeff is an architect, too, and although loaded with design talent, he's not nearly as good a businessman. He always wants home runs, yet they never seem to come. He keeps smiling though and would never turn his back on anyone in need. Jeff divorced and remarried after his kids were grown and now lives in Norfolk, Virginia.

My sister Kerry was the "fill-in" for my mom to get to six kids, which had always been her master plan. Our family adopted Kerry from Korea when she was eight years old. I was already in college when she arrived, so we never lived together as siblings. She is delightfully quirky and tough talking like Holly, but absolutely no one believes Kerry. At least I don't. The tough talk hides a mushy core. I admit this core is well hidden, but not from me. Unlike Holly, Peter, Jeff, or Julie, who I will talk about next, Kerry is not an evangelical Christian. That said, the wonder of Kerry is that underneath the tough talk and dismissal of dogma is an unbelievably caring individual.

Juliann, or Julie, is the baby, and was born thirteen years after me.

She is a nurse and was a supermom to five. With her husband, who started out Bobby, then Bob, now Robert, she has lived all over the world, including the Netherlands, Korea, Pennsylvania, Michigan, Iowa, and Virginia. Most recently, they transitioned to retirement and are now in Richmond, Virginia, with all five kids and their families living close by. They do family so well. Following their never-ending pictures on Facebook fills my heart with joy.

Child of the Sixties

I AM WITHOUT A DOUBT A CHILD OF THE SIXTIES, WITH ALL that that tumultuous decade brought and that this term implies. It was an amazing time to come of age. The election of John Kennedy in 1960 announced the dawn of a new generation. Someone assassinated him in 1963. His brother Bobby met the same fate in 1968. So did Martin Luther King Jr., just a few months earlier. The Vietnam War fractured our nation, and civil rights took amazing leaps forward.

Just as the sixties were years of rapid and far-reaching change, they were likewise for me. I entered the decade at eight years old and left at eighteen.

I have already shared the key parts of my persona. I was tall, kind of nerdy, decidedly unathletic, but leadership inclined. This package floundered a bit in junior high but worked much better once I got to high school. By then, my peers had splintered off into groups, each with their own center of gravity: jocks and cheerleaders; smart kids; band members; antiwar types, and hippies; student government junkies; joiners doing things like the play, the yearbook, debate club, etc.; and, of course, the popular kids. While I could have been part of no specific group, I discovered I could be well accepted by multiple groups. This became my plan, and it seemed to work.

After one last attempt as a member of the sophomore football team, I gave up being a jock. I kept up with something much easier for me, a kind of jock-lite interest in skiing. Friday nights skiing at Great Gorge, New Jersey's version of a ski mountain, were the social high point of winter weekends in my last couple years in high school.

I was, by taking advanced classes, automatically considered a smart kid. I added to this social circle by becoming a joiner, mostly as yearbook editor and a debater, but with lots of other activities, too. I was not really a hippie, but I was decidedly antiwar, and I soon came to be a leader of this group as well. Student government was then, as I suspect it will always be, inhabited by popular kids and a few folks who like to do stuff (that was me). My triumph was getting elected senior class president over a very popular football player and wrestler. I like to think it was my brilliant platform of priorities and projects that propelled me to success, but it was probably due to me being a part of numerous lower-level groups. No matter, with this accomplishment and my new Mr. President title, I occasionally hit the outer ring of the popular kids' group. High school was basically good for me.

Elsewhere you will read about my cornucopia of teenage jobs and budding dating life, but to set the scene, by the time of my senior year in high school, I was an ocean lifeguard in the summer and had a girlfriend. The summer of 1969 (isn't that a Bryan Adams song title?) was the beginning of my truly "child of the sixties year."

Unquestionably, the highlight of that summer turned out to be the seminal event of this entire time period, perhaps of my generation: the Woodstock Music and Arts Fair, known to virtually everybody as simply "Woodstock." It was not actually held in Woodstock, New York, but in the sleepy tiny farm town of Bethel on a farm owned by a guy named Max Yasgur. It all began for me when I packed up my mother's station wagon and, together with my good friend Tim Imbrie, headed to what was to be an outdoor concert in upstate New York. It was to last three days. We had tickets for the first two.

We first went to the wrong place, the actual town of Woodstock, nearly sixty miles away from the farm where the concert was held.

We encountered an unbelievable traffic jam getting there and had to park in a field miles away from the venue. The field grew so muddy it took twenty or more strong people to push cars out and would keep me stuck at the event for an extra couple days even after the music stopped playing.

When we finally got to the place where the music was to be played, it was fantastically overcrowded, and they were still building the stage. There was little or no food. There were just a few portable toilets, and they were hopelessly and disgustingly overfilled. The music started hours late and it often rained hard and got cold. Sounds pretty awful, right? Not so much. It turns out being in a self-created disaster area with five hundred thousand other people was absolutely the place to be.

The musicians found the overflow crowd inspiring and played their hearts out. All the adversity of too many people became a reason to suck it up and spread peace. During the day, the sun came out, and I got to swim naked with a couple hundred girls—no small feat for a seventeen-year-old male. A guy made love to his girlfriend so close to me that his leg hit me with every thrust. Yes, I also smoked a bunch of weed.

I have been talking about this event to the fascination of legions of listeners all the fifty years that have passed since I spent three cold rainy days listening to great music. I can't tell you how many cocktail-party and ice-breaker conversations this has taken me through.

"You went to Woodstock? What was it like?" These questions and the fascination started as soon as I got back to high school that fall. It turned out that just me and one other girl in my class of six hundred had been in attendance. We went from class to class talking about the Woodstock experience. My hippie cred went way up, even though I was still a student-council type, just as likely to show up in a tie than a tie-dyed shirt.

Now seventeen, I found my own moral compass and also grew increasingly political. This became a distinct problem at home. I am told I was always a well-behaved little child, old beyond my years. This did not change much as I grew up, at least until then. I was more of a nerd than any kind of rebel. My favorite activity was reading. Richard Nixon and the Vietnam War changed all this. My open rebellion, at least in my parents' view, came in this, my last year of high school. I had been taught from my earliest years to stand up for my principles, and those principles were the basics of the Judeo-Christian tradition, the Ten Commandments and the Golden Rule. This got complicated for my parents when, with my increasing political knowledge coinciding with a raging Vietnam War, these principles took me considerably left of my longtime and multigenerational Republican parents. I became very antiwar.

It turned out my dad was good with me as a young man of principle as long as my principles matched his. They did not on these issues. My father supported the war and, perhaps more importantly for him as a person who grew up with World War II and had served in the army himself, felt patriotism had little room for dissent. My reply, like that of antiwar folks all over, especially many young people in the sixties, was a howl of protest that the America worth defending must be one of free speech and defending the right to dissent.

The Vietnam War, to almost everyone eventually, was not just or logical; it was unwinnable. Years later, even my father arrived at this view, but by then, his personal view of history was rewritten enough that it didn't allow him to recollect his earlier views.

By 1969, my antiwar sentiments, activities in helping to organize protests, and intention to register for the draft as 1-A-O, a conscientious objector willing to serve as a medic or the like, pushed my dad to his limit. The last straw, as I recollect it, was my wearing a black armband to school. He forbade this. I ignored him and did it anyway. The result was not pretty.

My father had taught me to stand up for my principles, after all. My dad had protested angrily and eventually quit the school board over the school prayer issue. Now, he doubled down on his demand that I stop my activities and canceled a planned family vacation to Florida, lining up my younger siblings as his allies. All hell broke loose.

I was kept home from school. The family minister came to mediate, and in essence told me I should back down to preserve my mother's increasingly hysterical and vulnerable emotional state at this impasse. I told no one, but Alan Staver, this minister and longtime family friend, told me I was right but I needed to defer anyway. I begrudgingly took his advice and gave in, at least as to open defiance.

Now, almost sixty years later, I still think my father was wrong to make me abandon my principles. I felt strongly about this when it happened. After all these years, and now having raised children myself, I still feel my dad blew it. I have mellowed enough on this to be grateful that none of my daughters ever espoused Nazism, white supremacy, genocide, or something equally abhorrent to test me on this.

Despite the end to my open defiance at home, my antiwar activities didn't stop. All through high school, I had been involved in a YMCA program called Youth & Government. Each year, they would select several hundred students from different high schools and YMCAs to go to our state capital, in my case to Trenton, and run our own legislature in the real chambers and offices. During my junior year, the other students elected me as speaker of the assembly. I became youth governor during my senior year. As you might imagine, this was more student council than hippie. I already told you that I am complicated.

I got to use the actual New Jersey governor's office, gave speeches to the entire group, and they wrote about me in the newspapers. At the legislative session, we passed many thoughtful laws. As I recollect, I was a rather bossy and controlling governor, marking any bills I liked "Governor's Priority" and affixing my signature, requiring the same to get special attention.

Being youth governor of New Jersey gave me the privilege of representing my state at the National Youth Governor's Conference later in the spring in Washington, DC, and being a Yankee at a very conservative meeting of southern state youth governors in Stone Mountain, Georgia, a few weeks later. At both conferences, I aimed my bill and efforts at passing a law limiting the war powers of the president. I got my fellow youth governors to adopt the bill in Washington. In the Deep South, this Yankee and his bill went down to defeat. However, Congress finally adopted its own version of my bill, called the War Powers Act, in November 1973, about three years later.

At the same time I was doing all this national stuff, the war protest came home as well. The Kent State massacre, when students were shot by National Guard troops, happened on May 4 of my senior year. The country was in turmoil. Over four million students protested after Kent State, and most American colleges and universities shut down. I think it was on Tuesday, May 8, when more than 1,200 Paramus High School students walked out of school to a nearby athletic field to hear antiwar speeches. I was there; I spoke to the crowd.

Since I was the class president, I was asked to meet with the principal. With my student council hat on but my antiwar creds well established, I worked out a plan with him to convince the students to end the protest that day in exchange for a commitment to two school-wide assemblies where all sides could be heard. The big discussion was who could speak. He wanted just teachers. I insisted on others. In those days, these "others" were called "outside agitators." Somehow, I won. The principal, Joe McDonough, took some heat for giving in to the students, but the compromise worked. We did not end the war, but we found a way to discuss it at Paramus High School. The newspaper later wrote an extensive story called "Anatomy of a Revolt" that praised both the principal and me.

Not long after this, I had the privilege of giving the graduation speech to my six-hundred-member class and all our parents and loved ones, and we said goodbye to our childhood. Those of us with student deferments went off to college, for me Bucknell University; others with no deferment and low draft numbers were drafted and likely went to fight. The war went on until April 30, 1975, when Saigon fell.

Sex Education

My sex education came in fits and spurts. My relationship with the opposite sex as a child was, I suppose, typical: limited and voyeuristic. I remember at about age five talking a neighborhood girl into going behind the compost bin in my backyard to pull her pants down to show me "hers" if I showed her "mine." I can't actually remember what I got to see but it must have piqued my interest more than satisfy it, because I remained more than a little interested in female parts as my years advanced. In third grade, I engaged a female classmate to "go steady," a term I am sure I did not yet understand. I gave her a ring, only to have her give it to another girl, who held no interest for me. No parts were seen this time.

Years went by. Prepubescent hookups happened all around me but, alas, not for me. By junior high school, I was supremely afraid I would be the last twelve-year-old to get to "first base" with a girl, which of course meant touching a fully clothed female breast. In truth, the breasts of my classmates were not all that exciting at that point. When I finally got in close, the bra turned out to be full of tissues more than anything else.

Then at fourteen, I hit the big one. Lots of bases. No home run, mind you, but lots of bases. I met a girl from down the street at the shore. The shore is what we New Jersey folks call the beach. For me, this was Long Beach Island. I was staying for the summer, the young lady and her family for two weeks.

Separated from the rest of her family, my new friend was staying upstairs in a two-story house. Her room was connected by inside stairs, but a family cat had to be kept out of the attic room she occupied, so she and the family used only the outside stairs. These stairs made it easy for us to gain entry to her bedroom. Once we got there, we kissed a lot, like only young teenagers can, and snuggled and touched each other. In those days, this was called "petting." I wish I could remember the lines I used because they must have been good, as she easily consented to let the snuggling be sans pajamas.

This was the mid-1960s and it usually took a lot of really clever words by the guy to accomplish something like this. The act of undressing came in stages: as in over clothes, then under, then no bra, no pajama bottoms, etc. Ultimately, we were skin to skin, a general state I loved very much and have never lost my affection for.

Since that time in my life, I have never worn pajamas or anything else while sleeping, unless compelled by circumstances. I also, whenever possible, have a woman next to me. By "next to me," I mean just that. A cold room and a woman snuggled in close is a personal preview of heaven for me. I know most of the world, including many women I have known, like to eventually find their side of the bed for peaceful sleep. Not me. Fortunately, at twenty-one, I found and married a woman who likes this too, or at least likes me enough to pretend she does.

Back to my "second story tale," which at this point took a turn that changed my education on nocturnal activities quite a bit. One night, while kissing up a storm as usual, the young lady and I heard the sound of someone coming up the steps. I immediately leapt up, grabbed my clothes, and ran to the bathroom at the end of the room. It was my coconspirator's mother who had come for a visit. They talked for a bit, but I could not understand what they were saying. After what seemed like a very long time, I heard footsteps. Momentarily relieved, I then to my horror realized the footsteps were not going down the stairs. Instead, they were getting closer to me.

I was behind the bathroom door when the middle-aged woman in a dress walked in, lifted her skirt, pushed rather large white panties to her ankles, and sat down on the toilet. She could not see me directly but all she needed to do was look up and to the right a little and there I was, in full view in the mirror. I knew this, of course, because I had a full view of her, peeing and still chatting out the door with her daughter. I did not breathe. I mean really I didn't, not a single breath. I was sure she could hear my heart beating. Eventually, Mom wiped herself diligently, then, I will always be grateful, did not come to the sink to wash her hands as I was always taught to do. Had she done so, she would have been standing right in front of the mirror showing a trembling and naked fourteen-year-old boy, despite the catastrophic levels of fright with a full erection. It was hitting the door.

It now seems more than a little cowardly and little-boy-like, but when Mom left, I dressed fast then ran out of the bathroom, and the bedroom, and down the stairs. I didn't say a word to my partner in passion. Worse, I never saw or talked to the young lady again, not the next day nor any days of vacation, not ever. I think I went into hiding. Being scared shitless does very bad things to your manners.

My heart stopped beating hard a few days after her family car pulled away from its shore retreat for good. By September, I was ready to tell the deftly played skin-to-skin part to my buddies at school. The rest of the story, which you just read, has never been told until now.

My virginity disappeared—I was so pleased—fairly undramatically a couple years later when I was sixteen. Although I had my share of crushes and even some teenage true loves, the seminal event involved neither. It was what could safely be called a one-night stand. After a night of partying and drinking, I convinced a very pleasant and, as I like to remember it, attractive young lady to accompany me to the bedroom and double bed of a friend's mother. Mom was, of course, not home. I started through those same bases and met no resistance, and dimwit that I was, at some point realized there would be none.

I entered my conquest missionary style and condomless. This was before disease concerned any of us much, but the possibility of pregnancy certainly should have. I just had not seen this coming. I immediately and very excitedly came. I distinctly recall the young lady then asking me, "Do you like it so fast?" To which I right away responded, trying to remain the stud I now felt I deserved to call myself, "I like it all ways."

Day Jobs

IT HAS BEEN FORTY-FOUR YEARS SINCE I GRADUATED FROM law school in 1981 and began what was to become my steady day job of practicing law. I basically retired from active practice about five years ago. My path to the law was a bit circuitous, however.

During my junior year of college, my wife, Carol, and I opened a women's clothing store, the Gazebo. To finance this, I held jobs in a paper factory (two weeks at this and I decided it was too dangerous and I was just not enough of a redneck for this job) and as a classified advertising salesman for a daily newspaper (I quit after a week without even asking for a paycheck). Next, I was a Hoover sales representative selling vacuum cleaners and home appliances with Hoover nameplates to rural, local hardware stores. Although I was great at this and booked sales records, I was laid off after six months when the economy turned down in 1975 because I had the lowest seniority. They asked me to come back two weeks after I was laid off, but I passed.

These were all just "for the money" jobs, but each, although brief, gave me a never-forgotten insight into what a job that has only that purpose can feel like. I think often of all the folks who live like this for their entire working career.

The Gazebo was successful and lasted from when we opened it in 1973 until we decided to close it a couple years later when new competition moved into the market.

Next, I tried my hand at politics, working as the administrative assistant to a United States congressman, Allen E. Ertel, the first-ever Democrat elected in a mid-Pennsylvania district. This was cool and I learned a lot. I gave speeches in his place when he was in Washington, introduced him when he was in the district, and supervised constituent services. Not for long, however, as I gave up this job to start a company with two buddies called Central Pennsylvania Energy Savers.

The idea of the new company was to service the burgeoning new market for energy conservation devices. This was 1977, just about the time that then–Democratic President Jimmy Carter made it clear his glory days were ahead of him as an ex-president. It became apparent that despite his best efforts, he could not get an energy bill through an all-Democratic congress. Since he couldn't, we couldn't. Suddenly, law school, put on hold since college graduation, seemed like a good idea.

Count them up—four jobs and two businesses, from 1974 when I graduated from college until 1978 when I went to law school. However, there was one more. I went back and worked as a construction laborer in New Jersey for five months—again just for the money—after I was accepted at law school but while I waited for it to begin.

Even before all these post-college adventures, my attitude toward work, entrepreneurship, and myself had been forged by a bevy of teenage jobs. If I remember them right, I had nine jobs and started two businesses during my high school and college years.

My first job during this period was on a short-term paper route delivering the *Newark Star Ledger* on Sunday mornings. This paper, which never had any following near where I lived, tried to get a foothold in Paramus by letting members of the Paramus Boys Club, which from about age seven to eleven included me, sell subscriptions with all the money going to the Boys Club and us kids. As I recall it, they had us sell promotional Sunday subscriptions, much like the Girl Scouts sold cookies. In those days, the local paper, the *Bergen*

Evening Record, did not have a Sunday edition. So this is what they were selling.

At the peak I made about twenty-five or thirty deliveries. The Sunday paper was really big then (three inches thick) and I received, in a big pile thrown on a nearby corner, most of the paper on Friday, then the news section on Sunday morning. I had to put the paper together. My mom helped me deliver the paper most weeks, with the pile of immense papers—think lots of advertising circulars in the back of her station wagon. When my mom couldn't help, it was just me and a pull-behind red wagon. This job didn't last too long. When the promotion ran out, most customers said no more. There were not enough left to keep going. I was nine when I did this, but somehow I didn't feel discouraged.

By the time I was eleven years old, I had a thirty-four-customer paper route, delivering the daily paper, the *Record*, every afternoon and Sundays; by then, they had moved the Saturday paper to Sunday. I guess the *Star Ledger* edging into their territory got their attention. Delivery was from my bike, with most customers getting the paper folded and thrown onto the front porch. A few wanted it tucked behind the storm door. As this required dismounting the mighty Schwinn, these were not among my favorite customers.

In those days, the early 1960s, the paper cost 33 cents a week, which I would collect and note by punching a card on a ring with each customer's name on it. A typical tip was two cents to round up to 35 cents. Some gave a little more. A few folks would give the much-coveted two quarters. My favorite customer was the bar at the Chimes Restaurant where they gave me 50 cents and a Coke at the bar at almost every delivery. That was heaven for an eleven-year-old and I saved this delivery for last.

Then I got entrepreneurial and opened a business renting bikes I rebuilt called "Crazy Bikes." My dad shut this one down as soon as he learned about it. Something about insurance. He was right, of course.

When I was in high school, I was the grill chef at the local Dairy Queen and Brazier. I made $1.15 and hour then. Not bad, as my contemporaries were counter guys and made just $1.05. I did this until I went to college.

Most of my jobs as a teen were summer jobs at the shore. My first such effort was my first real business, Fresh Clams Taste Better. As the proprietor, I gathered clams from the bay at the end of my street by finding them with my feet in the muddy bottom. I then sold them door to door at thirty-five cents a dozen, three dozen for a dollar. I even had a recipe book I had written, which I included in every box. This business flourished, but there were only so many clams a twelve-year-old boy could find with his feet, and I never convinced anybody to work for or with me.

After that, I was a busboy at a little restaurant at the shore making $0.85 an hour. I confess I can't remember the name of the place. My job and the restaurant only lasted that one summer. I hope it wasn't anything I did.

The next year I spent a summer as the assistant in the meat department of an Italian grocery store. The highlight was hours spent stocking in the cooler, actually a nice place to escape summer heat. My least favorite job was collecting and mashing meat of all kinds and then pressing it into intestine casings. Yes, I was a sausage maker. I think that was the summer I also had the job as the "bouncer" four nights a week at a teens-only discotheque called Le Garage.

The next year, I passed the fairly rigorous swimming test and became an ocean lifeguard on 44th Street in Brant Beach. Although in reality, the job was boring. You stare at the ocean all day; this job defined me a bit. My otherwise brown hair was bleached blond after each summer. At night, I was an usher at the Ship Bottom Colony movie theater. I kept both jobs during college, advancing to theater manager and then district manager of three island theaters over the three years I worked there.

All through college I was the *Time Life* sales representative selling subscriptions to college kids. *Life* magazine closed down while I was doing this. I hope it was not my fault.

I also had a couple stints working as a construction laborer getting paid a spectacular $6.00 an hour, the union wage, which I got not because I was in the union but because my dad was the architect on the job.

Since I am sharing all this deep background, let me jump ahead and add that I worked at three law firm jobs when in law school, and for a big-city firm, then a local practice in New Jersey before starting my own firm that grew and prospered and still bears my name even after I retired.

Much later, even during my law years, my entrepreneurial efforts did not completely disappear. Six real estate partnerships, often with friends, clients, or law partners; service on the boards of three public companies; several trusteeships; and finally my entities owned with my wife: Deerleap Books, bought and lovingly run then closed after ten years; Wells Mountain LLC, a real estate entity with forty-four tenants, a country inn, and store; Wells Mountain Investments; and the one I hope keeps going forever, Wells Mountain Initiative, the charitable nonprofit I started in 2005.

That means I have had something like forty jobs or businesses over the years. Most, if not all, have been successful. Have I learned anything from all this? Well, to state the obvious, always work hard; give it your best effort whether you like the task you are doing or not. This applies just as much to making sausage as it does to perfecting a contract for an unreasonable and overreaching client. Your employer will appreciate it. If you are an employee, you will too. It makes the day go faster. The hardest I ever worked was a brief time when I was at a law firm one summer and I had not been given enough work; I had to pretend to be busy so I could put in the hours I needed to get the pay I needed.

Most of my experience has been on the management side, mainly as the owner. This is, I admit, a different animal, so my ideas are more about how to motivate and care for those who work for you than how to be a perfect employee. On this side, listen, pay attention, give praise, say thank you when it's deserved, and pay a little better than others. Even though you are the boss, do not be afraid to get your "hands dirty." If you want people to work hard and go the extra mile, let them see you doing the same, occasionally even shoulder to shoulder pitching in on their job, not just doing yours. Clean up a mess, and make a copy.

Over the years, I developed a tendency to look at people who work for or with me as falling into one of two distinct categories: creative problem solvers (CPS) and detailed task masters (DTM). Both types are vital to a smooth-running operation. The CPS is an idea person and visionary. When they hit a wall, they look for a path around it. They invigorate an enterprise and keep it moving forward. They ask questions like, "How about we reach out to such and such to find out how we can do that too?"

The enterprise goes nowhere, however, without the ability to deliver. For this, every business needs DTMs, the folks who focus on the details and make things happen efficiently and on time.

Occasionally, you will find someone who has a good measure of both CPS and DTM, but in my experience, this doesn't happen very often. Whether deep in the ranks or in the C-suite, most everyone favors one trait or the other. Although they need to appreciate each other, I would take one truly good at each over two folks with some of each. Both CPS and DTM need to be performed at full tilt for the enterprise to be successful.

Public Speaking

A FEW SIGNIFICANT EXPERIENCES, THE FIRST WHEN I WAS eleven, the second in high school, and, finally, as a young lawyer, have shaped my public speaking. Over my lifetime, I have done quite a bit of public speaking. I am good at it, but I am by no means great at it. I learned the cardinal rule: Just talk. Talk like you would to one person standing right in front of you. Forget the big crowd, the microphone, or the camera. Just talk, slowly if possible, and make your points logically and thoughtfully.

My first relevant experience was when I was in sixth grade. My class first wrote, then presented, a play. It was a satire, a new word we had just learned in order to produce one on TV commercials. The performance was made up of skits, each a comical interpretation of a commercial. I think there were six skits. *Saturday Night Live*, eat your heart out. This was 1963. We thought of it first.

I had four parts, each in a different skit. Most of the class had multiple parts. I think four was the most. Separate characters. Separate costumes.

We rehearsed and rehearsed. I was ready. I had learned my lines. When the curtain went up, the entire school was in the audience. I was a hit. I made them laugh hysterically. My classmates weren't laughing though. All these years later, I still remember the feeling of sheer panic as I tried, mostly in vain, to remember my lines. In the end, I remembered most of them, just not necessarily in the right order or for the right skit.

Imagine, if you can, my fellow budding thespians responding with their line to my excited utterance that made no sense in the skit being performed. That is what my classmates had to do. Add to that, the annoyance of having the audience loving the weird guy oh-so-sincerely spouting gibberish. To this day, I have never again delivered anything memorized. I am hopelessly phobic about even trying.

In my sophomore year of high school, I took an elective class in public speaking. Most of the class was seniors. The teacher, Mr. Morganti, taught English classes, not speech; however, he was a gifted and inspiring teacher and got us on our feet. He taught us the basics that I now share with others. Most of all, he got me past stage fright, to just talk.

As I relate elsewhere, my high school years were full of student government and the YMCA Youth & Government program, so I encountered plenty of chances to speak. At the end of high school, I went back to Mr. Morganti for advice when I gave the graduation speech. I still remember him telling me to slow down, look at the audience, realize, and take advantage that for just a few moments you have their complete attention. "It is yours to use or to lose," he told me.

Perhaps my biggest speechmaking lesson came in my first year of practicing law. By then I was twenty-nine. Remember, I didn't go to law school right out of college. Perhaps because of those four or five years I had on my fellow newbies, my law firm sent this fledgling first-year litigator off to two weeks of intensive training at a National Institute of Trial Advocacy conference in Chicago. I worked and lived in Cleveland in those days, so this meant a couple weeks in a hotel. It was a big deal. Really too big. The course taught at Northwestern Law School was taught by mostly federal judges—the good ones—and was populated with a cohort of about forty young lawyers all with five or six years of courtroom experience. Except for me, that is.

This intensive course was very hard for me. I hardly ever slept. I did all my meals by room service. I scraped by. Just making the right objections was a major challenge for me. Near the end of the second week, we took turns making jury opening arguments. They were to be ten to fifteen minutes long, which is a lot of talking. I will spare you all the legal elements that a good opening argument needs to have and avoid, but I will share the comment I got from the instructor we had who was not a federal judge; she was a college professor who taught public speaking.

This professor opened by telling me I was "no Clarence Darrow," shorthand for "you fall well short of a gifted legal orator." She then continued with what turned out to be great news. She said, "Tom, you are very believable. Your demeanor, your eye contact, your cadence, and sometimes lack thereof, and your occasional stumbles make you come across as very sincere."

Okay, I thought, *I can live with this*. Not so slick, but sincere. This turned out to be the takeaway from two grueling weeks of training. Not very long after I got back to the law firm after this two-week course, I decided I wanted to be a business and real estate lawyer, not a litigator. Oh well. However, to this day, I usually talk only from a few notes, never a manuscript, and I keep it loose, casual, and sincere.

Since I have had the privilege of doing so much public speaking over the years, I now get to teach it. My course is a favorite at Wells Mountain Initiative's Dream Big conference where I always teach it. The biggest focus of the class is getting each participant up on their feet a couple times, so they can get relaxed and start talking as if they were speaking to one person, not a room full of them. I also share tips on what I consider the basics of good public speaking:

1. Find and use your own style, but no matter what, be energetic.
2. Organize your presentation with a logical beginning, middle, and end, and then preview what you are going to do verbally as you go.
3. Generally, speak from an outline with just a couple of notes, if possible. Reading the speech should be avoided.

4. Try to start strong and end even stronger.
5. Make your speech personal. Use stories.
6. Work on smooth transitions that tie back to the opening.
7. Use quotes, ideally from someone the audience has heard of.
8. Don't be afraid to use visual aids or to ask questions of your audience.
9. Seek to make good eye contact—and do so with the whole audience, not just one section or a friendly face.
10. A touch of humor at the beginning and elsewhere in the speech is almost always a good thing.

On Being a Writer?

I SET OUT TO BECOME A WRITER ABOUT THE TIME I TURNED forty—over three decades ago. After all, I thought, words are no stranger to me; in fact, they are my friends. As a lawyer, these words were my stock and trade, and I had been spewing them from my mouth, and—with the help of a very good secretary—on reams of paper for years. Even better, although it is not good form to admit to any sense of personal surprise for this phenomenon, to my amazement, I was paid handsomely for all those words. Why not just skip the necessity for interaction with clients and solve real problems, I thought, and just focus on the words? How hard could it be? Damn hard, it turns out.

I scribbled down some of what you are now reading about this time, or in the thirty years since. Much of my efforts in those days was rather torrid fiction and is happily gone. But yes, the biographical stuff survives, and it took all that time for me to get around to finishing it enough to share it.

At the beginning of my writer phase, I sent myself back to school. My "education" started with Tuesday nights at the Dalton School on East 57th Street in Manhattan. Later, it moved to a big, old building on Washington Square in Greenwich Village, where I took continuing education classes at New York University. Despite the writer-like Greenwich Village surroundings, the building was an uninspiring hulk of sterile classrooms. I saw no signs of Edith Wharton or Henry James, both who had delighted their readers and inspired their tales so many years ago from roughly this location.

Although I was not an early riser then, I arose early and journaled random thoughts and story ideas. I did this almost every day for a while.

I also found myself a pen pal from an island in Puget Sound, who I would enthusiastically write to and amazingly heard from. Unfortunately, most of the correspondence consisted of a discussion of a horrible, all too autobiographical, story about a teenage boy and his first love. They say, write what you know. Well, some say this. I'm not so sure.

My willing and generous pen pal correspondent was actually neither, as *Writer's Digest* dispatched them to the task for a price—even writers have to eat—as part of one of the magazine's often-promoted fiction writing correspondence courses. "You, too, can be a writer!"

I lived and worked in northern New Jersey at the time this happened, so the diversion from suburban daytime to New York City nights was part of a primitive attempt at remaking myself into a writer. Perhaps this was a thoughtful response to vague feelings of uneasiness that seemed to creep into the male soul just on the north side of forty.

Picture this: I am holed up in the perfect wood, glass, and stone room in an equally perfect house of the same natural materials, fireplace burning, overlooking water, books around me, cardigan sweater, pipe, two-day stubble, polished fiction flowing from me like a fast-running spring into the keyboard and out of the printer. *Wait a minute*, I thought. *I don't smoke.* Okay, kill the pipe. The rest could work.

My decision to make myself a writer wasn't as tranquil as it now seems, cleaned up for this telling. Like others of my gender, I didn't just creep into middle age. Although I went to work every day and generally kept up appearances, and I did not thrust myself upon some young woman half my age, I was in some level of crisis. When I crashed through the tape into my forties, I developed out of nowhere, much like a glass of ice water on a hot day after a long hike, a primeval need to "do something."

I needed and wanted to do something dramatic, like bulldoze down a virgin forest. I am a tree guy, so I don't even know why I said that, but you get the point. I needed a new direction. Three of my friends bought Harley-Davidsons. I wrote. Lest you be too impressed with the inference that my response was mature alongside that of my contemporaries, let me confess I also bought myself a ragtop Jeep—a safer version of the Harley—*and* wrote.

I assumed I would write fiction, perhaps a novel. I had always enjoyed telling and reading stories. I burned hot with the desire to write for a couple years. Later, as I see more clearly by looking back on this enthusiasm and its subsequent falling off, what began as an itch, a trickle of an idea, emerged as a bubbling stream into a big slow river, into my mainstream life. Then it just went away, "dried up" to continue the now tormented metaphor. I can't point to a single event when this happened, but somewhere in there—about the same time the midlife Harley-Davidsons gathered dust in my fellow middle-aged buddies' garages—I started sleeping late again.

The result of my fiction period? A dozen stories, most of which have never made it beyond a continuing succession of hard drives as I bought new computers over the years. I made a backup copy of the fruits of this effort a while back on one unscheduled New Year's Day, when I printed them all out in a collection I called *Sketchbook*. My wife, Carol, who edits for me anything I have the guts to actually consider sharing with the world, hasn't even seen most of this stuff and never will. I have updated a few of the more biographical pieces and buried them in this book.

As I move to the end of this little aside, a thought occurs to me. The next generation—as in our kids—will have the nostalgic joy of cleaning out not only our attics and looking at old photos, assuming of course we are clever enough to die leaving them with the work of cleaning up our physical junk, but perhaps also our hard drives as well. In my case, unless I, in a final desperate act of anal compulsion, remember to wipe clean my computer's memory, this task could include the fascination of reading a father's unpublished and likely unpublishable fiction. Wait until they see how I deal with sex scenes.

My Gorgeous Blonde

I was nineteen years old. It was the beginning of my sophomore year in college. That year, I lived in the frat house of the Kappa Sigma fraternity that I had pledged the previous semester. Most of the upperclassmen had moved to apartments they shared with other fraternity brothers. These apartments and the fraternity house itself were party houses that boasted brotherhood and a place to live and share meals without the eyes of the university looking on.

The Kappa Sigma house was full of the sophomore pledge class ready to leave our mark on university life and fraternity history. Embracing a long-standing tradition of the day before classes were to begin, I strolled the campus with one of my brothers. We had trolled the freshman dorm areas to scope out the new crop of freshman girls. As I sit here, I can't remember much about how we did except that we got waylaid at the "new dorm" (this dorm without a name had apparently not garnered a big enough alumni contribution yet to get a name) mailbox by a girl from our class. Sophomore girls were decidedly not a target when the new class arrived. As a group, they were condemned to what was called the "sophomore slump."

My buddy knew this particular girl, and they started talking. I knew who she was but needed an introduction to make it official. I knew of her because it was hard not to. She was gorgeous. Blue eyes, exceptionally cute, and blonde hair literally down to her waist. Every freshman guy knew her—at least from her pig book picture.

In those days, the university created a book with every member of an incoming class, with a picture, name, and high school of each student. Everyone called it the pig book. Most often, the picture was from high school graduation, so it was usually a good one…sometimes a lot better than real life. In this young lady's case, the picture fell short; in person, she was even better than her pig book picture. This might have been because she was very sweet, unpretentious, and just plain friendly, besides being very attractive.

In that first conversation, the young lady and I discovered we would be in class together the following morning. The class was called Elements of Art. It was a hands-on adventure, mostly for non-art majors. I was on a liberal arts track, destined for law school, so I thought this introduction to the world of art made sense for my journey. Students in the class started with paintings, then moved to various three-dimensional art, and finally to a full-fledged installation piece. Not studying these mediums, mind you, but making them. The young lady was an art major. Somehow, this class was to be for both of us. I loved the class and so did she. Of course, this may have been because it's where we first came together, and like magnets, we slammed together, never to be pulled apart again.

The young lady had a name, of course: It was Carol Vitz. Instead of calling her Carol, everyone called her Vitzie. Many college students got nicknames in those days, although I never did. Vitzie came from Carol's last name, Vitz. When I got back to the fraternity house after the walk, I talked to my brothers about her. They told me she was from Scarsdale, New York, an upper-class Long Island suburb. I also learned she had been dating an upperclassman brother of the fraternity the year before.

When we both showed up in class the following day, I watched her closely from across the room. She was, as we already established, very pretty. No, she was more than pretty, a presence really. Somehow, quiet yet animated. Is that possible? I had to talk to her. I did. She talked back.

Despite my honed image of confidence—I was a student politician after all, class president by then—I had very little confidence with girls, especially one who was above my weight class. But even I could figure out she was downright friendly. Could it be she was even flirting with me?

I learned quickly she was not from upper-class Scarsdale, New York, but rather York, Pennsylvania, seventy miles down the Susquehanna River from our school. She was the product of a farm country high school. There, not surprisingly, she had been on the homecoming court and the star of the senior play. I also learned she was the high school newspaper editor and, get this, the Pennsylvania State Science Fair champion.

It only got better when on the second day of class she sat next to me, and she just kept being friendly. She started telling me about her social life. She was inviting me to be interested. This was amazing, truly amazing.

Ever since the summer before I went to college, I had a girlfriend whom I had met at the shore. A couple years younger than me, she was still in high school and thus not on campus, and what we called a "hometown." She was very attractive, sexy, and mature beyond her years. She was the type of high school girl who "of course" had a college boyfriend. I was thrilled to be with her.

My relationship with this young lady was pretty special. At home, in New Jersey, often accompanied by my five-year-old sister, we enjoyed playing that we were married, when people thought she was our child. At the end of the summer just past, I had negotiated the right to "date" at school—as long as I made clear to whomever I dated that my heart and commitment were elsewhere. I had not wanted or asked for this the year before. Instead, I brought my hometown to campus whenever I could and also went home often.

It turned out Carol also had a hometown. Her boyfriend from home was at Syracuse University and had been her steady for more than three and a half years. Carol had had the right to casually date the year before as well. She had made good use of it, dating not only the older guy in my fraternity but a few other guys as well, including, at the end of freshman year, a senior football star who, thank goodness, by then had graduated.

It became clear, I was slow at this stuff. She wanted to continue her social dating with me, and I was, should I say, excited to break out of my on-campus monkhood with her. Finally, the words came out—but only after an idiot would not have gotten the clues the answer would be yes—"Would you like to go to the football game with me this Saturday?"

I had a blue Volkswagen bug in those days. I picked her up for the football game that day, even though the game and the fraternity party were both within walking distance.

The game was not memorable except that in true college-boy style, I attempted to get us both drunk. I had brought a large thermos of whatever you call vodka and Tom Collins mix. My date, who had earned the freshman nickname of Vodka Vitz, because of some affection for this particular poison, drank none of what I served her because she was, unknown to me, hungover from partying the night before. I would not learn any of this until sometime later. Carol cleverly poured her drinks out in slow installments through the floorboards of the bleachers. I had no idea. Not wanting to be out-drunk by my date, I barreled on.

Usually, the combination of one of two people being pretty tipsy and the other sober does not bode well for chemistry, but we did fine because back at the fraternity house for more drinks and dinner—she may have been drinking by then—we were arm in arm, and I was later told by others we were noticeably a couple. Alcohol was the great socializer in those days, but as it was the early seventies, marijuana was also in abundance (though not so much for us, at least not that night).

The highlight of that first date was not the gridiron, nor the frat house. Ever romantic, I drove the Beetle to a lookout I knew, farther down the Susquehanna River. We parked and talked for hours. That mixture of personable, smart, and almost scary beautiful was irresistible. I was entranced. I was nineteen years old and my hunt for a partner felt over. What made it even better was that she seemed to feel the same way.

I am not even sure I kissed Carol that first night. Plenty of that would come later. Although I have exclaimed, "I love you only for your body!" many times in the years since, this was absolutely not true. I do really like it though, even now, the old-lady version. At first, I moved slowly. To be physical quickly seemed to me a sacrilege. I wondered what she thought of this.

About a week later, Carol was initiated into her sorority as a full-fledged sister. The girls wore white dresses, lit candles, and did all kinds of sacred things: ritual stuff—nothing stupid, mind you, like us guys. Then they got drunk (now they could be stupid), and as a group, caroused their favorite fraternity houses. As her sorority, Pi Phi, and my fraternity, Kappa Sigma, were close at Bucknell, they came to us first. This time she was the tipsy one and made sure I and my buddies were very aware of her affection for me. I was thrilled and even more so when she returned later after the carousing.

Sophomore guys shared a room that was so small, it had room for only one bed. Even the bed we had was a loft of sorts over the top of a desk. Loft is generous, really. It was a single bed—as in even smaller than a twin—six feet up in the air, with a rickety ladder leading up to it. It was in this special spot we spent our first night together. My roommate was safely tucked in his bed on the nearby sleeping porch where I would have been had it not been for my female visitor. That was the rule. If you had a girl, you got the room. This was good news for me, though it would later be a point of contention with my roommate when Carol stayed over a lot in his view, as he did not have visitors that year, ever.

Since that first night, we slept skin to skin. It was great. The only issue was her tangled, waist-length hair in the morning. Well worth the price in my view. Despite all the skin, although there was lots of foreplay, there was no sex. Notwithstanding the raft of guys the year before, not to mention the three-year-plus boyfriend, Carol was a virgin. I was more than willing to wait. I was totally smitten.

What about those long-term hometowns? How quick it was, we both knew right away we were on a track that made these other two impossible. I don't remember a lot of discussion on this, nor either one of us getting to this point first; we both just knew.

A few weeks after Carol and I connected so deeply, I went home to tell my hometown we were "over." I am not a cruel person, so I am sure I was as kind as I could be under the circumstances, but it was not pretty. She was devastated, and worse, her parents had determined I was the "catch" that her "old-school" mom felt she could not lose. Bizarrely blaming her for having done so, her parents were not very supportive. I felt bad, but, hey, I was nineteen and generally very pleased with myself.

Carol's boyfriend was a different story. I think it was three weeks after the above-related first date that he was due to show up for homecoming weekend. I was to stay out of the way—not so easy, I would add, because by then we were together literally all the time—and she would tell him. I did what I was told but must admit I pretty much stalked the couple.

By Saturday night, although the poor guy knew something was wrong and had heard Carol whispering about him with her roommate, she had still not told him. I am not sure what possessed her to bring the poor guy to a party at my fraternity house, but she did. This was all becoming too much in my view.

I introduced myself and took him for a walk through the streets of Lewisburg. Yeah, I know, what was I thinking? Recall I was nineteen and my hubris cup runneth over.

"Carol and I are together now. You two are over." Yup, pretty blunt. He took it amazingly well. No fight, just pretty quiet. The next day he was gone.

Carol later told me she softened my harsh words by telling him she needed to explore her relationship with me and that meant they could not be a couple "for now." Whatever, it worked. He took it well then, although about fifteen years later, he showed up at their high school reunion, after a couple divorces, and wanted to know whether she had made a mistake. The good news is all these years later, she told him, this time straight to his face, she had made no mistake.

The week after the hometowns were both disposed of, we opened a joint bank account at the local Lewisburg bank. Fifty-plus years later, our accounts are still joint.

Did Carol stay a virgin until we got married? Not even close. About a month after the momentous homecoming weekend, the two of us went on a two-hundred-mile trip in my VW bug to my family shore house on Long Beach Island, New Jersey. This is not that kind of book, so I will just say when the lights went off, our clothes did too. And in the morning, we woke up in each other's arms smiling.

It's the Law

ALTHOUGH BOTH MY BROTHERS FOLLOWED MY DAD IN BECOMing architects, I never had a desire to go this route. Later, I would jokingly call myself the black sheep, as the only male in my family who was not an architect. I design anything I build, but I can't draw. I loved talking and arguing a point, so the law always felt like the place for me. I liked those courtroom confessions on *Perry Mason*. Finally, at age eleven, when John Kennedy was elected president, I got interested in politics. The two seemed to fit together.

I did not arrive at my life's early ambition to become a lawyer until I turned twenty-nine. I had, at some point prior to that, after a stint of working in politics as the administrative assistant to a congressman, decided against the president gig.

Thus, after appropriate and well-intentioned delays through my other abiding interests of politics and business, in the fall of 1978, I arrived at Case Western Reserve Law School in Cleveland, Ohio. The four years of working before I hit the law books turned out to be helpful. By the time I got to law school, I was happy to be there and was a very dedicated and determined student, much more serious about studying than I had been a half decade earlier as an undergraduate. I was about as worldly as you can be at twenty-nine. I also had a wife and a kid. Unlike most of my fellow law students, plodding along right from undergraduate studies, I found being a student again fun after a stint in the trenches of the working world.

Although those years were a financial struggle, since I attended school full time and our oldest daughter was already one and a half and needed childcare by then, we made it work. Carol worked full time managing retail stores while I was in school. After the first year, I found part-time law jobs after school, and during the summers, I landed two great clerkships at big Cleveland firms. These were much sought after by law students, because they paid the same as first-year associates and often led to job offers.

The first year, I clerked at a firm called Burke, Haber, and Berick; after the second year at Hahn, Loeser, Freedheim, Dean & Wellman, which later became and still is Hahn Loeser Parks. Hahn Loeser gave me the coveted offer of permanent employment, beginning at graduation, at the end of my summer clerkship. It is really nice to go back to your third year of law school already with a job offer.

Once I graduated in 1981, I worked at Hahn Loeser for about two and a half years. This turned out to be my longest period of being an employee in my entire career. Even during that time, my drive and entrepreneurial approach helped me do very well, even if I didn't stay long. I soaked it all up. I paid attention. I worked very hard.

It was not hard to be a bit of a superstar as compared to the other newbies. My short career of owning businesses and politics had taught me some skills, and more importantly, how to play my role: confident and ambitious, but always deferential and humble. I recommend this strategy to anyone starting up the ladder. It worked for me, and I can say having spent many more years being the guy to be deferred to than the employee, it works from that end too.

I understood business. and I was learning the law. I knew exactly why it was significant when, working on a Saturday, which I always did, I found the managing partner opening mail in the mail room at the beginning of the month. By watching closely, I discerned he wasn't looking for a pleading or contract he was expecting—he was looking for checks. It seems a 120-employee law firm had to pay attention to cash flow.

I also paid attention when my billing rate was bumped up several times to that of lawyers at the firm several years senior to me. When I had my review, they said despite this, I could not be paid more than the other lawyers in my class. I knew the guy I was talking with realized he got out-argued on this one by the young lawyer sitting in front of him who questioned this practice, but his hands were tied. I think this would have changed had I not left.

My tendency to be entrepreneurial and my willingness to take on anything got me lots of interesting work and many great learning experiences. I was thought of as someone connected to the litigation department, but who also worked in the firm's large debtor/creditor practice, which was great business experience. I avoided being assigned as a junior member on one of the large litigation teams that had the big cases. These were considered plumb assignments, but not by me. Your work as the fourth or fifth lawyer was to research and, well, research. Instead of this, I tried small cases. No partner or even senior associates wanted those cases, especially since their billing rate would not make sense on the client's bill.

I won the cases. I got more. The firm sent me to expensive litigation training at the National Institute of Trial Advocacy, which I discussed in the Public Speaking chapter. Since I became the litigator who would do anything they threw at me, I did a couple divorces and defended a personal injury action. I learned from it all.

Perhaps the best demonstration of my tendency to jump into the scrappy jobs and avoid the big teams is demonstrated by two stories from debtor/creditor practice.

First, I should tell you what debtor/creditor means. For most of the world, this is usually called bankruptcy. However, bankruptcy takes many forms, especially in the business world. When a business goes bankrupt, the process is not just the financial end of a business and its liquidation. Instead, this troubled time for a business often involves some form of reorganization, new investors, or sale of at least some assets. Sometimes a debtor/creditor case is just helping a business get its act together and avoid the costly bankruptcy altogether.

My first experience in this practice was the slow and rather painful end of the White Motor Company. White Motor started in 1900. Based in Cleveland, but with plants all over the country, it had been one of America's biggest manufacturers of trucks, buses, and tractors. The company hit hard times in the mid-1970s. By 1980, the company slid into bankruptcy with several attempts to reorganize. It all came to an end with the sale of the last major assets to Swedish Volvo AB in late 1981.

When I arrived as a graduated but not-yet-licensed new lawyer in the summer of 1981 (I took the bar that summer but did not get the results until November), Hahn Loeser was counsel for the unsecured creditors. In bankruptcy, especially a big one, most every entity has its own counsel. The company itself, called a debtor in possession (or DIP) has one, secured creditors (mostly banks) may each have their own or share, unsecured creditors have one—sometimes employees, shareholders, and anyone else who thinks there is a piece of the pie for them will want to be at the table with a lawyer. The fees for all those lawyers—which in the end all get paid by the company—will kill you, even if your business is not already struggling.

So, by the summer of 1981, someone decided an analysis of all employee contracts and any claims the terminated employees might have would be a good thing. As soon as we got to the office, the two other brand-new associates and I, along with a few other relatively junior associates, were told to report back the next day in clothes that could get dirty. We were all sent to a warehouse in Cleveland to rummage through thousands of boxes of employee records from thirty-four White Motor facilities. The end result, many weeks later, was a dozen really big binders with summaries of all employee contracts. Were these ever used or even read? I have no way of knowing. My guess is no. This work was done because it was arguably useful—and it was billable, and thus made the law firm a fairly considerable sum of money. At a minimum, the work paid for a bunch of new lawyers at a time when we were not likely yet to be profitable. One of the two associates I hired on with, Larry Oscar, who was at my side in the warehouse, went on to become the managing partner of the firm and ran the entire place many years later. Law, you see, is a business too.

My other debtor/creditor story is about a small cement manufacturer in Akron, Ohio, run by two brothers. This was a much smaller operation, consisting of a showroom, cement plant, maybe twenty cement trucks, other equipment, and about twenty-five employees. Almost all these employees I ultimately got to personally terminate. I don't know what caused this business to flounder. I suspect bad cost control—read that as spending more than you're making. No phalanx of lawyers here. Just one firm, us, representing the company, the DIP. The partner on this matter was Lee Powar, and he had just one associate helping him: me.

While the company could operate for a while to see if they could reorganize to become profitable, it soon became apparent this would not work. Not much pie to divide and most, if not all, would go to the bank with secured debt. Few legal fees were justified either, so Powar left it all in my hands to visit these guys regularly and help them wind down the business, sell assets, have an auction, and, over time, let everyone go, because the two brothers could not bear to do it themselves. You can imagine how popular my visits were, since they all inevitably ended with my calling one or two employees in to give them the news. At the very end, it was just me, one brother and the bookkeeper. It was sad, but I made it just a little less so and kept it all organized, so I felt like I helped. Again, I learned.

The first of these two examples is a very typical use of a new associate in a large firm. The second was not. I gravitated toward the scrappy work. I already knew I wanted to have my own firm one day, and I was all about learning and doing as fast as I could.

In January 1984, I decided it was time to go home to the East Coast. I decided quickly that, despite having spent a decade at school and working in other places, Bergen County in Northern New Jersey was the logical place to start a law practice if I was going to do this. I had friends and connections there. My dad was, and soon my brothers would also be, respected local architects. It made sense.

A whole year before I moved, I detoured to New Jersey and took the family to Florida in a borrowed RV and took three days to take the state bar exam. I studied by doing a quick once-over review of my notes from the extensive preparation I had done before I took the Ohio bar. Passing the first time was life or death. This time, I wanted to see whether my destiny was back in New Jersey. As fate would have it, I passed it easily. It made me wonder if all the crazed studying I had done the first time had been necessary.

The path to owning my own firm took a short detour through working for a solo practitioner in my hometown of Paramus, New Jersey. I arrived in New Jersey six months ahead of the family and worked as an associate attorney for a man my father had gone to high school with. My new boss was a well-entrenched, successful, local attorney. He had occasional associates and by then, a son in law school who worked at the office, but he needed help. I needed a job.

This was not a job made in heaven. The boss was superficially nice enough, but more than a little set in his ways that were definitely not mine. Barking orders to secretaries, often from the throne of his private bathroom, and generally practicing law defensively with the clients almost seeming to be the enemy. In short, he was authoritative and very cynical. I was very much not, and had no desire to become so.

I remember the first day at my desk. It was a fancy desk in an office within an old colonial building. But the big change wasn't in how nice my office was. Rather, the utter contrast from being the superstar young buck in the big firm setting to being a protégé of this single man, who I was not very impressed with, brought me as close to tears as I have ever felt in an office setting.

However, right from the start, as I had in Cleveland, I worked hard, long days and nights. I paid close attention and soaked it all in. It turned out my new boss didn't enjoy doing the work that much and had me do everything. I was happy to do it. From house closings to wills, lawsuits to business deals, I did it all.

The big moneymaker in this office was an area of the law called land use. In essence, this was representing owners or developers who owned or put property under contract and wanted to build on it. Getting approvals in large populated and very developed Bergen County, New Jersey (just across the river from New York City), required hearings before a local planning board or board of adjustment and permission from various other agencies, including the state department of transportation or state department of environmental protection. All this permission and approval seeking had become a high art: difficult, often time consuming, and expensive. It was fertile ground for an attorney who would lead the effort. Done right, approvals added true value to a property, such as more square feet, a different use, less parking, greenery, and the like.

I learned every aspect of this application process—except making the actual presentations, which is where my boss took the glory. I did a couple small applications, but even better, everyone, including town officials, other professionals, and even our clients, figured out who did the work behind the scenes.

My boss liked what I was doing. For one thing, I was making him a ton of money. He also did not need to work nearly as hard. I did not begrudge him this at all. He was by then in his late fifties and when I started work he was able to go on his first big vacation ever, three weeks in the Far East.

After a year, he wanted to make all this permanent. He renamed the firm, which had borne only his name for over twenty years, to include my name. I was not anxious for this move and told him so, but he did it anyway. Whoever heard of a young, ambitious attorney not wanting to be held out as a partner, to have his name in lights? The partnership was in name only—I was, at best, a very junior partner—but I was paid quite well. My new "partner" had plans for me, but I had plans for me too.

It would have happened eventually, but this relationship crashed and burned out completely a bit sooner than it might have over a weekend in January 1986. I was working on a Saturday, which I almost always did. On my desk, I found a complaint that "my partner/boss" wanted me to sign. A complaint is the legal pleading to start a lawsuit. This lawsuit was initiated by my senior partner as the plaintiff against a business partner of his, who was also a client. It was full of what I considered ethical lapses and bogus charges, not the least of which were all kinds of conflict of interest. More importantly, the crazy lawsuit he wanted me to sign made no sense.

In response to my call to inform him I would not sign this complaint, he drove from his home to tell me in person that I had no choice. I stuck to my guns, and when he exploded at me, I simply announced, "Okay then. I quit." I told him he could consider this my two weeks' notice. I walked out of the room and the building, leaving him fuming.

At home, I told Carol what I had done. She was delighted, although a little scared. I met with my neighbor across the street, who was to be my accountant. Thinking about the aggressive nature of my now ex-partner, I then returned to the office that afternoon and emptied my desk. I took every personal item and everything related to clients who were mine. I knew in my heart, I would not be allowed back in the office once my erstwhile colleague collected himself. Sure enough, the next day, office keys, credit card, and even my leased family car (we only had one in those days) were all taken from me.

I opened my practice the following Monday, January 27, 1986. I know this is the date because it was the next day, January 28, when the Space Shuttle Challenger broke apart on liftoff, killing its seven-member crew. My dad was on a three-week Rotary trip, and I had called him, asking to use his desk and secretary to get up and running. At that desk, I took my handful of clients and built a practice. By the time my dad got home, I had rented my first office on Fairview Avenue in Paramus, hired a secretary, roughly furnished the place, bought computers, and was on the move. I also bought a used car from my brother-in-law and traveled to Pennsylvania to get it.

I did not take any clients from my former firm, other than those who had come to me while there, even though more than one asked to move with me. I had sown the seeds well, though. Everything worth doing quickly came my way.

Within six months, I hired a young litigator, Richard Garofalo, and ceased my involvement in the courtroom side of the law practice. Lightning quick, I grew the firm to include more lawyers and staff. As I added lawyers, I filled holes and specialties: real estate lawyers, land-use lawyers, estate lawyers, trust lawyers, and business lawyers. As the founder, I was the only generalist. While I filled all those holes, I learned to do everything.

While most of my notoriety and expertise in the big growth years were about pushing through large land-use proposals, I still had my fingers in other stuff. I continued to be a corporate and business lawyer, working with small business clients. Later, I worked with nonprofits. I always thought my initial years as a scrappy, do-everything generalist served me well as I specialized. Most other bigger firm lawyers don't have this chance, getting pigeonholed into a specialty sooner than I did.

By fall of 1987, I convinced a brash New York City developer to hire me for a project he planned for Paramus, New Jersey. The developer, Donald Trump, was not yet forty-one years old. I was thirty-five. When he hired me, I exaggerated the size of my firm and told him my firm was about to become a partnership. Mostly because of this boast, as of January 1, 1988, I made two young associates—Jim Jaworski, who is still my good friend and a partner today, and Rich Garofalo, my first hire—become partners in what we then called Wells, Garofalo & Jaworski. Like me at my previous firm, they were initially partners in name only.

If the firm had a challenge as it grew fast to more than ten attorneys and twenty-five support staff, its leader, me, had not yet turned forty years old. My hair was as gray as it got around our shop. I was ambitious and good at what I did, but really could have stood a few mentors and old-timers around.

I am not going to tell the full story of what is now the almost forty-year-old Wells, Jaworski & Liebman law firm, here but I will say it grew, became, and continues to be a great collection of lawyers and staff committed to doing quality work but not taking themselves too seriously. Once we hit the size of about ten to twelve lawyers, we consciously hovered around that size, deciding this was big enough to do anything we wanted to undertake, but small enough to stay "family."

I lured Stuart Liebman to the firm in September 1990. Stuart was hired as a partner on the first day and was added to the firm's name a few years later. Stuart is quite literally the best land use lawyer in New Jersey. Like me, and I guess all of our firm's land use lawyers, he does not believe in losing. He always out-prepares, out-thinks, and out-argues anyone who stands in his way.

Law firms are successful for a couple of reasons. First and foremost, based on the quality of the law that is practiced. They are also a business that must be run. I ran and grew the place by myself for the first ten years, from 1986 to 1996. In 1996, I moved to Vermont and began to practice long distance. Stuart became the managing partner. For this, I am forever grateful. He did not want the job. Partly to convince him to take it, from 1996 until just a couple years ago, I remained the CFO, and Stuart, I, and Jim Jaworski, also a great land use attorney and bedrock partner, became the administrative partners. We all shared responsibilities.

Recently, with my retirement, I was succeeded as CFO by a much younger partner, Mark Balian. As Stuart did in 1996, Mark now made my plan to push back even further a reality, which I appreciated.

As I write this, I am no longer a partner of the firm I founded. I am "of counsel," which is lawyer talk for anything other than a partner or an associate; in my case, it stands for retired founder and partner. Today, the firm has as its partners: Stuart, Jim, Mark, Jim Delia, Andy Kohut, and Jameson VanEck. These six guys, the associate attorneys, and the paralegals and support staff of WJL make me so proud. I'm proud of what I started, proud my name is still on the door, proud of what they have become, and proud of what they do every day.

I will leave most of the story of practicing law for more than forty years for another book, if I write one. However, I have a favorite story I'd like to share. It's as much a personal story as it is a law story.

* * *

Jim Jaworski started work at the firm on the last Monday of November 1987. On Thursday night of the same week, he shadowed me as I made a Board of Adjustment presentation for the approval of what was to become Pier One, a retail store, near the Ridgewood Avenue overpass on Route 17 in Paramus. It was a relatively tough approval, not a sure thing by any means. Jim, who is now one of the best land use lawyers anywhere, was totally new to this and was just along to watch. Halfway into the presentation, in a quiet moment, the entire room heard the pay phone just outside the council chamber ringing. This was before cell phones. Immediately, I knew who I had given that number to. Within seconds, the person who answered the phone announced to the room: "Tom Wells, your wife is at the hospital and having a baby right now. You need to get there." I stood there dumbfounded. Before I could say anything, a woman on the board announced, "You go now!" The other female board member nodded in agreement.

I huddled with my team of experienced witnesses—one was my brother, Jeff, as the architect, the other site engineer, Al Lapatka, and my very green attorney. I told Jim to skip the questions I would normally ask to prompt their testimony and just let these guys talk. "They know what to do."

I then went to talk with the chairman of the board. This very experienced chairman was Jim Huffman. Jim was "Uncle Jim" to me, as he and his wife, Nancy, were my parents' oldest and best friends. He had been at my wedding. He got it completely, including the newbie attorney who would now have to cover for me. I asked him to do me a favor. I told him the hearing would go on, but would he please, if he thought the board would vote no, just adjourn for the night and let the hearing continue in the future. The new lawyer would not necessarily be able to read the board this way, but Uncle Jim certainly would. He said to me, "I have it."

I left and headed to the hospital. My daughter Carlyn was born at 9:20 p.m., well before the hearing ended. They voted yes.

There is a reason Carol had the number of the pay phone. The day of the hearing was Carlyn's due date, December 3. Who is born on their actual due date? My amazingly punctual daughter, that is who. I knew this was a possibility and could have delayed the hearing for a month. My client, Sarkis Gabrellian, an old-school developer, told me straight out, "You're not having a baby. Your wife is. You don't need to be there. No delays."

I had rolled the dice. When I talked to Carol, just before heading to the hearing at 7:00 p.m., all was fine. Apparently, things started happening soon thereafter. So soon, in fact, she called our neighbor Marge Brightman, her backup ride plan, for a ride to the hospital. As it turned out, Marge wasn't there, so her husband, Dick, took Carol to the hospital and helped her get admitted. Even after getting admitted, Carol did not call the pay phone until it looked like the real thing.

I got there in plenty of time. Carol's blood pressure spiked and the whole process got a little tense for a few moments, so I was so glad to be there.

Sometime after the delivery, around 11:00 p.m., we were sitting in Carol's room reliving the last few crazy hours when the nurse announced, "The third father is at the nurse's station and insists on being allowed to see you." Apparently, the first father had been determined by the staff to be Dick Brightman who got Carol admitted. I was number two. Moments later, an excited Jim Jaworski poked his head in the door beaming. "We won!" he announced. Indeed we had. In more ways than one.

This story has a fun postscript. About five or six years after this happened, Carol and I attended a sixtieth birthday party for a client and friend. It was a delightful affair at the Ridgewood Country Club and included friends and business acquaintances of the man celebrating his birthday. Seated next to Carol and me were Sarkis Gabrellian and his wife.

Sarkis could be quite charming, and they were having a great time talking. At one point, when I was about to head to the bar to get us more drinks, I overheard him tell Carol I should prioritize my family time, and I shouldn't work too hard. I interrupted and said, "Carol, remember when Carlyn was born, and the client who said I did not need to be there for the birth?"

She nodded.

"You are sitting next to that client now."

I left for the bar confident that Sarkis would get an earful! He did.

Nonspecific D

"It sucks to be depressed. But then a lot of things suck. This is just the one I got." This is a quote from a journal entry written by me more than forty-five years ago. I was twenty-seven years old when I wrote it. It could have been written almost anytime during the ten years prior, or for that matter pretty much anytime since I actually wrote these words. The good news is that while depression does suck, it has been, for me, very much treatable.

What I had taken to calling "nonspecific D" was essentially an unexplained mental low that nothing in my life seemed to cause. I first noted the occurrence in my teen years. Happily, at that point, these lows didn't last too long or come very often. The lows were also, well, not that low.

This would change as to frequency, length, and, eventually, how low the low would get. By the time I was about thirty-five, it started getting ugly. I knew I needed more than my self-help coping mechanisms, which were elaborate and often didn't work well.

A big problem was it took a lot of energy to appear happy when I was not. By the time I came home, I often turned grouchy from all the effort during the day. My tolerance for anything out of order sent me spiraling—a mess in the front hall, something I had expected to be done that was not, anything not *Better Housekeeping* perfect. It triggered my temper and frustration. My wife and daughters probably felt like they needed to walk on those proverbial eggshells. Not probably. They have told me I wasn't easy to live with during those years.

I had a client who I was close to, who suffered from manic depression. I was used to his highs and lows and was along for his trip as his condition worsened and help from both therapy and medications became necessary. Although this condition was worse than mine, the parallels were instructive.

Finally, in about 1986 or 1987, I showed up at his psychiatrist's office, first to discuss his patient, my client, then to spill my guts. By then I was a virtual expert at my condition. I had read everything relevant and plenty that was not. I had gone on the internet and found a way to self-medicate with Prozac, the then go-to antidepressant.

When I finally went to the doctor, I was a horror as a patient, your basic know-it-all. Fortunately, this doc was very laid back and understood I neither wanted nor needed a lot of talk therapy. I just needed meds. He put me on some.

I got better. Better in the sense that the "nonspecific D" did not show up nearly as much, and when it did, the low was well within my coping skills. However, I did not like the idea nor the effect of the meds. I felt like they dulled me a little. They seemed to file off the point of my spear. My family loved this; me, not so much.

The result was that as soon as the lows went away, I went off the meds. This was not great because the meds, once taken, took about two weeks to work, so going back on them when a low hit wouldn't work for a while. I tried antianxiety meds. I tried going off only in the summer when lots of sunlight helped keep the lows away. Eventually, I tried moving from New Jersey to more laid-back Vermont, which is a different story told elsewhere, but even this big lifestyle decision did not fix the problem.

Finally, at about forty years old, more than thirty years ago, I gave up. I realized I should be grateful to live in a time when my broken brain chemistry could be fixed by regular doses of an outside chemical.

If this had some side effects, I needed to accept them. With a couple exceptions, mostly from accidentally forgetting the pills, I have been taking antidepressants ever since.

I do not talk about any of this, at least not much. My wife and kids, of course, know. I assume my daughters' husbands know, too, but as I said, we don't discuss it much. I told my sister, and by doing so, the rest of my siblings and my parents, when she was struggling with her own issues, only to have her declare at a group intervention session for her, "I don't have to listen to you. We now know you are crazy."

It is a big deal I am talking about this here. For anybody reading this book, the secret will now be out. My thought is because this book is about my well-lived life, it is probably good for my readers to know this dark corner was always there. I just learned to live with it. Depression sucks. But so do a lot of things.

Living Your Dream

WHAT CAUSES A SUCCESSFUL LAWYER, IN HIS MID-FORTIES, TO drop everything and start over, dragging his wife with her own career and kids invested in their own lives, more or less willingly along with him, to undertake what I like to call a midcourse correction?

First, we should define "successful." As in, if he was so successful, why would he want to give it all up? I believe I was successful, by any conventional standard. At forty-four years old, I was a well-respected and well-compensated lawyer and managing partner of the twelve-lawyer firm that I had grown from a solo practice in more than ten years. I was deeply involved in a myriad of community and civic activities, and I was a regular churchgoer. I had a great family, both my own and extended. I also had all the material trappings of success: a showplace house in an upscale community, a vacation house in Vermont, European vacations, western ski trips, new cars, etc. No problems at home either. There is no secret to tell here. No real dark clouds, except in my mind.

My wife, Carol, also enjoyed all the above, minus the law practice, but added a much-loved job as a school social worker. And we had each other and, I am happy to report, a strong, in fact, as close as you can get to a perfect, marriage of twenty-four years. We had for many years considered each other our respective best friends. My kids, who by then were nine, fourteen, and nineteen years old, were all great too.

So, what, if anything, was wrong? First off, all the material things came at a price. Big mortgages, lots of bills. I made a good living—many would say a great one. However, we spent most of what we made. It was also becoming increasingly clear the needs were growing. Lawyers, unlike business executives, make their living one hour at a time. More money usually requires more work, and there are only so many hours in the day.

Second, and perhaps more important, was time itself. There was never enough of it. Racing from one good thing to another became exhausting. How many lessons, how many projects, how many black-tie charity benefits, how many church suppers, how many demanding clients—all good things—become too much? Third, burnout, and maybe worse, a sense of personal malaise, began to set in. Carol was fine on this front, but then she pretty much always is.

But for me, always a double-A perfectionist type, it was becoming too much. Practicing law and the responsibilities of being the psychological parent for the thirty-plus people who worked for the law firm, until then a source of pride, was becoming not much fun.

My long-held desire to write had led me to some much-enjoyed time at the keyboard and then to a series of stimulating night classes. But a lack of time prevented any serious attempt to remake myself into a writer, something at this time I still desired to be.

Last, Carol and I found that we were losing ourselves in being ourselves. I felt this most acutely. I was so busy trying to be a good guy, to meet everybody's expectations of me, and worse, my own of myself, that it was hard to pay attention to those around me—to sincerely hear a friend in need and to be there for them. I had no time for serious, contemplative thought or prayer.

Prayer "on the run" had developed into a high art form for me, but serious, daily meditation and prayer—I truly believe necessary for all of us—as well as some form of daily exercise—also critically important—were always sacrificed to seemingly more important priorities on any day.

In the end, but certainly a big factor, was my long-term, low-grade clinical depression, my nonspecific D.

So, one day, I said to Saint Carol, "We've got to do something." I actually said this many days, but one day, I actually followed through. Her advice, as usual eminently sensible, was to look inside myself to see if it was me who created the problem, not our location or our lifestyle. Very good advice. Carol promised she would be introspective, not a simple thing when you are moving at one hundred miles an hour just to keep up.

The result of our deliberations, not surprisingly, somewhat proven out by the story I will relate here, is we agreed we were our own worst enemies, or at least I was, and she will go along. We were keeping ourselves so busy that our quality of life was getting lost. Could we change that?

The conclusion was difficult, and changing the circumstances would not be possible without a corresponding change of geography. A friend of mine, Mark Hatton, a psychologist, had once helped me understand we all have anchors on which we center ourselves—our friends, our spouse, God, our job. For me, it was a shock to learn that one of my anchors was my busy life itself. In short, my chaos anchored me. Could I let all this go and still be me?

I had always loved bookstores. They seemed the epitome of civility and culture—a pleasant place containing miles of printed words—well-written, thoughtful words, embodying exciting ideas, often thoughtful analysis, and wonderful stories, bound in conveniently sized packages, stacked neatly in sections. Just browsing the shelves was a kick for me. If I liked one of those packages of words, and often I did, I could take the package home.

How orderly. How civilized. Even the smell of lots of books collected together made me happy. The people who worked in a bookstore, at least in a good bookstore, were sort of librarians with pizzazz. I liked it all. It should be noted that every living room I have created has at least one wall filled with books. I know this is a little weird, but hanging out with books seems to make up for at least some stress-producing indignities we all endure every day. Even the new horizons of the cyberworld we were entering seemed okay. I feel challenged and excited when surrounded by an older, more venerable communications medium, text on a page.

Why did I find this environment so comforting? It is really tough to say. Maybe I just like the smell of books. Perhaps it is because all we leave behind is still there between the pages of those neat packages. However, so was all we have become, and the best predictions of what we will become. Perhaps the sheer overwhelming diversity of it all was part of the charm.

By the mid-nineties, when this was all happening, bookstores, as we had known them, began to not work for many folks. *USA Today*, in a little factoid published about this time, informed its readers that only 44 percent of Americans would buy at least one book a year, a paperback at that. Who even had time to read? Good question. My answer then and now is we all need to make time.

Way back in the 1980s, about fifteen years before we took the bookstore plunge, Carol gave me a gift certificate for my birthday to spend the evening at a local bookstore. This gift was much more than just money to buy a book. It was the whole night off to spend at the appointed spot. A babysitter had been arranged and the time allotted. Although we didn't have that much money in those days, as I was still in law school, it was the gift of time that makes this memory stand out. Even before we had money, we didn't seem to have extra time either.

The fifteen years that followed this memorable night were busy ones. Lots of good stuff, success in our chosen professions, three great kids, causes we believed in, and abundant material possessions. But always the unspoken and sometimes said-out-loud mantra, "If I ever find a bookstore for sale in a nice little town…"

I am about to tell you the bookstore story, but first I need a serious detour. There is another thread deep in my life with Carol that needs to be understood to appreciate our plunge into this midcourse correction. That thread is the state of Vermont, its unique people, and its special environment. Eventually, after ten years, we would let the bookstore part of the dream go, but certainly not that of being Vermonters. That die was cast.

As every school child *should* know, the United States traces its lineage to July 4, 1776. On that day, representatives of thirteen colonies, about to become states, declared their states independent and united. What most schoolchildren will not know, unless of course he or she goes to or went to school in Vermont, is that standing on the sidelines, refusing the privilege of joining with their fellow patriots, were the good people of the Green Mountain State. The people of Vermont, independent and tough, occupied land still claimed by the state of New York and were not invited to the party until almost fifteen years later, in 1791.

Being forced to spend the first fifteen years of the American experiment as an independent republic and joining the club only after paying New York reparations—a bribe of $30,000—may have something to do with the fierce independence that to this day characterizes Vermont and Vermonters.

Learning to deal with the rigors of a state dominated by mountains, hardscrabble soil, and long winters may have contributed to the independent spirit that epitomizes Vermont. While these adversities are, of course, not unique to Vermont, they are present in a unique combination, which, when mixed with eccentricities of Yankee New England, seems to affect everything.

Undoubtedly a cliche, many believe Vermont is not just a state but a state of mind. By the mid-1990s, already having spent ten years as part-time residents of Vermont, we had come to heartily agree: Vermont's people were just as unique as its geography.

In very simple terms, the Vermont we loved we found to be populated by two types of people: Vermonters who have always been there and, for lack of a better term, "dropouts." Others will tell you the two-part distinction is better described as Vermonters, those "born" in the state, and "flatlanders," which was everyone else. This analysis based on birthright makes for clever jokes and stories, but it just doesn't really tell the story.

It is the dropouts, the people who had made a conscious decision to live in this tiny state of mountains, hard winters, physical beauty, and an exaggerated sense of community, who came to define the state.

The immigration tradition was well entrenched. Although people have always migrated to the Green Mountain State—Robert Frost in 1920 is one famous dropout—the first real wave of dropouts came in the late sixties. These new arrivals were "flower children" who came looking for a freer, less-materialistic life. A lot of these folks started out homesteading with no water, no electricity, the full boat. Eventually they moved to town or at least into the twentieth century. There's nothing like a born-again materialist, many growing up only as they grow old. Howard Dean and Bernie Sanders, two of our best-known politicians, and Ben and Jerry, our hippie ice cream makers, all started their lives and grew up as New Yorkers.

The dropouts kept coming even after the seventies, of course, but by then they were a cleaned-up, slightly less strident version of their sixties and seventies counterparts. With the arrival of the eighties, a whole new brand of immigrant appeared. These folks, unlike their predecessors, had money and toys and many were only weekend adherents of the Vermont good life, looking for an alternative to the grinding "joys" of corporate yuppiedom. After a while, these latter-day converts quit their high-paid, high-pressure, sometimes thankless jobs and found their way to Vermont as permanent residents. A conscious decision to make a change.

Today's prophets, philosophers, and other assorted sages and public intellectuals tell us what is frequently lacking in modern American society is a sense of community. As daily lives become increasingly rushed, as both parents work outside the home, or nowadays in the home but in front of a computer screen or other smart device for hours on end, or, perhaps most significantly, as families scatter and spread almost routinely, a critical sense of belonging is disappearing.

Growing up in a community, whether it's a sleepy rural village or an inner-city neighborhood, helps develop a sense of identity, of self. It is true that sometimes, that self wanted to get as far away from the community as possible. That's okay, though. A self-image once well formed should seek fertile ground to grow to its full potential.

The problem is that when too many selves fly the coop, the coop is destroyed. If the community consists of several generations of family; community institutions, religious, educational, and otherwise; people who know you and your father and your brother, it can survive. There is still plenty of this in Vermont. Of course, even in Vermont, you have to work for it.

We bought our first house in Vermont in 1988, when our youngest daughter wasn't quite a year old. That's how I remember the year. It was a vacation home. It was down a dirt road and up the mountain in the tiny town of Orange, population 700. The nearest bigger towns were Barre, called the granite capital, and next closest, Montpelier, the actual state capital.

Our home was an old farmhouse at the end of the road that needed lots of work, which we tenderly gave it. Over the years, it gave back to us. Ski weekends, apple cider making, beautiful foliage in the fall, long relaxing visits with family and friends, and most of all, summers in Vermont for the girls and Carol. I commuted on Thursday nights and Monday mornings. For a few summers, we had live-in horses. It was a great retreat. Our neighbors, all full-time Vermonters, became our friends when we were in residence and they became caretakers of our home when we were away. Our friends and family from New Jersey, over the years, all visit and share this little piece of paradise.

After we bought this house, I retreated there, often out of season, with a briefcase and computer in tow, to undertake serious work and writing projects. I found the solitude—even though capable of instantaneous interruption by telephone, fax, and computer—therapeutic and work inducing. My middle daughter, Jordyn, and I often did these weekends as special father-daughter time.

During such a family weekend hiatus, I saw an advertisement for a bookstore for sale in Bristol, Vermont. Bristol was on the other side of the Green Mountains from Orange. Because of those mountains, it stretched into a long, scenic, fifty-four-mile drive. Bristol was a small town of about four thousand on the western foothills of the Green Mountains. It was at the edge of the best farmland in Vermont, an area known as the Champlain Valley.

Vermonters sometimes call the area on this side of the mountain as it stretches down to Lake Champlain the "banana belt," a name that strikes me as entirely too tropical for anything in this mountainous hardscrabble state. It is, however, far flatter than most of Vermont and has lots of dairy farms and orchards. Bristol had a great elementary school and was the home of a regional high school, Mt. Abe, which served Bristol and four nearby towns. The school in Orange was small and, sadly, not very good, so moving there full-time had never been a possibility.

Bristol was, from all appearances, very friendly—the Rotary Club sent me a note of welcome before I even got to town—scenic and complex. Complex because it had a mix of natives—the minority, I think—and folks who had consciously opted for small-town Vermont-style living.

We were surprised to learn that, of all places, New Jersey had a stunningly large number of people who had their roots in Bristol. One of the three local lawyers, the guy who owned the hardware store across the street, the local financial advisor, the guy who was owner and chef of the area's best restaurant, a guy named Kevin Harper who had made lip balm in his sink and now had a hundred-employee factory, the Mary Kay sales lady, and all kinds of other folks all came from our home state.

The bookstore, Deerleap Books, which was for sale, was named for the mountain just outside of town on which we would soon live. Although part of the downtown three-story connected buildings, it was uniquely one story and freestanding with alleys on either side. We bought the bookstore, and courtesy of the former owners, it looked much like an old schoolhouse, complete with a cupola on the top. It had a very open, friendly feel inside, which we improved by adding big front bay windows, a small self-serve café, stuffed chairs, and an excellent sound system.

Unfortunately, in its six-year existence before we bought it, Deerleap Books never made any money. Owned by a couple who also had a newsletter publishing company, it was kind of a stepchild. The couple allowed the employees to run the business, who did well enough to develop a loyal following, but who failed to make it a profitable business.

To be successful, as in making money, bookstores must be more than a place to shop. They have to be virtually a community center, and their owners must keep the special events flowing, the visibility high, and everyone happy. Oh yes, and along the way, sell books, in fact a rather lot of them.

Selling books in the mid-1990s was complicated because it seemed like everyone else was selling books too, from the grocery store to the internet, not to mention the superstores. Could we turn Deerleap Books around? We thought so, despite the challenges.

After I found the bookstore, having come to that point of midcourse correction related above, from all appearances, we rather abruptly packed up and moved to Vermont. Actually, it was nowhere near that easy. We had to put two houses on the market—the big one in New Jersey, which didn't sell until the following year, and the farmhouse in Orange, which we rented for several years and then sold. We had three garage sales, closed on the bookstore, and closed on a house in Bristol. All this occurred between June and August 1996.

We shocked everyone we knew with our announcement of moving. My law partners had the biggest shock. Not only had I started and guided the law firm since its inception ten years earlier, but I had also served as its only managing partner. Their initial reaction was thinking we had to shut the place down. Happily, this feeling dissipated quickly as my partners stepped up to the challenge with my assurance that while I wanted to "step back," I wasn't going anywhere, at least no time soon.

For the first four months that was true, as I continued doing my old job and working my old hours, even after moving. After that, I became a long-distance lawyer, long before everyone else figured out how to do this. I drove to the physical office in New Jersey two or three days most weeks and connected by computer the rest of the time. With the assistance of several great lawyers and staff who still hung out at the office in New Jersey full-time, I never missed a beat. I also had understanding clients, who only gradually found out I no longer lived in New Jersey.

My initial plan was to gradually phase out of New Jersey. This just never happened. First, it soon became apparent the bookstore would never support the lifestyle we had grown accustomed to. Second, the long-distance thing was actually not that hard. Go to New Jersey for a few days each week, work eighteen-hour days there, do the rest from Vermont. Although I did a clerkship to secure a Vermont law license, I kept doing the long-distance law thing and working on the New Jersey–based and national matters I had always worked on.

This continued for almost twenty-five years until the 2020 COVID-19 pandemic caused almost everyone to work from home for a while. As I was already in my late sixties, I decided it was time to let the endless commute go for good.

Back to the bookstore and the initial midcourse correction. Was the bookstore profitable after we made all our improvements? Not so much. Although we increased sales more than 200 percent, it was never very profitable. Although it made a little money each year, neither Carol, who literally ran the place, nor I, who did backroom stuff, including the bookkeeping, ever paid ourselves.

We eventually learned that bookstores were generally not destined to be big moneymakers ever again, certainly not the little independent ones. We worked hard at it though; luckily we also had a lot of fun doing it—events every Friday night, promotions of all kinds, our newsletter, young author's nights, a new Gallery at Deerleap, book groups, author signings, sales.

So why own a bookstore, if it didn't make money? Not a bad question. Well, why do any of this? Obviously, it was never about money for us. That is what I kept telling myself. Carol sometimes queried whether I knew how hard this would be before we got in so deep. I usually just grunted in reply.

We truly loved the bookstore. Carol maybe even more than I did. I had dragged her along on my dream, and now that we were in it and I pointed out it was a very expensive hobby, she was not about to abandon the ship. The staff we inherited when we bought the bookstore eventually figured us out and became our friends, as did our many customers. We hired more staff as the customers also became numerous.

At Deerleap Books we got to do it all. Carol out front and me in the backroom. Unlike the law office where others cleared away life's little annoyances so I could practice law, at the bookstore I attached the stamps, paid the bills, kept the books, and did my own filing. I also tore up the cardboard boxes and took them, along with all our garbage, to the dump once a week. What's more, I enjoyed doing it, almost all of it.

What I did not enjoy was starting over at home. Carol and I have owned, count them, five fixer-upper homes. We had never owned a new home. I confess that at forty-four years old, it was harder than our first fixer-upper at twenty-two. Our Bristol house was in a perfect spot, on the side of a mountain with a great view, within walking distance of the downtown area. Both girls could walk to school. The bookstore on Main Street was less than a mile away, so walkable too. Yet we lived on a dirt road among the trees. Unfortunately, the house itself was basically a mess, in pretty much every way.

Our last house in Ridgewood, New Jersey, also needed lots of work, but it was a grand old house built in stages in the 1700s, 1800s, and early in the twentieth century. It was worthy of being fixed. Our Vermont house on the hill fixer-upper needed work just as badly, but not because it was ever grand and had fallen into disrepair. Rather, it had been sloppily built just twenty years earlier and indifferently maintained after that.

It just did not seem worthy of all the effort. Of course, the lack of time and money engendered by the bookstore, which must necessarily be our primary focus, made the project more daunting. With the bookstore and home-front challenges, not to mention my long commute to New Jersey, we initially felt like we were fighting a multifront war.

Had the grand experiment at midcourse correction worked? Some positives were apparent. We thought our new hometown was great. Carlyn, the youngest, at nine years old, adjusted immediately. She flourished in a community that offered lots of friends and fewer pretensions. Our then-fourteen-year-old, Jordyn, adapted more slowly. The ups and downs of adolescence, which are without geographic boundaries, made her situation tough to evaluate, but moving a freshman in high school from a sophisticated suburb to a country school was clearly tough.

Both girls, however, did well in their new schools, with lots of friends, and they acknowledged that people "were more real here." For parents, this is no small blessing. Our oldest daughter, Ciera, was already off in a different world as a student in and resident of New York City when we moved, but she felt a little dislocated by the loss of her New Jersey home.

We found and joined a great church, welcoming and spirit filled. Carol and I made new friends too, but slowly. Becoming a good friend takes an investment of time, which unfortunately we still had too little of.

The best news for Carol and me was that our strong relationship grew stronger. At the very beginning of our marriage, Carol and I owned a business, the Gazebo. We worked together well then, but with a lot of rough edges. Not so much now. After years of supervising others, I saw Carol clearly for what she was, the most talented and dedicated worker I have ever known. She says the change was all mine, as in how I perceived her, not that she had actually changed. She might be right, but I think it was some of both.

Moving back and forth between my new life in Vermont and my

old life as a lawyer in New Jersey sometimes felt downright weird. Well-meaning friends at both ends had no real understanding of my other life, and I sometimes felt as if I were living two lives. A retired Episcopal priest in Bristol who I became friends with shared an article with me he had recently written opining that a change in life of any kind results in a grieving process. I thought he might be right. But grieving a life left behind is much more complicated when you keep visiting it.

What had I learned? Something I already knew: nothing is as simple as it seems. While we had begun a journey toward simplicity, we had actually made very little progress, maybe even fallen back a little. It took guts and determination to do this, and we felt good about what we had accomplished. As the bookstore would not make enough money to support our family, and that long-distance law was going to be how I supported us, I needed to adjust the plan, and I did.

As it turned out, a small-town bookstore in Vermont was not in the master plan for us, rather just another in life's many learning experiences. T. S. Eliot once said, "We shall never cease from striving, and the end of all our striving will be to arrive where we began and to know the place for the first time."

The bookstore plan came to its end in December 2006. We had operated Deerleap Books for ten years. Carlyn, the baby, had just moved on to college at Northeastern University in Boston. As usual, I drove the change, but, ever loyal and supportive, Carol would help make it work.

Since the bookstore did not make money, it could not be sold without overrepresenting its potential, which I did not want to do. For this reason we had to close it. I had a new idea, however. I wanted to create a family foundation to help students in the developing world. This seemed more worthy of the vast amounts of volunteer time we put into selling books. I thought I could still build a community, but now a bigger, more international one. With sadness by us, and by a community that had not responded nearly as well to our use-it-or-lose-it requests for support, we liquidated and closed Deerleap Books.

The space was quickly repurposed and has been the home for many years to Art on Main, an artist's co-op we helped found and set up a few years earlier. We still own the building and have offices in the back half from which we run our real estate businesses as well as support the foundation back-office operations.

Course corrections are hard. I have a dear friend who went from corporate HR to owning and operating roller rinks. Another went from law to stand-up comedy. Both loved the change. When people who would tell me moving to Vermont to own and run a bookstore was "living their dream," I would think, "Oh my, you have no idea." We love Vermont and being Vermonters. However, in reality, the midcourse correction went much differently than we thought it would. I never imagined I would do a long-distance commute to New Jersey for twenty-five years to make this work, nor that after ten years the bookstore dream would evolve into an international foundation dream, but both worked. Not easy, but great.

BIG GOD

God shows up everywhere in my life and thus is all over this book. Knowing God, living with God, and living in accordance with God's plan is really the essence of my approach to living—this and giving back in accordance with the blessings I have received from God.

So, who or what is God for me? Even a casual reading of this book will reveal I sometimes refer to God as He but sometimes He or She. I never use "it," but that would actually be correct as well. I am not gender confused. I actually do not think of God as having one. Sometimes with the support of a quiet, proud father, sometimes with overwhelming love of a mother, sometimes as a master creator, often with a universality of incredible natural beauty and the constancy of human conscience, my God is never mean, spiteful, unforgiving, or selfish. God to me is really undefinable, unexplainable, unfathomable. See how these words fail at even defining what God is not, never mind what God is.

The dictionary definition of God begins with the statement that God is the supreme ultimate reality. Elsewhere, God is the creator and preserver of all things, the spirit or being that controls the universe, the source of all moral authority. He is said to be omnipotent, omniscient, and omnipresent; to philosophers he is perfect, immutable, eternal, the apex of all being and knowledge. Even Albert Einstein, in many ways the epitome of scientific logic, who thought of the Bible as a collection of legends and fables, thought God was the explanation of the unexplainable creation of the universe. He elaborated, at one point relying on Baruch Spinoza to say God reveals Himself in the lawful harmony of the world but not concerning Himself with the fate and doings of mankind.

To me, God is all these things and more. My God is not as distant as Einstein's, not as jealous as the Old Testament tells us He or She is, nor as fire and brimstone as Dwight Moody and all manner of Puritan preachers declared Him. My God is bigger than all this, more universal, more all-encompassing, more understanding, and more forgiving.

For me, I love to commune with God, to pray to God, basically just talk to Him or Her quietly inside my head. This connection is a vital force in my life and makes me feel complete. I revel in God's grace and deeply appreciate that He or She lets me begin every day anew with a fresh slate.

I am very comfortable that God gets to judge me each day and at the end of my life. For me, this process feels very much like it should be very private. This relationship with God and even how I think of Him or Her is mine and only mine. Between me and God. I am allowed to share, but doing so is up to me. No one gets to dissect or judge my relationship with God.

All too often, the religions created by men and women seem to get in the way of all this. Once men and women start guiding each other in how to have a relationship with God, many start judging each other as well. When this happens frequently, God's grace, His most powerful of messages, can be lost.

For believers in God, I think it is fine to encourage others to also believe, and to gather with others of similar mind if they are so inclined. But in the end, I profoundly believe we must let all God's children find their own path and know their own glory.

I always seek to understand God's plan for me and to live it. That is my most important job here on this earth. However, I recognize and understand that God will likely allow me full knowledge and understanding of His or Her plan only infrequently. I freely recognize the plan may be just too big, too complex (or for that matter, too simple) or too magnificent for me to understand. I believe God is not likely to *tell* me what His or Her plan is. If I watch very closely, He or She may sometimes *show* me, and I should remain alert for the message. With this in mind, I am open to confronting the face of God everywhere and know that sometimes it will come when we least expect it.

I will talk a lot about my views on evangelicals later but here I should at least mention how I come down in the divide between those Christians who believe as did Martin Luther and later John Calvin, in solo fide, "faith alone" in Jesus Christ as the key to a relationship with God. I believe in faith for sure, but also believe as stated in James 2:17 "faith without works is dead." Dietrich Bonhoeffer, the German Lutheran pastor who resisted Hitler's nazification of Germany, is uniquely revered by both camps and in some ways exemplifies the sheer difficulty of this divide. Bonhoeffer made the distinction between easy grace (just believe) and hard grace but then in the end became part of an active conspiracy to assassinate Hitler, and just as the war was ending was martyred for his activities. In the end, Bonhoeffer took action. This is where I come out. Talking is good; walking the walk is essential.

Prayer is how I talk to God. While sometimes I feel the need to do this purposefully and with focus, to quiet my thoughts, mostly for me prayer is also constant chatter on the fly. In 1997, I was asked to preach a sermon at the church we attended in Ridgewood, New Jersey. I wrote a prayer to share, which incorporated a lot of my collected thoughts on this at the time. This effort has weathered well, and although I am not into recited prayer, rather just talking with God, if I were, this would be a good summary of how I would say what I have to say.

My Prayer

Lord, help me to always know I'm here to do your will, not mine.
Help me know your will.
As I plan my life, influence my plan.
Lord, help me to always appreciate my many blessings.
Help me to use my blessings and to give of, and from, them to others.
Help me to have a positive attitude, seeking out
  the best in everything and everybody.
Lord, help me to not overly focus on the annoyances of life,
  rather to revel in its special moments and special people.
Help me to cherish everything about our natural world, and
  work to preserve it for my children and generations to come.
Lord, give me the time to be a real person, to listen, to truly care,
  to really be there for friends, and for loved ones in need.
Lord, watch over my loved ones and bless my family; watch
  over them, give them peace, help them to know you.
Lord, thank you for your grace.
Help me to not take advantage of your never-ending
  willingness to excuse my many failings.
Lord, if it be your will, use me to do your work.
Lord, please help me to be the best person I possibly can.
Thank you, Lord.

Me and my dad, about 1955. I think I am three.

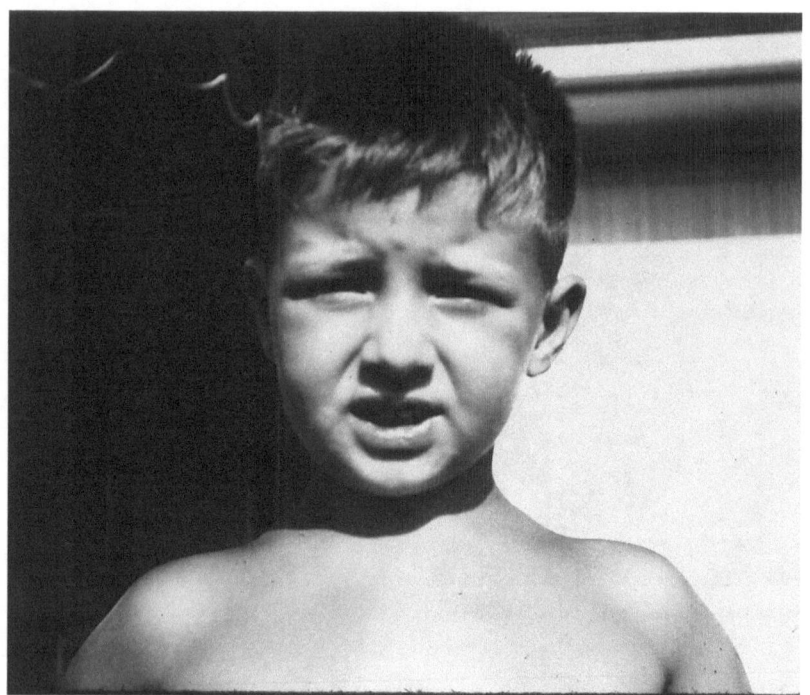

Me at five years old

Easter Sunday, 1965. My grandmother, Mamie, Holly, my mom, baby Juliann, Peter, Jeff, and me. Kerry did not arrive until !972. My dad took the picture.

Confirmation Sunday, 1967. Note me towering over my mom at age fifteen.

Front page of *New York Daily News*, August 16, 1969. Me and my buddy, Tim Imbrie, in my mother's station wagon on our way to Woodstock.

Carol, me, and my mom, 1972

SECTION II

Giving Back

When I met with my editors to talk about writing this memoir, they wanted me to focus it on a single overriding message. I had the idea of making this message "giving back." This is as close as I get to an abiding life philosophy. If anything is a common thread of my actions and beliefs, this is it. However, I decided since this book was about other things as well, and occasionally more lighthearted, it made no sense to tie every chapter to this message. With this in mind, I chose to divide my "giving back" story into the following four chapters. The first tells where all this "giving back" philosophy comes from and how it has guided me. After that, I spend time talking about my first trips to Africa and then to Haiti, two places where I have labored hard at giving back over the years. The last story is about the foundation I started twenty years ago and all that it has become. Maybe this all should have been in its own book. I just had so much more I wanted to talk about and no inclination to write a multivolume tome.

God's Gifts

I BELIEVE IN GIVING BACK. IT IS, IN MANY WAYS, MY LIFE PHIlosophy. When I was a kid, my mom had a wall plaque in the kitchen that said something like, "What we are is God's gift to us. What we become is our gift to God." I did not discover until much later that this quote, one I took on as a core belief, was not the distilled thought of a great theologian or philosopher. It is attributed instead to a mid-last-century dancer and actress, Eleanor Powell. Her other famous quote is, "I'd rather dance than eat!" Which just proves wisdom is everywhere if we just pay attention and look for it.

So, inspired by Eleanor, or at least her words, from when I was just a little kid until right now, I have always felt very grateful for my blessings and just as strongly obligated to give back. I know my more evangelical brethren pronounce that it is not about "acts," rather our love of God that demonstrates our faith, but to me the former demonstrates the latter. This said, I sometimes think I am less a good guy than one driven by a sense of guilt, or perhaps tradition. No matter what, I always try to care for others and give back, so the result is good.

I do not carry this good-guy behavior to what I believe would be an illogical extreme. I do not reject all materialism, not by any means. In fact, I live rather well, and I have some pretty big toys. This troubles me sometimes, but not so much that I change. However, I do not believe he who dies with the most toys wins. I am much prouder of what I have done for others than what I have.

I believe a sense of balance is the best. To me, and I suspect to almost all of us, this struggle between serving others and taking for ourselves is a daily one. To really win this struggle and be at peace with your role in the world is to know God, as He or She manifests Himself or Herself in us.

Stop. Read that sentence again. I think it is important. Maybe one of the most important things I say in this whole book. I am profoundly grateful I get to continue this struggle and every day do my best. The struggle between our best and worst selves is what life is.

I think all religions, especially mine, Christianity, can be distilled into the profound wisdom of the Golden Rule. The simple words of Jesus Christ, "Do unto others as you would have them do unto you," literally say it all.

Don't get me wrong. I am not a complete Goody Two-shoes. I can fight hard, I am notoriously blunt, I often impatiently talk over others, but my sweet spot is I absolutely love to give back of my blessings and to help others.

Public service came early to me and by example. My mom was a Girl Scout leader, PTO president, hospital volunteer, and more. For my dad, it was the Jaycees, then Rotary, the school board, and for many years a Sunday school teacher. Public service was mainstream in my family long before President John Kennedy asked us all to "Ask not what your country can do for you—ask what you can do for your country."

As I grew up, I followed all this with zeal, joining everything in sight. Because I liked to talk and perhaps because I was always tall, I also easily fell into leadership positions of anything I became involved in. For me, in school, this was student government, the newspaper, the yearbook, and debate club; outside of school, it was Boy Scouts, the YMCA, church, and church youth group. Later, like my dad, this took the form of service clubs, particularly Rotary, once I was in the working world; I also helped lots of nonprofits and the YMCA.

The YMCA is worthy of special mention. I first found the YMCA as a camper at age nine. By my teens, I was in the Hi-Y service club, then a volunteer leader. I joined what they called Youth and Government and progressed from legislator to speaker of the house, then finally youth governor of New Jersey in my third year.

After high school graduation, my YMCA connection kept going. In college, I joined a group called Concern & Action, which was the secularized version of Christian Association cleverly utilizing the original first letters, from what even earlier had been the campus YMCA. In law school, I was active in another renamed but similarly valued offshoot. The law school version was aimed at keeping all their budding professionals, lawyers, doctors, and nurses mostly grounded in moral principles, including my favorite, giving back.

As soon as my legal career brought me back to New Jersey in the early 1980s, I joined the board of directors of the YMCA I had belonged to as a kid. I had served on the very same board fifteen years earlier as "student representative." This time, while I loved all of the Y, my passion became World Service. Unlike the gym and swim and so many regular YMCA activities, the mission of World Service was focusing on helping Ys in the developing world.

When I was the chair of the board of directors and president of the Y, I brought our CEO with me on a trip to Kenya to observe our Y's mission efforts and those of another Y. I was hooked and have stayed active in this initiative ever since. My work with the Y eventually developed into the Wells Mountain Initiative (WMI), which I discuss in greater detail in the upcoming chapter.

Besides giving back through the Y, I found ways to give back through my law firm as well. Helping nonprofits became an important part of my day job as a lawyer. Over the years, I represented many nonprofits, from hospitals to social service agencies, mental health providers, churches, synagogues, and volunteer fire departments. These were usually paying clients, although often at a substantial discount.

At some point, I made my legal expertise in nonprofit formation, organization, and governance a personal program of giving back. I put the word out that I would help new nonprofits get started. The plan was simple enough. I would do all the paperwork to form the legal entity, usually a corporation, get the 501(c)(3) tax exemption from the IRS, and then help set up the governance. This would normally cost from five to seven thousand dollars in legal fees and filing costs. Most times, we donated this money.

The governance piece—figuring out how the organization would run itself, how it would raise money, what it would spend, how to put the funds it raised into an endowment—I would handle by staying on the newly formed board of directors for at least one year. I did this over and over again, for schools, hospitals, libraries, and even one museum. When the underlying organization was supported by public funds—schools, for instance—the nonprofits were usually some form of "friends of" organization to provide the extra stuff. This was great fun and gratifying.

That last point is key: "fun and gratifying." This is what I preach to our WMI Scholars. This is what I believe. Elsewhere, I will tell you that relationships are so much more important to creating a great life than are acquisitions. Giving back from your blessings has always been the critical element for me.

White Guy in Africa

DURING AN EIGHT-DAY VISIT TO KENYA IN 1989, I HAD THE opportunity to visit nine YMCA branches. Not only was Kenya a new destination for me, but I had never set foot on the continent of Africa. My eyes needed opening—big time. They were. On the surface, I learned that black people, as I always thought, were just the same as white people, but as to skin color in Africa, black people were more often just that, black, not the many shades I had become accustomed to in the United States. Until I visited Africa, I never understood how much twentieth-century African Americans had interbred with whites. I immediately knew I needed to know just how much of this had resulted from slave ownership, or perhaps other unhappy Jim Crow events. Skin color was and always will be a meaningless distinction.

I also learned that poor people in Africa outpaced what I thought of as poor in America. I had read this, of course, but now I got to see it and feel it. This kind of poverty meant a staggering degree of lack of opportunity, possessions, or even basic sustenance. It did not, however, mean an automatic loss of spirit, compassion, or even contentment.

There was so much to learn for this middle-class, middle-aged white guy from America. I tried to take it all in, absorb and comprehend. It was a lot for me.

The YMCA, in Kenya as in most developing nations, is not so much the gym and swim family institution we know in the US. Instead, it works to help local people provide very basic social and human services. As such, I visited vocational schools, agricultural projects, safe latrine programs, safe spring and well projects, health programs, and day care centers. The highlight of the visit was the village of Kondo, where the Ridgewood YMCA had been working with villagers for eight years to install a water system.

The various YMCA projects sometimes had "partnerships" with YMCAs and other organizations in the developed world. The Ridgewood YMCA partnership with Kondo was a good example of this type of partnership. Over the years, more than $20,000 of Ridgewood YMCA financial support and Kondo labor had built first a school and now the first phase of running water to the center of the village.

As representatives of the US institution that had supported this village, we got the royal treatment. When we arrived, the entire village was out on the dirt road leading to the village to greet us. As "Mr. President," I was presented with a walking staff and seated to watch a presentation of dance and welcome and then fed abundantly. I quickly observed in the local culture I sat with the men, who seemed to do a lot of that—sit, that is—and the women did all the work.

We toured the village and the water project we had funded. Much of the pipe had not been laid yet and, worse, the pump we had supplied had been stolen. The water project was simple enough. Take water from a canal, perhaps a mile away, pump it into a storage tower of sorts, and then pipe it to several spigots located at the heart of the village and its school. This would eliminate hundreds of hours of women and girls carrying needed water in containers (usually on their heads) from the canal.

The need of the villagers was plain enough, a better supply of water. My plan was not just to give money to help this happen but to send groups of high-school-age US "campers" on service-learning experiences to help dig the trenches and lay the pipes. To me, this was a win. Over the years, I was involved in setting up these types of service-learning experiences, first here, and then in western Africa,

Mexico, the Dominican Republic, and Haiti. Both daughters, Carlyn and Jordyn, went on these trips, Jordyn later leading trips. The win-win produced much needed local improvements and simultaneously broadened the perspective of some US upper- or middle-class teenagers. We repeated these trips whenever they could be done.

For me, another highlight of this first Kenya trip was a visit to the largest slum in Nairobi, a place where my daughter Jordyn would spend several years working two decades later. Kibera was a slum along the railroad tracks in central Nairobi. It had an estimated seven hundred thousand inhabitants (some say in the millions). At this time, there were few permanent structures, just shanties. There was no electricity or plumbing. Sewage ran down the middle or side of a dirt road, in an open ditch. Children were running everywhere. There were few, if any, schools.

One of the infrequent yet somewhat permanent structures was a small YMCA compound in the middle of the area. Unfortunately, it had no running water. Staff spent several hours each day carrying water to the compound. The YMCA had a small vocational school that taught a dozen women and girls how to sew. It also had a day care center with 140 small children and two teachers. On the day I was there, 110 students were in attendance. They had just finished their meal of rice and beans. In most cases, it would be the only meal they would have that day, and it was the reason their parents had sent them to the day care center. It was nap time. All 110 children crowded into a small room, lying sardine-style for a nap on the concrete floor. Only about thirty of the children could share a few torn, soiled mattresses. The day care center had no furniture.

The Kenya Central YMCA was working to either run water to Kibera or to dig a well. This was a priority as it would allow staff to bathe children who badly needed it and eliminate the hours of staff time diverted to carrying drinking and cooking water to the compound.

When I got back, Carol and I and our daughters were committed to raising the necessary funds to purchase mattresses and furniture for the day care center. It was in many ways a drop in the bucket, but it significantly improved the lives of these children. By working the YMCA network, I found a way that the furniture could be built in a local YMCA vocational school by students learning carpentry and joinery skills. It would be well built but inexpensive and would give work to these students. The total cost would be about $4,000—$10 per mattress, $22 for a table, $13 for a chair.

I included this appeal in our annual Christmas letter. I was gratified to quickly raise the money from a dozen friends and family members. I think Christmas felt just a little bit more meaningful in all the households of those who helped.

I did several more important things when I got home. I wanted to have a continued impact on the community. The goal was to send groups of high-school-age US "campers" on service-learning experiences. I reported back to the Ridgewood YMCA and began deep partnerships that lasted many years. Within a year, we began annual visits of service-learning groups of a dozen US high school kids going to Kondo to work on the water project and later the school. The villagers benefited and so did the middle-class American students who were part of this experience.

I also went to my daughter Jordyn's second-grade class. The class was studying Africa, and I brought it alive with stories, pictures, and many craft items I had brought back. This first exposure to Africa and later visits to our home by African students piqued her interest. This led to her interest in visiting the continent in high school and a career that has had Africa at its center after that. It's a bigger story though, and hers to tell, not mine.

Visiting Africa, my first trip to what we then called a "third-world country" changed me. My eyes opened wider to the world and the people in it. I developed more perspective on what it meant to be an African, but also on being black in America. I saw real profound poverty. I saw community and gratefulness when there was little to be grateful for. I saw many opportunities to help. I became determined to do more and to make sure others, in particular young US teenagers, could learn what I learned. It was a beginning.

In This Truck...a Haiti Perspective

IN SEPTEMBER 2001, JUST TWO WEEKS AFTER THE 9/11 ATTACK on the World Trade Center, I went on my first trip to Haiti. This trip made quite an impression on me and would become the first trip of many. What follows next are my words written then, reflecting my very first impressions of the country:

> When you are over six feet tall, standing in the back of a rack body truck, even sometimes a fast moving one, is a great vantage point. From eleven feet up, there is not much you don't see. This is how I saw Haiti when I first visited this year, or at least more of it, and in Haiti, our hemisphere's poorest country, there is a lot to look at.
>
> The truck of which I speak, a 1976 vintage 3/4-ton box truck converted to its present use as the lifeblood of orphanage transportation. It was this truck that met us at the congested Port Au Prince airport, a welcome sight for sixteen travelers with forty-five giant duffle bags of clothing, tools, medicines, and supplies and our own backpacks, in the process of being overwhelmed by a throng of would-be helpers desperate to make

some money. This is the truck that somehow had room for the mountain of luggage and for most of us travelers on top of the pile.

In this truck, we traveled across Haiti for a promised four-and-one-half-hour trip that took seven-and-one-half hours, the last three hours in the dark, over roads that varied from bad to nonexistent. We saw wrenching scenes of poverty and smelled a world where meals are prepared over open charcoal fires and garbage is left to rot. We saw Haitians end their days, gather to eat, and then converse in a world without television, radio, or the internet and hardly any electricity.

From this truck, we saw the horribly smashed remains of the other orphanage vehicle, in which its assistant director and three passengers died in a head-on collision the day before, on their way to meet us at the airport. We contemplated this unspeakable tragedy and the realities of truly scary third-world driving, with bad lights, rutted roads, no signals, no guardrails, few signs, and aggressive passing in both directions.

The next morning, in this truck, we first saw the orphanage and its sea of smiling, hopeful, little faces. We saw and smelled street after street of open markets, produce, meat, and grain lying open for inspection and the bugs and heat of midday. In this truck, we saw Mother Teresa's mission and sensed its healing peace in the midst of poverty. We rode to a cinder-block factory to buy blocks to build shelves that would not submit to termites, and sitting on top of the cinder blocks, we rode home. We picked up supplies, and in this truck, we went to the dump filled to overflowing with the detritus of areas, from within the orphanage grounds, that, were it not for some overzealous North Americans, would have stayed where it landed.

In this truck, we rode back and forth to the Project Hope (*Proje Espwa*) orphanage every day, finding comfort in a breeze that miraculously seemed to cool the air, otherwise so heavy with heat and humidity that it made even Haitians sweat. In this truck, we experienced the unspeakable joy of seventy orphan boys, together with a couple of us "Blancs," stuffed like sardines and yet hanging out all over, driving down city streets then over country roads, through a river, and over an unimaginably decrepit bridge to journey to the beach, and we made a wild, naked dash to the ocean.

In this truck, a big white guy and his companions were worthy of stares, and with eye contact sought and made, and waves exchanged, a mountain of differences disappeared, and worlds connected.

I wrote what you have just read shortly after arriving home from the trip. The "In this Truck" theme strikes me a little forced now as I reread it, but I left it for you. This trip was the first of more than thirty visits I have made to this country. It began a deep connection for me with the people of Haiti.

Talking about Haiti brings me to a discussion of two dear friends with which my life intersected and was made better by our common connection to this country. The first of these is my Haitian brother, Gwenael. As a "brother" is how I always refer to Gwenael Apollon and how I think of him.

I met Gwenael not in Haiti but in, of all places, Indianapolis, Indiana. In the fall of 2002, I attended a World Service conference, which gathered YMCAs working on this common mission from the US, Canada, and Mexico. Not all Ys do world service, and those that do like to gather periodically to share ideas. The three-country gathering, which occurred every other year, was always special.

Gwenael was new to the YMCA and had come to learn about possible partnerships. He had a table where he stood, telling his Haiti story. It was not a long one at this point. A year earlier, the YMCA of Quebec had offered to be the financial supporter if he would restart a YMCA in Haiti. Previous YMCA efforts in Haiti had long been dormant.

For both of us, the reason you go to these conferences, for ideas and synergy, were accomplished by our meeting. I went right to his table, having made my above-described visit to his country the prior year and now fomenting a plan to go back and bring others.

I told Gwenael of my upcoming, already-scheduled trip and intention to bring with me a friend, client, and active philanthropist, David Bolger. David, often hard to impress, had remembered the Mellon family work in Haiti and had agreed to come with me. I made a breakfast date for the three of us at the Hotel Montana in Port-au-Prince when we would be there. I scheduled this meeting with Gwenael at the end of a trip, which would also include the orphanage in Les Cayes.

I went back to see Gwenael and the YMCA again only a few months after the trip with David. This time I brought with me Ridgewood YMCA CEO Rick Clayton and friend and super volunteer Bob Dill. As a result, we three started an official partnership between the Ridgewood YMCA and the YMCA d'Haiti and began supporting its soccer camp. In future years, this camp would grow to be a countrywide event with hundreds of campers and US coaches and supplies. My law partner, Jim Delia, went to Haiti to run this for two weeks every summer for nine years. The camp was magnificent, and so was his commitment.

Over the years, Gwenael and I came together many times. I went to Haiti. He came to the US. Sometimes we met in Montreal, his other home. We did projects: book drives, clothing drives for the Y, computer collections, disaster relief, and, of course, the ever-growing summer soccer (now multisport) nationwide camp that moved around to different locations.

Gwenael and his wife, Marie Lawrence, were what I consider very special Haitians. They were Haitians by choice, not because they had to be. Both had family roots in Haiti, but both had grown up outside of Montreal, Canada. Both were Canadian citizens. They had moved to Haiti together as a young married couple after getting their education in Canada. For a country where the diaspora is distinguished by its support, those who have stayed to live in the country, but where the clamor for a passport to leave is never-ending, this is extraordinary.

Marie Lawrence spent her entire career working for the Haitian central bank. Gwenael started in business, but in 2001, he took on the YMCA job. I say job, but most years he never paid himself, though he certainly had a job title and plenty to do. This extraordinary couple lived in Petionville, a suburb outside the city and up the mountain from Port-au-Prince. They raised their three kids there. One by one each of these children went off to Canada for their university education. One by one they chose to stay in Canada where opportunities were better and safety was much more assured. The pull to leave Haiti was relentless.

On January 12, 2010, Haiti experienced a horrible earthquake. It was a 7.0 on the Richter scale, frightening enough, but which does not tell the full story. Structures in Haiti, particularly housing, were never substantial. The earthquake took 250,000 lives and left 1.5 million people homeless and living in tents and other makeshift accommodations for years.

When this happened, I wanted to help. I knew I was not in the first-aid business, so it would need to be some other way. I decided to run a food and supplies drive, mostly clothes. I put out the word. My idea was to fill a container (eight feet by eight feet by forty feet) with clothes and supplies and ship them to Haiti.

I was accidentally way too successful. The story of what had happened in Haiti was compelling, and Americans are generous. When the dust cleared from my outreach, I had to borrow an empty twenty-thousand-square-foot warehouse from a client, Paramus Building Supply, and I filled it up! We had enough stuff for not one container but twelve of them.

Along the way, Do Something, a nonprofit my daughter Jordyn then worked for, had arranged for a donation from Aeropostale, a young-woman-focused retailer, of, get this, 200,000 pairs of jeans. The lesson here is to be careful what you wish for. This whole project, which I started with a $10,000 budget of mostly my own money, took a year to get the stuff to Haiti and the budget grew to more than $130,000, which required lots of fundraising.

When we realized how many containers we needed, I also shifted from renting them to buying them and thought of what we could do with them in Haiti. Our first thought was housing, but later we thought about utilizing two containers parallel to each other, ends facing forward but spread apart and building a large room between them. This design would create a very functional freestanding YMCA, one that was pretty much earthquake proof as well.

The first container Y was planned for Laboule, Haiti, in Petionville. Gwenael secured some land on top of a mountain and started planning. I had the design worked out and hunted for volunteers. My friend David Bolger gave $25,000. It took a whole year to get the containers of clothes and supplies to Haiti. I organized two groups to go down. The first group would open the containers and distribute the clothes, and a separate group would build the first container Y. Our first major distribution of clothes, which would continue an effort that would go on for more than a year, was on our final day at Laboule. We had a great circle of tables and so many grateful recipients.

Among the supplies were a great number of doors and windows that Paramus Building Supply had donated. Mostly mismatched and left over from customer orders gone wrong, they were perfect for the containers. We also brought tools and the supplies we needed to build the entire building.

The Laboule branch would be the first of six container YMCAs we built. Over time, the design evolved. The width between the containers grew from sixteen to twenty feet, three containers became just two, and the steel superstructure for the roof trusses got stronger but lighter. Each time a work crew of eight to twelve American volunteers arrived, they, together with other Haitians, placed the containers; cut steel; welded miles of angle iron; installed doors, windows, and interior partition walls; and built the roof trusses in about two weeks. They finished up the electric and plumbing in a bathroom, installed the metal roof, and poured and tiled a floor after we left. All this was completed by volunteers or Haitian contractors.

To do one of these container Ys required a $25,000 donation, the donated materials and tools, and all the volunteer labor. The volunteers paid for their own travel costs. Gwenael worked miracles with the donation and turned the good start into a completed YMCA—not just built but painted and furnished. A fully functioning YMCA by my best calculation for about $50,000, or $30 a foot. We did this in Laboule in 2011, Croix Des Bouquets in 2013, Dessalines in 2014, Caracol in 2015, Laurent (near Les Cayes) in 2017, and finally Jacmel in 2019.

I can't say enough about the volunteers who helped over the years. Long, hard days of hot, sweaty work, but also a sense of comradery. Special mention goes to those who came back again and again. My friend Andy Topp, the minister contractor whom I will talk about in depth in a minute, was there with his truck and tools for every trip except the last one. My brother, Jeff, worked on the initial design. My nephew, Phil, also an architect, took over and helped on every trip, bringing friends. He repeatedly led the design and construction teams with Andy. Among Phil's architectural school friends who returned many times were Mike Taglivia, Jennifer Bennet, and Andres Spinney. Pete Reyer, Kevin Schloerb, and his daughter, Carrie, returned three times. My dear friend and YMCA and WMI buddy Bob Dill never missed a trip. Brian Hughes, YMCA board president and later chair of the trustees, came three times and also brought his son. My son-in-law, Dave Jones, came back three times and also paid for and brought one of his employees, Moses Villanueva.

There were no shirkers on the crew unless you count me; I was more a facilitator and procurer than any kind of skilled help. Somehow, Phil, Andy, and Dave got the dirtiest and were the hardest to get off-site at the end of each day. I cannot say enough about everyone who helped. I am grateful for all those who I named here and everyone else who was ever on one of these trips.

After years of steady progress and growth, the YMCA d'Haiti story has taken a sad turn as I write this. Arm in arm with Gwenael and supporting his leadership from our first meeting in 2002, we kept building. I was privileged to serve on the Haiti Y's board of directors for much of this time as the one non-Haitian. From one small branch in Port-au-Prince to more than twelve branches throughout the country, we served thousands of members, young people, and families.

Then came COVID-19 and the assassination of Haitian President Jovenel Moise in July 2021. After the assassination, this always-struggling country descended into chaos. Unsafe streets forced many into their homes. Schools and institutions had to close. Anyone who had a way out of Haiti left. After struggling to keep something going all year and then finally having the Port-au-Prince national office ransacked, in December 2022, the Board of the YMCA d'Haiti voted to close all operations and tried to maintain its facilities. As I write this, only four branches have reopened, and the Y is a mere shadow of what it had grown to be.

Beginning in 2021, Marie Lawrence suffered major health issues that required hospitalization in Miami, and ultimately, she and Gwenael moved to where care was more easily reachable. With the Y closing, Gwenael and Marie Lawrence are now back in Montreal, at least most of the time. The idea of him not being in Haiti to lead the YMCA is sad, but as his friend and brother, so is the idea of him going back. It makes me heartsick to think of all this.

Turning to my dear friend Andy Topp will not lighten this story, especially if I start at the end. Here I go. I was sitting in the kitchen of our Vermont house at 3:00 p.m. on the afternoon of May 4, 2018, when Andy's wife, Milande, called me. Milande had grown up in Haiti and had lived in the US less than a year at that point, so she was not always easy to understand. She was also crying, sobbing really.

The news was the worst possible. Andy had died in a plane crash just minutes before. On hearing the news, Milande did what Andy had told her to do if things went really bad. He said, "Call Tom." I was gut punched. Andy had been flying in his single-engine plane for years, and although I, as an ex-pilot, always told him how crazy that was, I felt God watched out for Andy. I must have believed this because I once let my son-in-law Dave join him on one of his over-the-ocean single-engine flights to Haiti. I often flew with him myself.

I had first met Andy about thirty-five years earlier in 1986. He was then the part-time assistant minister at the Old Paramus Reformed Church. That's the church I grew up attending, and that's where Carol and I returned when we moved back to New Jersey. Andy was a half-time minister, half-time contractor. He was maybe five years younger than me, and we became friends. When we put a small addition and deck on our house, Andy was our contractor.

The senior minister changed at the church soon after we arrived. As is typical with ministers, just like CEOs, the boss makes decisions about their team. The new guy thought a change in Andy's position would be a good idea. By then I was on the consistory, the governing body of the church, and as a lawyer and a friend, they gave me the task of telling Andy. I did it over lunch, and it went reasonably well. He would take my suggestion and treat this as his idea and announce that he would be leaving.

I stayed pretty connected with Andy thereafter, mostly through Rotary. Although we were in different clubs, we were both involved in district projects, like Youth Exchange and Gift of Life. It was through Rotary we got close again. The In This Truck trip in 2001 was sponsored by the Ridgewood AM Rotary Club, of which Andy and my brother were both members. He was on that truck with me. Unlike me, it was not his first trip, and his connection with Haiti was already building. From helping *Proje Espwa* (Project Hope), he helped another school and orphanage. Later, he got involved with hurricane relief, water projects, water wells, and you name it.

Eventually Andy formed a 501(c)(3) nonprofit, International Humanitarian Aid Foundation (IHAF), to support his activities. I always supported Andy, both generally and during his regular pleas for funds. I came to understand IHAF was really just Andy doing Andy things, but this allowed those of us who believed in what he did to deduct our contributions. Eventually, IHAF facilitated Andy's other love, flying, when he bought a four-seater Cessna plane that he used on mission trips.

Andy was a natural choice when I started the container Y project.

If he would come and help and bring the truck he kept in Haiti and his tools, I would pay for him to fly back and forth. I also had to buy lots of tools, some expensive welding equipment, generators, and eventually a laser cutter. The Y was very bad at keeping this kind of stuff. It would all seem to disappear between trips. Eventually, whatever I bought for each trip I just gave to Andy. He had trouble keeping the tools and his truck going too, but he was generally more successful. I also paid to have the truck fixed more than once.

Andy was not only an incredibly head-down-and-work type of contractor, he also knew his stuff and had a MacGyver-like ability to fix equipment and to jerry-rig solutions. He made a perfect partner for my young nephew, Phil, a newly graduated architect and thus very careful about all structural issues. Andy, like me, was about *reasonable compromise* in the name of quick progress.

Lest you start thinking Andy was a saint, he wasn't. Like many driven guys, he may not have been too easy to live with. His first wife and three of his now-adult kids, all of whom I knew from the church years and Rotary Gift of Life, no longer spoke to him. His second wife came and went within a couple of years. None of this made him happy.

Eventually, in 2014, he let a good friend in Haiti choose a niece to be his third wife. This was Milande. They married and had a daughter, Elena, within a couple of years. Then it took another eighteen months to get them visas to come to the states. Honestly, how that was all working out was still in play when Milande called me that fateful afternoon. Only one of his four older kids had any relationship with him or them.

Two big hurricanes, Irma and Maria, hit the Caribbean in September 2017. Haiti was not hit, but the US Virgins, British Virgins, and Puerto Rico were. Andy had an old connection with Virgin Gorda, one of the British Virgins. This was where we also kept our sailboat out of the water during hurricane season. When the hurricanes hit, Virgin Gorda was devastated and our boat was totaled, even while on the ground. This fifty-foot 32,000-pound boat was lifted and smashed to the ground forty feet away on top of a boat with a third boat on top of it. Andy first found it for me that way.

Soon after the hurricane, Andy planned a trip to Virgin Gorda, first stopping in Charlotte Amalie in the US Virgins. I raised and gave him $5,000, and with the help of JT Bolger, he got a load of hospital supplies donated by Valley Hospital. I also lent him our place to stay in St. Thomas (no water or electricity except for a couple of hours each day at this time) and my truck. He went to Virgin Gorda and helped build for a couple weeks. He then picked up a wealthy guy on St. John, did some work on St. Thomas, picked up some homeless dogs, and came home. It was an Andy kind of trip.

The following May he had a plan to go back. By then Carol and I had been back and forth to our place in St. Thomas, as well as to Virgin Gorda to see the boat, which was declared a total loss by the insurance company. I told him I thought these places, while devastated for sure, unlike Haiti, had the economic strength to come back, so I would pass on contributing this time. He still wanted to go, so I said he could use my house and truck again if he went. He somehow got another trip together. It was on a check ride for a repair that had been made before he went on this trip that Andy's plane crashed. He was due to leave three days later.

This chapter seems different from the others. Most of my memoir is full of God's grace and accomplishment. Lots of success. Not here. Haiti is still broken, badly broken. Gwenael is rightfully tired, and like me, perhaps a bit sad and discouraged. Andy is no longer here.

However, seeds are sown. We do not get to know God's big plan. So, for Haiti, I say only stay hopeful and stay tuned.

Dream, Plan, Do!

It was June 25, 2015. I stood at the front of the room in a convent we found to hold our conference in Nairobi, Kenya. I was assigned as the keynote speaker to kick off the first-ever Dream Big Conference of ten-year-old Wells Mountain Initiative, called WMI by all of us. More than fifty Wells Mountain Scholars from twenty-two countries were in the audience, as well as our staff and guests. My goal was to inspire these young people to give back to their communities, to plan and execute a meaningful life, and to be their best selves. I looked out and felt proud. I took a deep breath.

What I told the assembled audience that night, the message simplified here, was really four things. First, I told them that education was the all-important key to the kingdom. I shared Nelson Mandela's quote, "Education is the most powerful weapon you can use to change the world." Next, I shared my belief that "giving back" was the way to live a fulfilled life. Again I used a quote, this time from the plaque on my mom's wall when I was growing up, "What we are is our gift from God; what we become is our gift to God." I added to these two principles my abiding belief in the words of cultural anthropologist Margaret Mead, who had proclaimed, "Never doubt that a small group of committed individuals can change the world…

indeed it is the only thing that ever has." I closed by telling them my enthusiasm for the Madison Avenue sports manufacturer, Nike, "Just Do It!"

I embellished this fourth principle to mandate that the audience "dream big," then "plan well," and finally to "just do it." The shortened version I declared would now be the official motto of WMI: Dream, Plan, Do! This has been our mantra ever since.

Just three years later, in July 2018, I presented to this group again, or at least some of them, now at a second Dream Big Conference with more than one hundred scholars in attendance, this time in Kampala, Uganda. I elaborated even further. I gave them twelve principles to think about. There were the original four—education; giving back; power of small groups; and Dream, Plan, Do!—but now I made the list longer and more comprehensive. It was one of my lists again, but perhaps the best one I have ever made.

TWELVE PRINCIPLES TO GUIDE YOUR LIFE

1. **Listen more, talk less.** Yes, listen, really listen. Don't be busy planning what you want to say in response while you are listening. If what you heard was particularly valuable, write it down.
2. **Learn the difference between urgent and important.** Admittedly, some things are both—a fire in the room, for example. Most things are not. Education, training, and a friend in trouble are important. Many phone calls and interruptions are not. The key is to stay focused and prioritize.
3. **Education is the most valuable tool you can use to change the world.** Nelson Mandela went further. He called his education not a "valuable tool" but a "powerful weapon." The key is to never, never stop educating yourself.
4. **We are a product not of our circumstances, but rather of our decisions.** There is no question some have it easier, a lot easier, just by their birth circumstances. I include myself in this group. However, hardship is opportunity. Wealth is not success. Decisions matter.

In the end, we all must take responsibility for our own destiny and what we accomplish.

5. **"They thought they could bury us, but they did not know we were seeds."** Wonderful words from a Mexican poet. Seeds grow. The takeaway here is to never, never give up. As I tell folks facing adversity, "When a door closes, a window opens."
6. **Seek first to understand, then to be understood.** Yes, education, again, listening, again. Do both, again and again.
7. **Never doubt that a small group of committed individuals can change the world.** As the quote from anthropologist Margaret Mead continues, "Indeed it is the only thing that ever has." I believe this. I have lived this.
8. **What we are is our gift from God; what we become is our gift to God.** This is the plaque that hung on my kitchen wall when I was growing up. Be grateful for your blessings. Give back. Pay it forward.
9. **Fake it until you make it.** This one sounds a little out of sync with much of my advice. What it really means is believe in yourself. Become who you want to be. If you want to be a leader, act like a leader. If you want to be a professional, act professional.
10. **Fail again, fail better.** Don't be afraid to fail. Learn from failure. As WMI Student Scholar Alpha Habib Bangura said at our conference, which I like even better than my "Fail better," is "Fail forward!"
11. **Do unto others as you would have them do unto you.** It really has never been better said than these words by Jesus Christ. This concept undergirds most all of the world's religions. To me, it is the ultimate show of faith and respect. Live it. When you miss the mark, go to bed and get up the next day and try again.
12. **Finally, our very own, Dream, Plan, Do!** In long form: Dream big! Plan well! Just Do it! By all means, do it over and over again. It works.

* * *

Since in a way I am ahead of myself with this story, let me now back up to the beginning, thirteen years before the second Dream Big speech. In 2005, I founded Wells Mountain Initiative with the goal to help young people in the developing world by leveling the global playing field for education, opportunity, and justice. At the start, our name, Wells Mountain Foundation, was a bit less ambitious, and our mission and purpose was simple: give scholarships to young people with potential, who happened to live in the developing world. Long-term support, emphasis on giving back, and community building would all come along pretty quickly thereafter.

Through a study-abroad program in her Vermont high school, my daughter Jordyn had become friends with Victoria Galley, a fellow high school student in Ghana. Victoria was one of the most driven students in her village and went out of her way to help others. As young women, Victoria and Jordyn talked a lot about how they could make the world a better place—so more girls could be leaders, and so there would be enough resources for everybody. I met Victoria when I visited Jordyn while she was staying in Victoria's village. As the only Christian in her family, she memorably took me to church with her on Palm Sunday during that visit.

While in college, Jordyn returned to Ghana. She quickly discovered that Victoria had not had the same opportunities that she had to pursue their shared goals. Victoria could not continue with college because her family did not have the funds for tuition. Jordyn asked me if I could help her. I said yes. And with that action, what is now WMI, with more than eight hundred WMI Scholars from fifty-four countries, was born.

When Jordyn asked me to help Victoria, I had been working in Africa and Haiti through YMCA World Service, and had met many young people like Victoria with big hearts and lots of ambition, but who needed financial help, particularly in pursuing education. Victoria's specific ask was just the impetus I needed to bring all this into an action plan.

At the beginning, it was just Victoria and me and wires of money when needed and lots of emails. It soon became apparent that some structure was needed. I also realized that much more could be done if I went beyond what I could do personally. I sought the support from others, believing I was giving them a chance to make these life-changing contributions as well.

With the help of my friend and longtime client David Bolger, a "business bonus" due to me for helping him buy a bank was turned into an even bigger gift of startup money, and I formed a nonprofit charity. I asked Jordyn and a young friend and work colleague to serve on the board of directors. The rest of the board were clients and friends, all old white men, who I could count on for help and financial support.

I rolled into this a charity called Book Angels, an annual book donation program that we had run for ten years through Deerleap Books, which we had now closed. When I first set up the foundation, I also included other important work I had been involved in under its umbrella, including literacy support in the form of free books to many programs, countries, and projects in Haiti.

For scholarships, it was no surprise at all that Victoria was not alone in needing help. The number of students supported grew from just Victoria to four the next year, then eight the following. This was the point in time when being my friend got harder. At first, I had been an easygoing asker, but I then became an increasingly relentless fundraiser for this cause. If you were really a good friend, I would talk you into joining our board, which gave you the privilege of not only giving but also getting others to give.

The number of students kept growing each year…fourteen, twenty-six, thirty-seven. We were like the commercial where the internet startup gets orders, then more, and more, and more. We soon needed the involvement of our third "founder," my wife, Carol. Early efforts were run by just the two of us. Then we got office help in our Vermont real estate management office. When we cleaned up the founding story years later, I was labeled the founder and both Jordyn and Carol were co-founders.

The first formally designated WMI-only employee was Nicole

Baker, who was hired in 2013. Until then, other than Carol's and my efforts, we used employee time from folks working in the other businesses.

Nicole was a great asset since the day she started. We celebrated her ten-year anniversary with WMI at the 2023 Dream Big Conference. Now our executive director, Nicole has had experience in every aspect of our organization. Beginning part time, then becoming full time, she stayed with us even while moving to Macon, Georgia, then to Curitiba, Brazil, and after an extended stay in St. Petersburg, Florida, to most recently Merida, Mexico, not to mention months at a time of world traveling. She declared herself a "lifer" a while back. I so hope she is.

As the years went by, the core program of WMI, Empowerment Through Education, evolved not only to include far more students and a more sophisticated application process, but also through enhancement of the community service requirement to a requirement of one hundred hours per year for each active student. I have always given credit for the "one hundred hours" to Nicole. This requirement of "giving back," often met with less than total enthusiasm, became a bedrock of WMI. It truly became who we are.

Later, we created fellowships, the Dream Big Conferences, community development grants, and finally, an academy for extra skill building for recent graduates. This provided continuing support to WMI Scholars and encouraged networking after their initial education experience. In a very real way, WMI over the years evolved from a scholarship program with emphasis on community service to widen and refine our focus to help motivated young people become true social change agents. Today, twenty years later, WMI not only funds scholarships, but we seek to build the next generation of change makers. Our last major program enhancement was the creation of a community development grants program that allows our WMI Scholars to apply for and receive (if worthy) grants to help start non-profits or needed businesses generation of changemakers in the most impoverished and under-resourced areas, and we have a particular emphasis on women and girls.

Although I loved literacy, book projects, and the early work we did in Haiti helping to build container YMCAs, as WMI grew, we needed to streamline our core mission. Eventually, our focus became just three main program areas: Empowerment Through Education, global collective action and networking, and community development grants. Through these, we became a small but mighty and growing global community of engaged young leaders and social entrepreneurs tackling issues, such as gender inequity, educational access, health disparities, healthcare, agriculture, climate change, and social justice.

Our logistics obviously needed to grow, as our program did. We started with Carol and me managing everything as volunteers and have now grown to an impressive staff running the show. I remain a very proud chair of our board of directors. As such, my primary responsibilities are to work with the board and on fundraising. Carol, who in the first ten years we gave the fancy title of director of operations, continued to run our annual online auction, which she did for twelve years. During that time, the annual event has raised more than $200,000.

One of our annual duties, which we gave up just three years ago, was the final selection of the scholarship awardees. The process, which winnows down usually 1,600 to 1,800 applications through the fantastic work of more than 150 volunteer reviewers, would leave us with about one hundred applications to read. We would then select sixty to eighty finalists who would receive scholarships. Nothing in my life has been more gratifying nor as hard as doing this at the end of every July. Each applicant feels immensely deserving, and knowing the decision is life-changing makes this selection feel like a religious experience.

This final review is now handled by staff, more than half of whom were once applicants themselves. So, I pass this along knowing it is in the best of hands. Carol and I now join the sea of reviewers doing initial reviews.

In our early years, while I kept going with day-to-day operations of WMI, I had a lot of help from Carol and borrowed staff from our other businesses. Our third founder, Jordyn, spent nearly a decade working for several leading NGOs across Africa. During this time, while Jordyn stayed on our board and helped when needed, she learned from her positions at Do Something based in New York, and Kenya-based Shining Hope for Communities (SHOFCO), the on the ground realities and the global policy context of what WMI could do.

Jordyn developed a deep sense of the importance of the need to be humble and to listen to the expertise of people like Victoria and those who followed her, who led change in their home countries. In 2018, after she led a long-range planning effort for us, I talked Jordyn into becoming WMI's first managing director, at first part time. Eventually, she was hooked, and soon she became our first full-time executive director. I very happily relegated myself to my board chair position, my "vision-thing," and of course, fundraising.

When Jordyn took over, we already had several long-term dedicated staff. Things took off. WMI became much more professional, both in reality and appearance. Jordyn expanded the staff, especially in Africa, and grew our programs. Not only would we fund more scholarships, better facilitate networking and training of our scholars, and assist more social entrepreneurship projects, but we sought to elevate the voice and leadership of WMI Scholars to become effective changemakers at all levels.

In 2021, Jordyn was approaching forty years old, and at long last started to worry about her life other than WMI. She met and fell in love with a great guy, Ray, during the COVID-19 lockdown, and that prompted her to consider having children and getting married. She also felt, and I agreed, that WMI needed a leader at its helm who knew and loved development and had the skillset to gather the financial support we needed to keep growing.

In 2022, Jordyn told me, with lots of notice, that she wanted to step down as executive director and leave the staff. Her timing was actually good, as WMI was ready to enter its next big phase. It was time for a major push. Our budget had grown to just over $1 million a year, and now we needed to solicit major foundations and corporations for our continued growth. My friends, many of whom had become board members, had been so very generous over the years and were at or close to their limits. We needed to reach for a new plateau again.

We waited until December 2022 to tell the board about this upcoming change and then we launched a search committee in January. Using an outside search consultant, we started a process that included ninety-six applications, which eventually led to four, and then two final candidates. We interviewed them more than once, made them do a thought exercise, and grilled their references. Then I got to do one final one-on-one interview with the last two candidates.

Our choice for the our next executive director, Lisa Meadowcroft, started in June 2023 and by August was leading our staff to our third Dream Big Conference in Nairobi, Kenya. This time we had more than two hundred scholars from twenty-five countries and forty presenters and visitors, including six board members, in attendance. Lisa would turn out to be a poor fit for the position and a year later we reorganized our development team and the board enthusiastically elevated Nicole to the executive director position. Proof for sure that nothing is easy.

* * *

Our third Dream Big Conference, always and increasingly a momentous event, opened on Friday, August 18, 2022. I stood at the podium, once again, doing the welcome address. My plan is to keep doing this until they kick me out.

Because it was exactly fifty years to the day that I had married my beautiful oh-so-special co-founder "Mama Carol," I ended my address by inviting her to the stage and announcing the milestone. I thought it would be a surprise. I guess not, as we were soon joined by a gigantic cake and everyone in attendance. I doubt anyone has ever enjoyed an anniversary like this. Two hundred wildly enthusiastic scholars cheered us on. I will never forget that moment.

While my speech started with a restatement of my Twelve Principles, I also pitched my latest idea: "Tell Your Story." I told the scholars

I would write a book about the history of WMI, who we were, and what we stood for. I invited them to become contributing authors by writing and submitting a personal narrative "Dream, Plan, Do!" story. Not every story could be included, but I promised that several stories would be at the heart of the book. So many of our superstars had persevered through adversity to achieve a goal. I told them that sharing this could inspire others. When I asked who had such a story to tell, many hands went up. I knew my next book, after this memoir, would be a success.

* * *

Sometimes when you do good things, it goes unnoticed. Not so with WMI. Not even close. The scholars themselves tell me all the time how grateful they are. Their sincere gratitude is so special and means so much. I also received, along with Carol, a Distinguished Citizen Award from Bucknell University in 2015, and with Carol and our daughter Jordyn, honorary doctorates in humane letters from Middlebury College in 2023.

I am profoundly proud of WMI and all we have accomplished. The scholars make me giddy with pride. I have been blessed with professional success, a wonderful wife, kids, families, financial security, lifelong special friends, and also a lot of toys. However, there is nothing in my life that makes me prouder than WMI and the unbelievable world-changing young people we have been able to help. I love it when they call me Papa Tom, and I love passing along lessons and matters like our simple slogan: Dream, Plan, Do! and my Twelve Principles. They make me feel truly blessed.

Accepting an award in Dakar, Senegal, 2000

Kay Espwah (Project Hope), Les Caye, Haiti, 2001

In Haiti with nephew, Phil Wells, 2013

Finishing the sixth container YMCA in Haiti, 2019

Carol and me being filmed for WMI video, about 2015

Dream Big Conference, 2015, Nairobi, Kenya

DBC, 2018, Kampala Uganda

DBC, 2023, Nairobi, Kenya

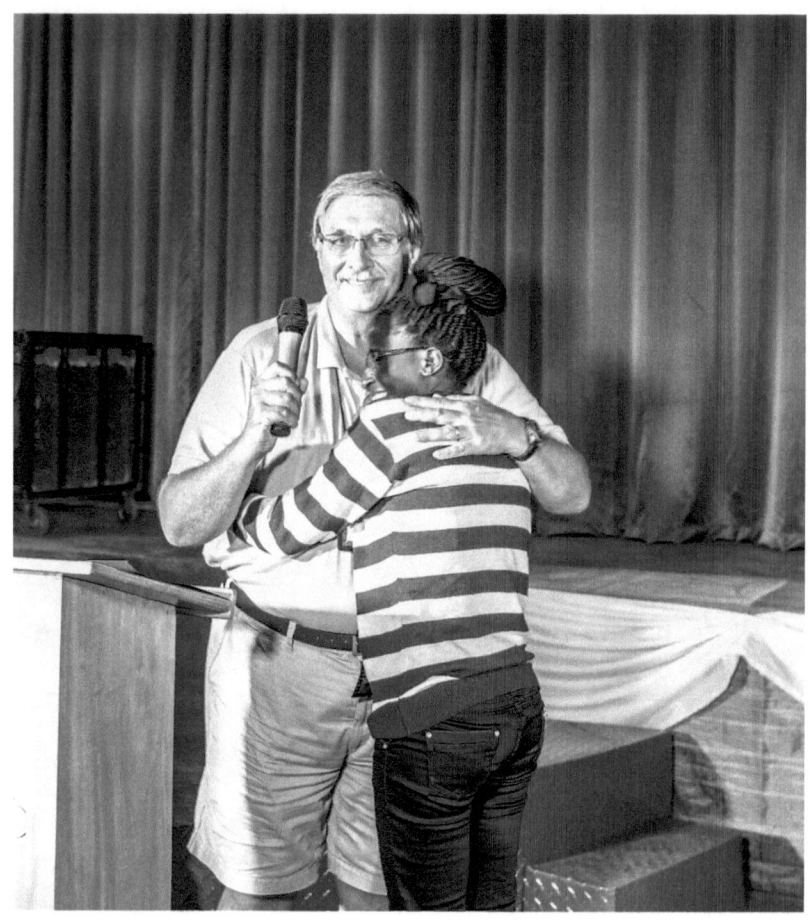

Presenting Founders Award to Dr. Catherine Nagadya Kiruyi at DBC, Kampala, Uganda, 2018

SECTION III

Just Living

I am neither David Sedaris nor Mark Twain. Although a century divides these two, they are both gifted storytellers. What divides me from these two is literary talent. What follows is my humble attempt at telling some of my stories. Many written when the kids were small and I was deep in family life, they capture real life as I lived it. Sometimes cocky, sometimes insecure, I bumbled through. Some stories appeared in a newspaper column I wrote for a few years. One story, "The Fire," I used at jury trials when I needed to convince the jury of the power of circumstantial evidence. Some I just like to tell and have told many times. A few I have never shared before. The last one, "Evelina," I wrote on the morning I met with the editors I decided to do this book with.

Alone at Sea

My relations with wind and water and the natural combination of the two created by the fine art of sailing have lasted all my life, a sometimes spotty yet enduring affection, if not a full-fledged love. I began my sailing in a pram, a rowboat with a single sail, and continued with a sailfish, a seventeen-foot surfboard-like contraption with a dagger board and a big triangular sail. I took to the water over the years in a series of ever larger boats: sixteen feet, twenty-eight feet, thirty-six feet, and finally fifty feet. The last two of these could best be described as a nice RV with sails. As to true actual sails, after the pram and the sailfish, there were two of them—a mainsail and jib—three if you count the spinnaker, and on the last two, we also had a diesel engine for when I got tired of sailing.

As with skiing, I had good equipment and went to good places, but I never became truly accomplished. I am an okay sailor, but by no means a top drawer. Although I tell Carol I keep the boat well in control—as in no heeling way over in strong winds—entirely for her sake, I am quietly not that brave either. They say part of the joy of sailing is getting through the tough spots and out-of-control experiences. A storm on the water can be damn frightening. Truth be told, I would just as soon sail around these experiences.

One of my earliest sailing memories is actually one of my youth's all-time-most-frightening experiences—without justification, it turned out. But it had me, at one point, peeing in my pants and deep in prayer.

I was ten when this occurred. I had sailed out in the sailfish as part of an early season race. Sailing in a race usually consists of following a course around three buoys in such a manner as to experience all kinds of wind: at your beam, as in blowing directly into the side of the boat allowing you to "reach," "running," the wind at your back with the sail out as perpendicular as possible to catch the wind; or "tacking."

Tacking is perhaps the real art of sailing, as it requires you to sail toward or into the wind, or as close into the wind as possible. I can't explain here all the lift-and-drag forces that make this possible, but suffice it to say that if you do it right, pull your sail in real tight, and have a keel—the long, skinny, heavy thing that sticks down from any respectable sailboat—or in the case of a sailfish, a dagger board—which is a piece of wood you lower into the water amidships (the middle of the boat)—you can sail into the wind. If you are any good, you can get up to about fifteen or twenty degrees away from directly into the wind. This distance, going both ways, from the direction the wind is blowing from, which by simple addition totals, say, thirty to forty degrees, is the "no-go zone." You guessed it: You can't go there.

To take your boat to a point into the wind, you must alternate tacks, pointing as close as you can to the wind, each time advancing closer to the point you desire to reach, or, in the case of the buoy, you wish to sail around. Alternate tacks implies two, and indeed there are two tacks: starboard, when the wind is coming over the right side of your boat, and port, when it is coming over the left side.

What makes the race stuff fun is deciding how long to stay on each tack before "coming about" to the opposite tack. Figuring out when to do this is what often distinguishes the winners from the also-rans. Until you round the buoy, it is often hard for everyone, even the sailors, to tell whether the guy with just one long zig (tack) and one long zag will do better than the guy who does many. Different combinations of zigs and zags can put boats on a collision course, which only adds to the fun—and the strategy. The starboard boat, by the age-old rules, has the right-of-way, and the port boat must get out of its way, even if it slows him down.

There are oh-so-many such rules and, as you may have gathered, lots of arcane lingo that come with the sailing experience. The back of the boat is the stern or aft, the front is the bow or fore. If there is a kitchen on board, it is a galley; a bathroom is a head. The surfboard-like sailfish had neither…hence, no easy solution for my eventual need to pee.

I knew all this and more at the age of ten because I had by then already taken sailing lessons for a summer or two at the local yacht club.

I don't remember much concerning the start of the race I am about to tell you about, other than that there were about a dozen of us lining up. One of the other measures of a skilled skipper is how he gets his boat off the line. The key is to be sailing as fast as possible, heading toward the first mark (buoy) at the point along the starting line closest to the buoy and upwind of your competitors. Upwind is almost always better, since he or she who "has the wind" almost always goes faster than he or she who has his or her wind blocked by the guy or girl upwind of him or her. The skipper wants to do all this, but under no circumstances be over the line when the starting bell or horn rings. If you are, you must turn back.

I don't remember the start as I write this. However, I can tell you I was well back in the group. I know this because I always was. Once or twice I even started dead last, a place usually reserved for the real losers, which generally I was not.

I rounded the first mark about a mile out into the bay in good shape. I didn't count all the boats, but I was sure I was in the front half of the fleet. Cool, I thought.

Two things happened almost immediately that made this day the memorable one it became. First, the wind died down, completely. The sailing term for this phenomenon is "becalmed," which of course means sailing is what you will not be doing.

Becalmed I was, and if that wasn't enough, fog descended. After a while, this was not just routine fog that didn't allow me to see another nearby boat or perhaps a friendly if unsubstantial island. It was full-fledged pea soup, a fog that would rival the equally disconcerting experience of being in a whiteout on a ski slope that literally makes you ill. The fog and no-wind combination lacks the hysteria-producing high-speed effect of also being on two thin strips of fiberglass speeding down a mountain, which feels roughly like falling through space, but it is still not much fun.

The present situation was not that bad. Clearly not dire enough to scare you to death, at least not right away. What I learned that day is that eventually the slow drip can become as effective as the fire hose in the face.

After what felt like an eternity, call it two hours of no wind and seeing nothing, my sense of being anywhere I wanted to be was distorted. Eventually, I irrationally convinced myself I had slipped out from behind the eighteen-mile sandbar island that created the bay I started out in this morning. I reasoned that I had somehow found my way into the vast Atlantic Ocean.

Two more hours passed. Increasingly strident silent prayers went unanswered. Eventually, the bargains offered became rather aggressive. I would never be mean to my sister again. I would never again tell lies. Finally, "God, just let me find my way home. I'll do anything." During this last prayer, I was on my knees on my thin surfboard with a luffing sail.

It all ended, not in a dramatic mid-sea rescue of a small boy lost in the Atlantic, as I had conjured, but with a lifting fog and my first view of land, what looked like an island. It turned out to be a swamp-like appendage of the mainland about three miles away from my point of origin. As I had by then been gone a long time, soon after the fog lifted, I was discovered by a race patrol boat that had been searching for me and offered a tow in. Stupidly, however, just back from the depth of despair, somehow the idea of being towed in brought a full measure of ten-year-old macho and I refused the tow. The wind was also picking up and I would sail in. Mercifully, I did not have to tack.

Later, just under six hours after the race began, I sailed into the shore to a chorus of cheers and, of course, some jeers from my buddies. The race had ended some four and a half hours earlier and apparently, I now held the club record for longest time out in a sailfish race.

The lessons learned this day: First, always be logical and rational. Panic should never be allowed to take this power away. Logic, even for a ten-year-old, should have made it clear that I could not possibly have found my way to the ocean. The closest route to the ocean would require sailing more than nine miles, thus even if I had sped along, sailing perfectly, I could not have covered this distance…and remember, I was becalmed, as in not moving at all. Duh!

Also, be careful what you promise God. If you have a well-developed conscience, like I did, these promises will have to be kept, or many hours of rationalization and compromising deals are ahead for you.

The Fire

It was 1963 and I was eleven years old. In those days, my family lived in a house with a little brook and some woods off to one side. Not deep in the woods or in the country, mind you; think developments and suburbia. Our lot was, however, a little oversized and we had this patch of mini wilderness.

The brook is key to my story, so let's focus there for a minute. I call it a brook, but this river of no return was frequently not too much more than a trickle of water—sometimes in the hot summer, not even that. In a big rainstorm, however, it was torrents of water, sometimes overflowing its banks. Remembering that I lived in suburbia and learning that my brook went through sections where it was piped underground for a shopping center, you will realize the cute little brook through my yard was actually better described as a drainage ditch, mostly for rainstorms.

For our purposes, all you need to know is at the time in question, it had shallow water running maybe about six feet wide with grass and weeds on both sides. It was the summer between fifth and sixth grade and eleven-year-old boys like me spent our days, all of them, outside. Most of that time, for me and my buddies, revolved around the little patch of woods and the aforementioned waterway—forts and boats and the like.

John Kennedy was president, and my Republican parents were not all that impressed, but he was young, with kids like they had, so I guess a little more than they would otherwise be. They took me and a friend to see the movie *PT 109* when it came out that summer. The movie was the story of World War II Lieutenant Kennedy as PT boat commander, and the movie was playing at all the theaters that summer.

The big scene in the film, at least as I remember it, was when the PT boat patrolling at night was split in half when it was rammed by an enemy vessel. The big takeaway for me was that the water was on fire. This really amazed me. When the film was over, I wanted to know how it was possible that water could burn. I accepted with fascination the explanation that it was not the water that was burning, rather fuel that had spilled from the boat that lay on top of the water. How the fuel lay on top and did not mix with the water I found particularly intriguing.

Two days later, I decided to run an experiment. I took the gas can from the garage that my dad used to fill up the lawn mower. My idea was to pour the gas into the brook and see if the gas and oil mixture would separate from the water. If I had stopped there, all would have been well enough. I didn't. In addition to the gas can, I secured a large box of stick matches from the kitchen drawer. My mom kept them there to light candles and, once in a while, the oven, when it wouldn't light itself.

I poured gasoline on the water. I then stood back and threw a match. It was glorious. Leaping flames.

My sense of glory faded quickly. I had forgotten a stream does not just sit there. The water moves. In this case, the water topped with fuel on fire was moving downstream.

Worse, almost immediately, it was lighting the dry grass on the banks on fire. I was no experienced firefighter by any means, but my first instinct was to stomp out the fires. I tried to do exactly this.

In case you have now assumed the next thing coming is clothes on fire and a near-death experience, what happened was the fuel-covered water quickly started more fires than I could hope to put out. They immediately spread off our property to the much larger field across the street. So, I did the decidedly unheroic thing…I ran away.

By the time the fire engines arrived, it was a pretty big brush fire endangering nearby woods, if not homes. I heard the sirens from my hiding place in a four-foot crawl space under my house. I watched firemen do their work. I was physically shaking and engulfed in sweat. I saw my neighborhood friends, their parents, and then even my mother out there watching the action. I was too afraid to even think about returning to the scene of the crime.

Several hours later, I showed up in my mom's kitchen and nonchalantly began a discussion of current events. But Mom interrupted my speech and asked if I knew anything about the fire.

At this point in the story, telling it to a hushed courtroom, with even the judge seemingly paying close attention, I would usually walk right to the middle of the jury box. I would slowly and deliberately look right at the jurors. I had been taught to do it this way. In support of the power of circumstantial evidence, which I was arguing to them could be convincing in the case before them, I would slowly and deliberately ask, "Ladies and gentlemen, did my mother have any doubt, looking at her son's soot-covered face and singed eyebrows and hair, that my declaration, 'Mom, no,' was totally untrue?" She, just like all of you today, knew "beyond a reasonable doubt" I was not telling the truth. She also had a pretty good idea exactly what happened.

My Russian Friends

Most historians now believe that the summit held in Reykjavik, Iceland, in October 1986, between then-President Ronald Reagan and Soviet leader Mikhail Gorbachev marked the end of the Cold War between the United States and the Soviet Union. About that time, we all learned two new Russian words: perestroika (restructuring) and glasnost (openness). They were related concepts, both the brainchild of Gorbachev and his followers. The result was the effective dissolution of the Soviet Union in 1991. It was not remotely anticipated at the outset. Gorbachev sought only badly needed economic openness and an end to the nuclear arms race.

I turned out to be an active participant in this beginning with a, for me, historic visit to Moscow and a summit of my own in Yalta in 1987. I was part of a group of five YMCA young adult leaders, accompanied by sage older folks to keep us in line, who visited with and discussed issues with five Soviet contemporaries. Their youth credential was symbolized by their status as Komsomol members, which was the young leader's stepping stone to becoming a full-fledged Communist party cardholder. Both statuses were a form of elite level and were not widely held in the Soviet Union. About this time, the USSR population was approximately 280 million. Card-carrying Communist party members numbered about nineteen million, or about 15 percent of the population.

Our delegation was between thirty and thirty-five years old. I think I was the oldest at thirty-five. We had a very experienced older couple as our mentors and guides. We started with briefing papers, then two days of meetings near Dulles International Airport outside of Washington, DC, before we flew to Moscow. We were all about the theme of the times, glasnost, and getting to know the people as opposed to the government.

We met our Russian counterparts at the airport. They were at first quite reserved. A member of the group, Tanya, who was the youngest, was also assigned to be our interpreter. Although this group all spoke some English, many folks we would be with did not. It was Tanya's job to tell us what was going on and being said, and to interpret for the others what we said.

I immediately knew Tanya would be a good person to be close to, so I endeavored to make this happen. I sat with her, not my delegation, on the bus ride from the airport. This began a quick friendship between us, and soon thereafter with her whole delegation. It also began what would become my rogue status in the eyes of the delegation I had come to Russia with.

I would later learn that, ironically, what speedily advanced the budding friendships was a quick decision among my new Russian friends that I was the best candidate among the visiting Americans to be corruptible. This corruption would take three forms. When I said I wanted to get some rubles to spend in their country, they quickly volunteered to trade theirs for my much-coveted dollars. As I think about it, they may have actually asked me to do this before I got around to needing local money.

Second, in Russia, at least in these times, they had what were called Beriozka stores. They were state run, took only foreign currency, and were filled with things everyday Russians could not get easily: foreign alcohol, cigarettes, luxury goods—pretty much what we think of as a typical duty-free store inventory. They also had the absolute best matryoshka dolls. My new friends very much appreciated my willingness to buy cartons of cigarettes and the like for them in exchange for their rubles. The dolls were left for us tourists.

This was all illegal, mind you, a private currency exchange. I would assume it was illegal at the parking violation level, but in the Soviet Union at that time, who knew? No matter, I had no particular fear of a Siberian transfer and was happy to oblige. They were right on this kind of stuff: I was low-level corruptible, especially for a good cause. Go glasnost!

What sealed the deal for my new friends was my third corruptibility: my willingness to buy refreshments for evening get-togethers. I assumed the beverage of choice would be vodka. Russians are known for their vodka drinking, aren't they? No, they wanted me to buy "whisky," preferably from Scotland, what you and I would call scotch.

Most of the bottles were gifts from me—solicited gifts for sure, but still gifts. I was happy to oblige and looked at the drinks as a well-spent personal investment in friendship. I quickly got invited to share in the whisky at otherwise all-Russian informal gatherings to drink and relax at night.

Thank goodness for Tanya, by now a fixture at my side interpreting up a storm for me. Strangely, in just over a week of hanging out with a group who spoke only Russian, unless someone was talking directly to me, I followed many conversations; if not the details, certainly the general subject under discussion.

All this was fun—a lot more fun than the meetings we would have during the day. I was the most popular I have ever been in my life. My Russian friends who were stern-faced pseudodiplomats by day, were loose, and often drunk, fun folks at night.

All this camaraderie came with a price. My delegation and our leaders were furious with me. You see, not only was I partying with the enemy, or at least quasi enemy, I was missing our nightly delegation meetings to discuss our strategy for talks the next day.

I am usually a very responsible guy, and all this disapproval would ordinarily bother me, a lot. But, I thought then, and still do more than thirty-five years later, that getting to really know these people was far more important than what we said in the daytime talks. Besides, they liked me so much!

Our visit began in Moscow, where we talked a little and mostly went sightseeing. They took us to a Russian Orthodox Cathedral to celebrate five hundred years of this church in Russia. They took us there because we were representing the YMCA, we assumed. YMCA had Christian right in its name!

None of these young Komsomol members were supposed to have any interest in religion but all wanted to prove that in the Soviet Union, even the much-disapproved church was respected.

The formal "talks" between our delegations were to take place in Yalta, a resort city on the Black Sea, made famous, at least for us Americans, because it was the location of a summit between Stalin, Churchill, and Roosevelt near the end of World War II. Yalta was the jewel of the Crimea region.

Yalta was part of Ukraine even then, but it was also part of the Soviet Union. In 1991 with the breakup of the Soviet Union, Russians lost their Black Sea resort, but they later stole and annexed it back in 2014.

When I was in Yalta in 1987, it was picturesque, much more so than Moscow, and felt both historic and like a tourist destination. The hotel we stayed in was modern, yet a little shabby. I remember tiny elevators that fit two people, maybe three people at most. The hotel was near the water and beach. We had to take the stairs to get to the beach.

The rooming situation differed markedly for the two delegations. We Americans all had our own rooms; actually, we all had suites with a living room and bedroom, and all our rooms had ocean views. I learned from my friends, although they never took me to their rooms, that the Russians were packed in anywhere from two to four to a room. No views and often no windows.

In the 1980s, as it would remain until an unfortunate skiing accident in 1993, jogging was my everyday stay-fit obsession. In Yalta, I jogged on the beach every morning. The idea of running for no particular reason seemed rather odd to my Soviet friends. Soon Tanya asked to come along. The next day, there were four of us.

I was initially shocked to learn—but soon it made loads of sense—that they came because on the beach they could talk freely. Apparently at the hotel, at our meetings, virtually everywhere, they assumed someone could and often would be listening. Wow, I thought.

The jogging conversations were often much more personal. I can replay in my mind, like it was yesterday, the big one, "Do you really believe in God?" I did, of course, but I was never much of a preacher or witness of my faith with words. I like to live it, not so much talk about it. I told my new friends, "Oh, yes, I really do." This they accepted with fascination more than confrontation. Although we debated each day about the differences between capitalism and communism, the group seemed almost in awe that this American guy, who they actually liked and, I think, thought was pretty smart, was a believer in God.

This religious curiosity took another form when our delegation was asked what we wanted to see in the area, and a visit to a Russian Orthodox church, perhaps even a service, came up as a possibility. Interestingly, it was my running companions who urged me to make this happen because they would get to accompany us, and they had never been to a service. We went, of course.

The last night in Yalta the entire group went to a beautiful country restaurant. The food, the company, the atmosphere, and the wine, which was ample for many toasts, were all wonderful. Toasting was a big deal on this trip. A toast was usually a quasi-diplomatic speech of, say, three or four minutes in length, followed by downing whatever was in your glass. We often traded compliments. By the last night in Yalta, the trip was beginning to wind down and everyone felt cordial and relaxed. My delegation was still not pleased with me, but many of them joined me and the Russians when we sat together, rather than sitting off on their own at the other end of the table.

By the time we got back to the hotel, many of us were intoxicated, certainly I was. On the way out of the van and just inside the door, one of my friends whispered, "How about you buy some whisky, and we will come to your room?" I said, "Sure." I went off and found the hotel store open and purchased the requested alcohol.

I barely got to my room when it became full of Russian friends, and not just the delegates, but a few of the keepers as well. Almost immediately, the furniture was pushed back, and we all started dancing in a circle. I am no dancer, but I was happy to oblige after some basic instruction. The dancing was punctuated by toasts. Unlike at dinner, the glasses were bathroom-sized and typically filled with scotch. It seemed that almost every toast this night was to be directed at me. I remember that every toast, whether given or received, required me to bottom-up a glass of scotch.

When I woke up the next morning, I found myself in a totally empty room, in a state of partial undress. I wore only my boxers, maybe socks. My first thought was that I was in a Russian jail. I was terribly hung over.

After a while, I recognized the room as my hotel room—but stripped of all furniture. I crawled to where I was pretty sure the bathroom was. After a very long shower, I staggered into the main room and looked out the window. Piled up on the little balcony overlooking the sea was the furniture for my room.

It was 10:00 a.m. The schedule had been for us to leave our rooms, bring the luggage downstairs, eat breakfast, and then take a shuttle to the meeting place. We were scheduled to arrive by 9:00 a.m. for a protracted last day of discussions on the joint statement we would issue later that day.

When I walked into the session at almost noon, having stopped since leaving my room twice to throw up in a nearby bathroom, I was surprised, yet I guess really not, to see every one of the Soviets who had been with me the night before sitting around the table, seriously going about their duties. No one but Tanya even cracked a smile at me.

Back from Yalta, we had just one more night in Moscow before our delegation left to fly home. This night my Russian cohorts invited me to go out with them to Moscow nightclubs. Now all but the most conservative of my American colleagues asked to join and did. Glasnost had finally thawed out my colleagues.

Perfect Me

I ADMIT IT. I'M A PERFECTIONIST WITH A "TYPE A" PERSONality. Actually, I might be a double-A but isn't that a battery? The rub for me is that all this perfectionism was not necessarily a good thing in a house full of women.

First, consider what being a perfectionist means: I work like a maniac, drive myself and others practically to exhaustion, am never completely satisfied, and always, always have a long list of uncompleted projects. Worse, despite the inevitability of my state of perpetual partial dissatisfaction, part of my perfectionism is to expect it to go away. The fact that it won't bothers me. So does anything out of place, less than perfect organization, messy bedrooms, lint on carpet, toothpaste in the sink, and anything not in its proper place.

My advice to those who share this affliction is to marry only if you must, and then only someone just like yourself. If you do, you will live in a house that could be photographed for *Architectural Digest* at any hour of the day or night—a good thing. Another approach is monastic life. However, if the lack of material possessions or perhaps celibacy doesn't work for you—it didn't for me—by all means, at the very least, you may want to consider not having children because with kids comes a house and tens of thousands of toys and other possessions. The resulting clutter is the enemy of any real perfectionist.

Since children bring joy along with all their clutter, you must learn to cope. I eventually did. That's where the groove in your tongue comes in, a sore subject with me. I no longer have a groove, you see. But of course, my tongue is shorter now and it's harder to talk. This is okay since speech is the enemy of any red-blooded perfectionist who must live in an environment cluttered with hair curlers, every conceivable facial and hair care product, and enough clothing to dress an entire third-world country, mostly maintained in an unfolded state in countless baskets strategically placed throughout the house.

Humility is the key. I simply had to gain a more worldly perspective, to focus on the eternal truths of peaceful coexistence, and to understand the essence of quality family life. In short, I had to accept that what I think simply does not matter. Biting my tongue right off also helped.

Armed with this considered worldview, I could no longer accompany my careful shoppers as they surveyed every aisle of every gift and clothing store at every destination. The old me had to repeatedly fight the temptation to point out—thereby deepening the groove in my tongue—that every store had basically the same stuff, and we didn't need any of it anyway. That's how I lost my tongue. Now I peacefully sit on the bench out front of the store reading newspaper stories or on my phone. It seems to soothe me, and I get to sit on some great benches.

Yup, I got a little carried away here and I may be exaggerating a little. However, you get the point.

Organize the Pictures

Remember photo albums? I do. I realize these mostly no longer exist, or if they do, they are likely prepared for you from your social media posts and delivered to your door. Anyway, in the old days, organizing and pasting in place actual pictures was a monumental job. Worse, in our house it was a two-front war. Straight ahead was about ten years of pictures stored in envelopes, and frequently mixed up, that we had been too busy to put in an album. To make matters worse, the flanking action was the existing albums that were falling apart and over the years have been looted of favorite pictures by the happy camera subjects. It made me wish I had never given up slides.

Since most pictures taken in recent years have been digital and are hanging out on the same hard drive as this essay, we continue having this problem. The issue for all these shots is whether you print out the good ones or just lug around the iPad to show them off.

Going through old family pictures is a powerful experience. The images conjure up strong feelings that transport you back to the moment when the picture was taken—and just as frequently, and sometimes with the same picture, a shocking sense of disconnect. Could that really be me in this picture? Thousands of images of me and my daughters, hugging, holding hands, smiling at each other or at the camera. Such loving scenes, yet I don't really remember feeling so loved. Does the camera lie? The pictures look real enough.

Would pictures taken today look just as loving? I bet they would. Pictures capture special moments. They are taken in moments of happiness and, more often than not, posed. There are no photographs of the walk in from the parking lot, the scene in the car with tense parents in the front seat, and three bickering girls in the seat behind them, of me distracted at a dinner table, my companions in earnest conversation, or of the late-night waits for an overdue daughter.

But in some ways, the photographs are real life too. They are us at our best, projecting our good feelings and best smiles onto film or into the binary language that now allows an image to be stored digitally. The best thing about the pictures is they help your mind search its hard drive for the events behind the pictures, those mental images stored only deep in the biochemical recess of the same.

House Full of Women

I HAVE THREE DAUGHTERS. THIS FACT IS MADE MORE SIGNIFicant because they have no brothers, me, no sons. I am not complaining, mind you—one of them might hear me. I am just making sure you know what kind of world I live in, my wife also being female, of course: a world that is decidedly female.

In the early years, before sons-in-law and now grandsons, my world was always surrounded by women. Beautiful women, thanks to my wife's good genes. However, the long run in from the distant open spot in the parking lot, after dropping off the passengers at the entrance, was always alone. Worse, although I really believe my four women love me dearly—well, I'm not sure all the time—I was always the odd man out. They are a team. I was usually just along for the ride.

Was family life ever easy? When Pa Ingalls spoke to his family on *Little House on the Prairie*, didn't they all seem to pay attention? Of course, that was television in the 1980s re-creating the 1880s, and we know history reconstructed by prime-time television may take some license. Times have also changed since the 1880s. Heck, they have changed a lot just since I grew up. In addition, I'm no Pa Ingalls—he had a son to balance out his three daughters. Three daughters with no son makes all the difference. With Mom, that makes four against my one. The neutered dog doesn't count.

In the fast-paced nineties, when my girls were all in the house growing up, most family life seemed to be on the run. Family "discussions" took place at the dinner table, if at all. At our house, the brief breakfast gathering at the same location, hours earlier, did not allow for anything but cursory exchanges. Usually, not even that. "I want more Honey Nut Cheerios," my youngest would announce to no one in particular. So, of course, no one listened. This resulted in a repeat of the announcement, but this time with more volume and a higher "whine factor." Again, nothing. You would think one of her big sisters would respond. They didn't. But then, neither did I. I had a newspaper that must be read. The demand repeated. This time the volume was truly frightening. The light over the table shook. A grunt, a glance up, several glares in her direction, but still no Honey Nut Cheerios.

Happily, help was on the way. One floor away, Mom, who had not yet made it down to breakfast, being otherwise occupied with critical last touches on morning makeup, pricked up her "mother's ears" and discerned her baby was in distress. The next announcement was in stereo, the treble line from across the table, the bass from the bathroom above. It worked; the message got through. I staggered to the pantry. Daughters number one and number two never missed a beat. Middle daughter's nose never moved from the book and Nancy Drew would not have to solve her mystery unappreciated. Big sister had partially emptied my wallet and was running out the front door to school. Anyway, serious discussions would have to wait until later in the day.

But by dinnertime, 7:30 p.m. at our house in those days, because of Daddy's inevitably late arrival, we were ready to tackle and solve all world problems. It all started simply enough. I always asked the same question.

"So, how was your day?" Although which daughter was the target of the inquiry varied, the initial response was always a highly predictable "Okay." If I had been smart, I would have accepted this answer and finished the newspaper story that had been interrupted by the Cheerios run twelve hours earlier. But of course, I didn't. First, I was not allowed to read the newspaper at the dinner table. Second, for the millionth, nay billionth, time, I was foolish enough to think I could get a reasonably concise answer to a well-articulated, extremely concise question. Unfortunately, a woman, once fully triggered to speak, just does not answer questions that way, at least no woman who lived at my house.

What unfolded was a begin-at-the-beginning, end-at-the-end, seventeen-chapter novella with no discernible plot. I said end-at-the-end; I take that back. In truth, there was really no end. The story just finished out there somewhere in the outer reaches of the Milky Way. Remembering it was my question that called up this elaborate response, I was in a tough spot. If I let on to my dinner companions that I was not rapturously interested in said story, I would be the object of untold scorn. "You're sooo rude," the chorus would announce.

There was a way to avoid all this, but it would take cunning and cleverness. The trick was to sneak in a mid-story question under the cover of feigned interest. Of course, pulling this off was difficult. It was all in the eyes and the set of the jaw. The right question would rapidly advance the story. If the technique worked, chapters would mercifully whiz by or, better yet, disappear altogether.

But my daughters were clever too. Most of the time, just before reaching the end of the now-abbreviated tale, the storyteller would sense she had left something out, sigh, and dutifully recap the whole story, this time filling in any details somehow missed the first time. I did not just lose at mealtimes. When you live in a house full of women, defeat waits for you around every corner.

Cute Dollars

"Daddy, can I have a dollar cause I'm cute?" This ritual, started long ago by me, was during our child-raising years, a well-honed, time-tested, money-raising device at our house. Eyes appropriately widened and smile set on angelic, what father could resist? Not this one. At last count, this single device, despite the meager size of the prize at stake, cost me $11,342. But who's counting?

However, nowadays having grown up, all my daughters have long since given up on soliciting "cute dollars." A dollar just didn't go that far. More relevantly, when they became teenagers, having to compromise oneself by use of this technique for a meager dollar just didn't seem to cut it. After all, they had entered the world of boys, rock music, and fashion.

That's not to say that later Miss Newly Sophisticated would not be a most willing participant in the prototype for all government programs: the financial assistance from Dad plan. While they gave up the magic phrase of their youth, all were still willing to compromise themselves enough to apply for grants, the denominations of which have left lowly cute dollars in the dust. One request I recollect was roughly equivalent to a year of my grandfather's wages.

Another variation on this was "the lip." The lip is admittedly heavy artillery. This device, inherited from Mom, or perhaps genetically passed to all females, uses no words. It simply combines the above-discussed angelic smile with a focused stare and a slight quiver of the lower lip.

"Sure, I'll buy the Brooklyn Bridge—a bad report card, an accident. You want to study in Europe, *again*—no problem." Add tears and it only gets better. Have you ever apologized for having something of yours broken? I have.

My daughters growing up were an absolute joy. They were also very smart, especially when it came to financial matters. They taught me many things, among them the power of block voting. With their mom as an ally—she always was—all major decisions at our house seemed to be determined by a four-to-one vote.

Lest you worry about me too much, let me say that fortunately there were political forces available other than democratic rule. Take brute force, for example. I'm much bigger than any two, perhaps three, of these ladies. Only kidding—not that I am bigger—but the inference is that I might use this physical advantage to get my way. However, I am not so principled with money. I was only too happy to resort to basic capitalism. I was not too proud to use my enhanced economic power, as the family's primary breadwinner, to buy votes or otherwise corrupt the process. I know that doesn't seem very fair. It bothers me too. But I had to hold my own somehow.

You Can't Prove It!

A bunch of years ago, mid-1990s as I recollect, I had one of those unsettling experiences one can't easily shake. My youngest daughter, then ten years old, and a friend came running into our bookstore to tell me the friend's little brother had just broken the windshield on my Jeep. By the time I arrived at the scene, the young man and his friends had scattered. I gave chase and soon encountered the six-year-old culprit hiding behind a nearby building. The rock thrower looked up at me with a practiced look of nonchalance, that, even at a young age, he had mastered well enough to allow him to claim ignorance to minor mishaps. But the gravity of this situation was too much for his poker face. Eyes, mouth, literally everything on his face, began twitching. Out of breath, I delivered my message, that breaking a window is a serious matter and I would need to talk with his parents. The rock thrower looked relieved. I think he thought I was going to hit him.

Happily, I have insurance for this type of mishap, less one of those nagging $100 deductibles. So, what was I upset about, the $100? No. I was upset about the conversation, if you can call it that, I had with the rock-throwing young man's father a few minutes after the incident. It was a stunner. Dad was upset with me! "How dare you accuse my son of breaking your windshield? Did you see him do it?"

"Well, no, I didn't," I had to admit. But half a dozen kids did, including his daughter, who was the one who came and told me. Well, it seems in the interest of family unity, her story had now changed. A mere half hour after the incident, the party line had been determined and was being aggressively pronounced by Dad, "You can't prove it."

I have been to law school, so I know all about probable cause and admissible evidence. However, the thought of disturbing a quiet afternoon at the Bristol police department with a request that an officer be dispatched to question a bunch of kids was more than I could bear, even if angry. Actually, I was more sad than angry. The father kept talking and I ruminated. Finally, I said to the dad, who by now was deep in my personal space—and I am a big guy—"Is that the lesson you want to teach your son, to lie his way out of a problem?" Apparently it was, because having faced me down, Dad turned on his heel and departed.

"You can't prove it." In a society that increasingly seems to reward its "victims," was it becoming the "American way" to tell the truth only when you could not find any other way out?

Now, I realize as a lawyer, I am in a class with society's great truth manipulators. After all, what is advocacy if it is not massaging the words so much that truth becomes like pasta, straight and stiff before the boiling water, bendable to any shape after. Look at what our politicians and their spin doctors are dishing out to us. This said, I firmly believe honesty and integrity must be taught and modeled. This may be one of the most important principles of parenting.

When I was very young, I used to go with my dad on Sunday mornings when he picked up the papers on the way home from church. On one particular Sunday, when I was about six years old, the same age as the rock thrower, I quietly pocketed a package of candy cigarettes. Even at this young age, I knew better, but I proceeded guiltlessly.

Several hours later, when I was discovered eating my treasure, my dad asked me where I had gotten them. I lied. I think I told him something about a friend having given them to me. In those days, my dad was not afraid to use his considerable power over us kids to let us know how he felt about things like lying and cheating. It was the fifties and fathers then were known to give a "whipping" to a misbehaving child when it was warranted. Although it may have been warranted in this situation, my father chose a different course. He calmly said, "Son, let's go back to the store."

When we got in the car, I coolly sat back with legs and arms crossed. But as we got closer to our destination, my counterfeit composure failed me. This wasn't going to work. I bet my face started twitching too. Finally, I started to cry. Eyes on the road, my dad just kept driving. I wailed out a confession. I begged not to have to face the store owner. My dad kept driving. What followed wasn't pretty, but a valuable lesson was learned that day.

The Eyes

THIS IS THE STORY OF A SET OF EYES THAT HAS STAYED WITH me all my life. All memories that stay with us are not happy—and this one is decidedly not—but it is also one I have never let go.

During my first year of college, when I was eighteen years old, I volunteered to work one afternoon a week at Selinsgrove State Mental Hospital. They do not have these types of institutions anymore these days, opting instead for group homes and other solutions. But in 1970, the profoundly disabled were placed together in wards in large state institutions. I worked on a ward of young ladies so profoundly disabled (in those days the word we used was *retarded*) that the skill I would teach each week was basic hygiene, as in washing one's face or brushing teeth. We also would do creative play.

This was upsetting enough for a young, privileged, and, in many ways, naive college boy. However, it got worse for me when I wandered down the hall to what was called the crib ward. Here the patients, who were not destined to live to be even my age, were crippled, with badly twisted limbs and bodies.

I happened upon the bed of a twelve-year-old girl whose age I knew from the label on the side of her bed. Before I could fully take in how badly deformed her stunted little body was, her eyes locked with mine. They were bright blue, and they were alive. She stunned me with her intense stare. I am sure I verbally gasped. We then stared back and forth at each other for what seemed like forever. I can't actually remember how long this went on. What I do remember was crying on the way home in the van, and again that night, and again and again every time I thought of her all that week.

When I went back to the hospital the next week, I could not help myself, and, of course, I went back to the ward. I did it all over again. I did this at least four times more until, all of a sudden, I went, and the girl was not there. I wasn't supposed to be in this ward, so I was not allowed to ask what happened to her. I would never know.

Although a churchgoer since I was small and a very real believer in God, I thought at this point in my life, I was still figuring out what this belief meant. The connection I made with this girl was initially my all-time low point in this process. For weeks, I railed at God as to how or why He could create the tormented young people who inhabited this hospital, and, in particular, the girl with the blue eyes trapped in a hopelessly twisted body. I was really mad about this.

I was so mad this would take a while, quite a while. At some point, I guess God decided to tell me, and I knew the answer, deeply knew it, such that I have never doubted it for a second since this revelation.

The girl with the blue eyes had a purposeful life too, a powerful purpose. She was there, at least partially, for me. Her job was to humble me, to make me grateful, to give me compassion, and to never let me forget that her eyes would always be watching me. They still do. Every day. Apparently, God's plan is often much bigger than we get to understand.

Miracles

Do you ever think about miracles? I do. At Sunday school when I was a kid, every week we heard about new ones: burning bushes, parted waters, miracle healings of all types, and of course that a few fish and a couple loaves of bread always seemed to feed a big crowd. What's most disappointing about these miracles is that none of this stuff seems to happen nowadays. When I am in a big crowd, I always have to find the refreshment stand, and if I have the family with me, I have to part with a sum roughly equivalent to annual wages of, say, my grandfather, to get what everyone wants.

Does it ever offend you that the Bible seems to be chock-full of miracles and our modern experience is utterly devoid of them? It does me. To be honest, instead of filling me with awe, all those miracles trouble me. I am not just talking about the skepticism that is the inevitable by-product of lots of education, as if this were not a formidable enough hurdle to believing these stories. I'm talking about fair play. It seems to me that if all the miracles really happened, then why isn't God paying closer attention these days? Couldn't we use a few miracles in our screwed-up modern world, if they are really so easy to come by?

Well, I have a theory. You knew I would. Perhaps *most* miracles, even the biblical ones, are like the faith healings that pepper the evangelical side of today's church: at best, the power of positive thinking (which I like), at worst, fraud (which I do not like), or somewhere in the middle, as in creative storytelling to make a point worth making (I can live with this).

Let's deal with the fraud first. Have you ever turned into "Christian television" and heard the folks sit there and announce, "I am thinking of (reading a name off a card) who has pain in her leg," and then with an expression of shared pain and soap-opera-quality compassion, announce, "Through the power of God, your pain is gone." Ugh. Even if you believe, as I do, that God has the power to take away someone's pain, could this possibly be His chosen vessel? When the TV healing time is followed by invitations to send money in support of all the good this particular program is doing, this version of modern-day miracles gets even harder. Well, thank goodness I think God has a sense of humor and is not inclined toward lightning bolts. If He were, it wouldn't be just the lights that would be hot in this television studio.

So, let's eliminate the money-raising miracles. Tainted stuff. If God answers these calls, it is either a coincidence or because even He feels sorry for a victim. But all this begs the bigger question: If God is available for miracles on request, how come He makes His or Her believers suffer so much and keeps them in the dark on how the whole process works? How does God decide when to deliver a miracle? There is lots of theology here, but my humble, not-so-theological view can be stated in short order. I think God simply abides by His own plan, not ours. And I think His plan is pretty much to leave us alone to figure it out ourselves. Does this sound familiar to you parents of teenagers? It should.

We parents often, as God always does, know how to do it better, but how is our teenager going to learn if they don't try? Even more fundamental, in God's plan, a sickness, a death, poverty, loss of a job, or a relationship, no matter how fervent the prayers in opposition, may be the right thing, not something bad. Why do we humans so emphatically and continually presume to know what is best for us? That is the question I'd be pondering if I were God.

Now that I have doused this whole subject with a healthy dose of my pseudo-intellectual skepticism, I will undertake a spectacular flip-flop and confess I believe miracles are indeed very possible. Not when we want them, necessarily, and not always for what we perceive as important. The key, as in so much in life, is to pay attention so you won't miss them when they occur.

My miracles, both of them, were pretty garden variety; both have to do with finding something. The two miracles occurred about thirty years apart, and both had the everyday quality that loudly proclaims nothing is too small to escape God's notice. Neither had importance in the larger world, nor even were known by anyone but me. Ironically, on the day of the second miracle, as I took an early morning walk, I had been thinking about the first of the miracles, how long ago it had occurred, and that I wished God would send me more of these simple signs of His presence. Apparently, on this day, God's plan intersected with mine.

My oldest daughter is a city girl. On this day, she was to graduate from a great city institution, the prestigious and very large New York University. Emphasis here is on very large. The NYU graduation is held outside by commandeering historic ten-acre Washington Square Park in Greenwich Village and all of the surrounding streets. The year was 2000, and Ciera was graduating along with the undergraduates and graduate students in NYU's fourteen colleges. In all, there were 13,000 graduates decked out in purple caps and gowns.

To fully comprehend the event, you have to add to all these graduates twenty thousand proud parents and guests, and more, thirty thousand folding chairs—yes, fewer chairs than people—squeezed into the otherwise ample park, most behind dog runs, children's playground equipment, and park benches, few with any meaningful view of the platform. The procession of graduates started blocks away and took one and a half hours to wind itself to the center of the park and their assigned seats of honor—actually, the only seats with a really good view.

Carol and I had already attended Ciera's graduation from her own "college" three days earlier, which, while still large, almost filling three-thousand-seat Carnegie Hall, was manageable. Ciera processed to the stage, and I have the picture to prove it.

For the second graduation on a beautiful June day, with Carol back in Vermont, my then seventy-year-old mom was filling in, anxious to see the oldest of her eighteen grandchildren graduate. I had some trepidations about taking "Nana," but she was determined. We arrived an hour and a half before the speeches were to commence, surprised to discover streets already blocked off, people everywhere, and a river of purple-gowned students having begun their march toward the center of the park.

I quickly developed a plan. As I encouraged a now less-sure grandmother out of the car and into the crowd, at the closest point that I was allowed to park the car—many blocks away—I handed her an official entrance ticket and one of two walkie-talkies from my glove compartment. I pointed to a nearby entrance and told her I would park the car as close as I could and then call her on the walkie-talkie. She could then talk me into wherever she had located two seats. The parking went fine once I offered a "premium"—roughly equivalent to another year of my grandfather's salary—so as to not have to return to New Jersey for a parking space. Okay, this will work, I thought.

However, congratulating oneself too soon is always dangerous. As I walked toward the park, fumbling with my walkie-talkie, I discovered that when I had hastily turned them on and checked the volume a few minutes earlier, I had failed to check if the two units were set to the same channel. Apparently, they were not. This critical omission was going to render my high-tech solution useless for finding my then seventy-year-old, five-foot-two mother in a ten-acre city park presently overrun by more than thirty thousand people.

When I got to the gate where I had dropped off Mom, the guard told me this area was full and I would have to walk to a completely different entrance around the corner. Had my mom been told the same thing fifteen minutes earlier? Likely not. When I found the entrance I had been redirected to, I began anxiously navigating through thousands of people. A very long four minutes that seemed like four hours later, I handed over my admission ticket and dove again into the sea of people, now at least among those admitted with tickets. I began to cut up and down aisles, methodically swiveling my head back and forth, trying to take in thousands of faces, looking for one. I was sweating and breathing hard.

Although I am not very comfortable praying for specific personal requests, preferring to leave myself in God's capable hands, at this moment, my prayer was focused, direct, and immediate: "God, please let me find my mom." When I raised my head, my eyes were drawn, first, to the area behind the fenced-in crowd, to the river of purple streaming down the street to join the purple ocean at the center of the park. Then my gaze focused on the crowd directly in front of me. There, to my shock, was my mom, standing next to two open chairs ten yards ahead of me. She was fiddling with the walkie-talkie. She saw me too. As I walked toward her and returned her smile of recognition and relief, I glanced up to the street over her shoulder. Not twenty yards behind her, in the middle of the endless flow of purple, I looked directly into the eyes of the precious daughter we had come to watch.

The other miracle, the one that occurred thirty years earlier, happened when my parents bought me a high school ring, which instantly became a cherished possession. Tellingly, by the time I went to law school ten years later this ring was by then not so important and I sold it along with some other unused jewelry to raise money for my oldest daughter's day care tuition. However, in 1969, there was probably nothing I owned as important to me as this ring.

Not long after I got the ring, I lost it on a massive sandy beach at the edge of the Atlantic Ocean. The area of search was never-ending sand. I marched back and forth between the jetties a couple of football fields apart, with only late-sixties male macho holding back tears of disappointment. Finally, I asked God for help, and then there was the ring at my feet in the sand. That little miracle, utterly insignificant in the big picture, was so real and personal for me that it carried me through all manner of crises in the years that followed.

As I type this, it seems to me what I really found on these two days thirty years apart was not the object sought, but some understanding of my place in a world that might indeed occasionally experience divine intervention.

Sailing Through Life

SOME FOLKS PLAY GOLF OR TENNIS. THESE ARE GOOD SPORTS to start when you're young. They allow you to continue playing into old age. Not me. My adult sports were my kids' activities. Skiing and sailing became my passions. Tennis was my sport for only a year or two in my mid-thirties. Doubles were in and joining a tennis club was the right thing to do. It was mostly just embarrassing.

Golf, especially if you like and get somewhat good at it, to me seems a perfect storm of diversion. Under the cover of building business connections, you can play with your friends for hours, not just on weekends, but during the week as well. I made a passing attempt to become a golfer. But all the time and frustration never really made much sense to me. What was all this desire to hit a little white ball hundreds of yards, often into the woods, streams, sand traps, and the like?

I enjoyed golf as a social event. You know, a friendly foursome playing for the American Cancer Society, the chamber of commerce, or Rotary. I would carefully choose the foursome, comprised of friends and clients who could accept my erratic play. The idea was to hit a one hundred on a good day.

My golf career ended on a Monday in August 1997. I remember the day. New Jersey was at its hottest and most humid and, as "real golfers," we walked the course without using golf carts. This foursome was not my choosing. It had been delivered to me as a gift by the CEO of the bank that sponsored the outing—a client, I might add. These three guys knew each other well; I knew none of them. My companions were big-ego developer types. They were also scratch golfers. In a word, they "hated" me.

The ski accident you will learn about elsewhere was a year and a half behind me by then, but my occasional limp and one-inch-shorter leg was not. This day the limp became a gimp and, eventually, by about the fifteenth hole, I was dragging my right leg behind me. My drives that day seemed to be either to the ladies' tee or another fairway. My best shots on the fairway were those when I missed the ball completely. My putting did not become consistent until my companions let me flaunt the rules and just pick up my ball when my score hit eight. After that, I was a consistent eight.

I seriously considered faking a heart attack. I didn't even stay for the ritual dinner when prizes were given out so abundantly. When I got home that night, I put my golf clubs at the curb with a sign marked "Free." Happily, they were gone in the morning.

Sailing was something else, altogether. This I always loved despite my becalmed race story related earlier. Although I read and enjoy all those stories about people who have chucked their land-based obligations to cruise the world with a willing spouse, this was not me, if for no other reason than I had no willing spouse. Carol was the absolute best and my partner in almost everything. However, I think her support for my pronounced enthusiasm for sailing, which came in our late forties, was only because she compared it to all the couples our age riding around on Harleys. When I had cleverly suggested a motorcycle along with a new sailboat as possible post-kid diversions, she said, "Let's look at boats."

Carol became a more-than-able first mate as we cruised around Lake Champlain, and later around the US and British Virgin Islands and on bareboat charters in exotic ports as far away as New Zealand. But she drew the line at sailing across an ocean. I even tried telling her

I would have to find some beautiful young sailing bimbo to accompany me if she declined. She quickly announced, "Good luck with that." Then she said she would meet me when I docked on the other side. Presumably, her job would be to pick up the pieces.

Carol is tricky this way. When we first got into serious sailing, we took an advanced cruising course. Although I had years of experience, I took the class with her, "to keep her company." At the end of three days, there was a written test as well as the need to sail a course. When the score came in, my chest swelled when the instructor congratulated me on my ninety-six. My moment of glory was smashed a minute later when he revealed my mate had scored a perfect one hundred.

Our first big sailboat was a twenty-eight-foot O'Day. When we bought it, it was twenty-five years old and cheap. After a few years of sailing this boat, *Chapter II*, around Lake Champlain, we decided a more substantial investment was in order. We traded it in for a practically new thirty-six-footer, this time a Hunter. It had all the bells and whistles, including a self-furling mainsail as well as jib, and, of no small importance, a comfortable main cabin. You see, in the twenty-eight-footer, Carol and I slept in single bunks on either side of what during the day was our living room and kitchen. Buy a new sailboat so you can sleep with your wife, instead of across the room from her! Sounds kind of stupid, even to me—but in this case, I am guilty as charged.

Sailboats nowadays are big and beamy—"wide" for you landlubbers. They are basically RVs with sails on top. Even the sails' rigging is made to be easy. I mentioned the sails self-furl. This means you can raise and lower both sails from the cockpit. Actually, you can do pretty much everything from the cockpit. Down the companionway (stairs to the inside), you enter the cabin (living room) and galley (kitchen) area and then, of course, there is the stateroom (master bedroom) with the queen-sized bed. All the comforts of home.

Our last sailboat was *Epilogue*, a fifty-foot Beneteau, and it had everything all the others did, just more of it. I will leave the story of this boat to the Epilogue of this book. Epilogues are unique. They need to stick together.

On Being a Guy

SOMETIMES MEN NEED TO BE WITH EACH OTHER. NO WOMEN. The activity doesn't matter. It's the companionship, bonding, support, and holding each other accountable, or sometimes not doing so, that is important.

Let me put my credentials on the table to make such a statement. Despite being male, I am in many ways a card-carrying feminist. At least, nowadays I am. Actually, it has been quite a transition. I was raised in the 1950s by a wonderful, hard-working dad and an equally wonderful stay-at-home mom. When I was a kid, fathers almost always served as the family boss. Despite this role modeling, by the early seventies, when I met and courted my wife, I had loosened up a bit. By then, my liberalized view was that a perfect male–female relationship would run on, say, a 60/40 split of authority. Carol still married me despite this view, but she had her misgivings. After fifty years of marriage to this competent, compassionate woman, and a world that has changed around us, we are both very much devoted to the beauty and workability of a 50/50 relationship, a true partnership.

I feel the same about the workplace. As the father of three daughters, who worked hard educating themselves for their lives and careers, I cherish the idea of a world where a woman can do anything she wants to do. I want no glass ceilings holding down my daughters in the working world.

So why do I think men need to spend time with other men? While I believe women and men should enjoy total equality of opportunity, I also strongly believe men and women are inherently different. I am not just talking about anatomy. In my view, males and females approach the world differently. Many women, dare I say most women, look at the world a little more emotionally and often more compassionately. Whether this is learned or bred into the gender that bears children and must endure the hormonal and physical cycles that go with this privilege, it is a reality. A hug, a gentle touch, or just listening, will frequently work better with a woman than an oh-so-logical plan to solve the problem; it is a fact of life. To me, this more feminine approach is to be valued. I, for one, would like to see more of our elected officials have it. I am not suggesting the halls of government need more hugging, only that a little more compassion and basic fairness at the expense of cold logic might serve us all well.

There is a flip side to a world where the role of women is changing. All this change can be hard on us men. Many of us are struggling just to keep up. Our entire society has trouble figuring out the changing roles. Take television and movies, for example. Gone are the strong, respected father figures we grew up with. Now sitcom fathers are the clueless butt of family jokes they never seem to get. At my house, happily, it was never this bad. But dinner with three daughters and a wife can be a little rough going. Disagreeing with any one of them can bring down a chorus of "Men don't understand," that leaves me outvoted, outgunned, and wishing for the son I never had. Carol says I am outvoted not because I'm male, but because I am wrong. Maybe, but maybe not. Perhaps I am outvoted simply because I have the perspective of a man.

This brings me to my central point. We men need to help each other. We need each other for support, to compare notes, to help us learn how to be good husbands and fathers in a world where our fathers' good examples, when they were good, no longer seem relevant.

I had two brothers and a father. My father has now passed. As to my brothers, we talk, not enough, I suspect, because like most men, we have trouble getting down to the "personal stuff." This is yet another challenge for us guys.

Every Monday morning from 7:00 to 8:00 a.m. for about twenty years from the mid-nineties until the teens, I had a group of ten or twelve men who met at our bookstore, and then later down the road in a different place. We called ourselves Men Under Construction. Sometimes it was a Bible study, sometimes it was just talk, but always it was brotherhood. It was a good thing and the men needed it. I miss this group.

I also had a group of eight guys with whom I have gone on a western ski trip in the first week of March for more than thirty years. I first put the group together from good friends, including some who were also clients. Jim Jaworski was my law partner; Lou Capuano, a plumbing contractor, was a friend from church. Brent Edmonds, a general contractor, was a friend and client. Terry Beltramini, a landscape contractor, was Brent's best buddy since high school. Dean Cerf, a veterinarian and businessman, was also a friend from church, and a client. Harold Knutsen, who managed his family-owned health club, was a client. And finally, there was Al Lapatka, a civil engineer and good friend who built his business alongside of mine. While we are all friends—and some of us have done business deals with each other—we often do not talk except during that once-a-year trip.

Only one of these guys, Dean, bowed out of the group a half dozen years ago. The rest of us just keep going on the trip. I did all the planning for the first twenty years. Jim then took over, and he has, if anything, surpassed me in picking fun locations. During the thirty-plus years we have done these trips, it has become a little like *Same Time, Next Year*, a movie about a couple who had a one-weekend-a-year, longtime affair. So much life has happened, and we share it all for one week every year. Three guys are married, one is divorced, one dropped out of the group, and tragically two years ago, Al Lapatka died. The seven survivors cried like babies when this happened.

Over the years, we have drunk a lot of drinks, smoked some great cigars and a bit of other stuff, skied, enjoyed tens of dozens of superb meals, and shared thousands of stories of our sixteen children, the grandchildren, and our wives and girlfriends. We have endured each other's current diet or exercise programs or latest business schemes. A while back we decided to keep the trip going forever.

Sometimes being a man is not easy. No longer the kings of the world, we need more than ever to sometimes nourish each other. In my cherished world of no glass ceilings, I hope there will still always be places and times where men can be with men.

December 1959

ON THE LAST DAY OF 1959, I WAS SEVEN YEARS OLD. ON THAT day, I vividly remember being in the attic of my parents' house, listening to a crystal transistor radio I had received as a Christmas present the week before. Transistor radios in those days were nothing like today's high-powered stereo counterparts. They had just been invented and were small, cheap, and plastic. They boasted scratchy AM reception, and this was only if the radio's antenna wire was clipped to something metal, like a pipe.

On the afternoon of New Year's Eve, and the end of a decade, through the static roughly equivalent to a hard rain on a metal roof, I was treated to a countdown of the best music of the closing decade, the 1950s. I wish I could tell you the songs. But alas, this information, if it is still in there, is stored in one of those dark, musty closets of my brain that lately I don't seem to open. What I remember from that afternoon in December 1959 was the radio disc jockeys talking about the New Year's event forty years in the future, at the turn of the century. He was happily contemplating what he predicted would be the party to end all parties. Because the numbers were big for someone only halfway through third grade, it took me a few minutes to figure out that in the year 2000, I would be forty-eight years old. Forty-eight! Almost dead, or I might as well be.

Well, before I knew it, it arrived—the year 2000, that is—and I was not dead. But my seven-year-old past self could no longer read small print without glasses and had started to move somewhat slower.

This particular turn of the calendar, being not just another year, but a decade, a century, and the millennium, was supposed to be a big deal. I can report that my expectations were not too high. I would be awake, of this I was sure, which I had not been on some New Year's Eves. I would not stay up because I thought the world would end, either because God had given up on us; because our computer cyberworld has turned on us, imploding our utilities, ATMs, and Nintendo games; or because I thought an atomic war would accidentally be triggered by a computer frustrated by not knowing whether it was 2000 or 1900. Remember all those crazy ideas?

In the mid-1990s, Carol and I celebrated New Year's Eve at what was our most exotic year-end locale, Chamonix, France, in the French Alps. That year our eldest daughter was an exchange student in Europe, and my youngest sister and her family were stationed in Holland. We all decided to gather at a European ski location. On the train between Paris and the little town in the Alps, we made a list of our past twenty-five New Year's Eves. Even with Carol's better memory for this kind of thing, we had many blanks on the list. Quiet nights at home, I guess. All and all, not a bad way to spend the night.

Every year when we enter the holiday season, beginning with Thanksgiving, followed by Christmas, and finally New Year's Eve, I grow philosophical. It's not easy to be philosophical when you're so busy that most of the time you can't remember what day it is. However, as the season progresses, I find myself in equal measures grateful for my many blessings, overwhelmed by all the secular joy that has attached itself to Christmas, looking forward to and then always a little disappointed by family traditions that seem to miss the mark, exhausted, and finally optimistically making resolutions to do a little better in the new year.

The year with the millennium change was really no different in the end. I confess I had been a little awed by the sheer number of years that had gone by. Forty-eight seemed like a lot, then. Should I do something momentous? Would I enjoy some astonishing enlightenment? Not so much.

Here's my New Year's Eve contemplation, written in my backyard writing house on the last night of 1999, the year the millennium changed:

> Every day is a new day to do my best; attitude is more important than ability; people more important than things; God loves me; time is precious; life is a journey not a destination; we should all talk less and say more; feeling good is good; love is the answer; and finally that I can work harder, know more, understand better, persevere longer, sacrifice more, move faster, sit quieter, find more contentment, and be a better person than I think I can, so I better keep trying.

At this point, my best guess is I will likely finish each of my remaining calendar years kissing Carol as long as we are both here, and comfortably contemplating a few important lessons I have learned in the years since 1959 when I first thought about this big night.

Evelina

I came to Austin, Texas, for a three-day meeting with the editors I had in mind to help me create, write, and publish the book you are now reading. I flew in from St. Thomas the night before. Really the whole day before. This distance, with two long flights including a changeover and time change, took all of Tuesday.

I got up at 6:30 a.m., early for me, and organized myself in the hotel that would be home for the next three days, a nice seven-room inn near the meeting site. Since I don't walk well these days, I had rented a car to cover what others would call a healthy walking distance to get me back and forth. I drove to the meeting place, then kept on driving to look for a place for a quick breakfast. The highway revealed a lot of bars, now closed. A Tex-Mex vibe was everywhere.

I did not drive far before spotting a low, neat, blue building with a big sign at its front, Pete's Bakery. There were lots of cars, always a good sign. I found a parking space easily. Inside, I was met with a sign to seat myself and a full room of diners. There were lots of those prefab plastic booths with the seats on both sides of the table, and the table itself formed a single unit. From past experience, I avoid these, as my large size and ample girth inevitably leave me with the table cutting into my stomach. I found an old-fashioned table for two with chairs and sat down. Scanning the room, I was delighted to find the crowd very local. Working types, mostly Hispanic, all engaged, unlike me, a solo diner, with someone or in a group talking as well as eating. The room felt nice, the crowd comfortable.

A youngish, but on the edge of middle age, waitress arrived with a menu, and soon after, coffee. I studied the menu, taco breakfast items. I picked a combination of scrambled eggs, taco shells, cheese, and beans.

As I ate, for some reason, I reached down to touch my front pocket where I always keep my wallet. Nothing. My mind raced right past how or why I left it back in the room to, Do I have cash or a credit card in my bag? No. Money in the car? No. It was a rental. Race again, through all the places, all the pockets. In seconds, I knew I had a problem. I was due at the meeting in ten minutes.

Flash to a recent time when I had also forgotten my wallet. Is this forgetting money incident becoming a sign of my aging mind? I had not done this—forgotten my wallet—in decades; now it had happened twice in a month.

That other time, Carol had suggested I see if the restaurant took Apple Pay from my phone. I have this feature but barely know how to use it. What the heck. I would try it again. The first time I tried it, the waiter took my phone, and moments later, he was back, letting me put in the tip.

One look around the room and I thought, That won't work here. But then I was skeptical when my wife suggested I try it the first time. I flagged down the waitress. I had barely started the breakfast, so her look said, Is there something wrong? Embarrassed, I confessed, "I forgot my wallet. Do you take payments from the phone?" She looked a little puzzled, and then said, "I don't know. I can check." Then a smile crossed her face, and she said quietly, "Don't worry about it." She was telling me I did not need to pay.

I was shocked. Gobsmacked really. I sputtered, "I will pay tomorrow." She did not seem to care but said she would be off the next day but would be back the day after. In my mind, a deal had been made. I asked her name. It was Evelina, but she was called Evie. I was immensely relieved. Evelina scurried off to the next table.

I thought about this waitress more than once in the next couple days. Before I left, she had given me the bill I did not pay. It was $16.00. I decided Evie, who I had not really even focused on while I was in the restaurant, was quite attractive. Was she, or was I just so damn happy with her act of kindness?

I came back two days later, as promised. I made sure I had plenty of time. I sat down and I had a different waiter promptly show up. This time, I got two bacon, egg, and cheese tacos. The taco shell would have been good enough to eat by itself. I asked my waiter if Evie was here. She was.

"Can I see her?"

Across the room I saw him find her. I imagined him saying, "Some guy wants to talk with you." I saw her look over his shoulder at the guy he was referring to, initially a bit apprehensive. Then she broke into a smile of recognition. When she arrived, I gave her the unpaid bill I had been carrying around in my pocket for two days and a $100 bill. Her face became radiant. She hugged me and then she kissed me.

"Thank you so much," she said.

"No, thank you," I replied. The chemistry and magic of the moment was palpable.

Evie came back twice while I was eating. The first time she thanked me again and asked my name. The second time she brought me a bag of baked goods and gave me another radiant smile and another kiss. The world is still full of real people. How nice to be reminded of this.

Me with daughters Ciera, Jordyn, and Carlyn, 1988

Making cider on Main Street in front of our bookstore in Bristol, Vermont, with Carlyn, 1996

Me and my brothers, Jeff and Peter, 2018

My ski buddies and me. L to R—Al Lapatka, Jim Jaworski, me, Terry Beltramini, Brent Edmonds; kneeling—Lou Capuano, Dean Cerf, Harold Knutsen, Sun Valley, Idaho, 1996. Trip still going strong today, after thirty-four years.

Sailing in the Virgin Islands on my sixty-fifth birthday, 2017

Me and my mom. I was being honored by the Ridgewood YMCA, 2019.

At my desk at the law office in 2013

SECTION IV

On the Soapbox

I am nothing if not full of opinions. Sometimes, I wear them on my sleeve; often, not so much. Anyone who knows me well certainly knows my politics are left of center, although I try to emphasize my pragmatism to those who are less comfortable with this. My lifelong belief in giving back comes up over and over again.

In the last section, I often used humor to tell my stories. Here, I am more about logic and passionately felt ideas. I try to keep myself grounded in facts—real facts, not those slanted to a particular point of view. My interesting and somewhat unique love of compromise, strong convictions, my take on God, religion, and giving back, are very much exposed here for your enjoyment or to debate, something I also love to do.

Just Do It!

NIKE, THE SNEAKER PEOPLE WHO LATER EXPANDED INTO A sporting goods colossus, years ago—in 1987, I checked—coined a phrase that has stuck with me then and ever since. I suspect I am not alone in this. This phrase, born as just one more clever Madison Avenue advertising slogan, was at once startling in its simplicity and yet complex, powerful, and wise. I am speaking, of course, of the "Just Do It" campaign.

"Just Do It," proclaimed the Nike commercial, either in a voiceover or in block letters, after illustrating many human endeavors, usually physical. I suspect the campaign sold a lot of sneakers. As it is difficult to overstate the sheer power of a decision made, whether to exercise (the message of the commercials), to run down to the mall and buy Nike sneakers (the campaign's real purpose), or stripped of its commercial overtones, to get virtually anything done, the nifty little three-word slogan will, for me, always be a classic.

Why? Just doing it is how things get done. What the words at the end of the commercial never told you, but I will, is that this frighteningly simple concept is almost always the vital ingredient of the secret formula late-night television hawkers and internet memes use to make you rich or get you thin.

It is axiomatic to state that nothing happens without the will to do it. The concept is more complex, however. How many times have you met a successful person, successful at what doesn't matter, and thought, I'm smarter than he or she is. Why didn't I think of that?

Often, you probably were and did. However, because you are smarter, you also thought of a lot of reasons why the idea could not succeed. And worse, you may have been absolutely right. What you did not know is that determination and ignorance are sometimes first cousins.

Now I am not knocking knowledge. Knowledge and preparation, especially gained at the knee of someone who knows what they are doing or perhaps from a book or two, a plan of some kind, or maybe even good instincts, can all be very helpful. You know from the earlier chapter on Wells Mountain Initiative, I teach this "just do it" philosophy to the WMI Scholars in our cleaned-up version, Dream, Plan, Do! Not only does this idea make my "twelve principles" but it, along with "giving back," is one of the two most important ones.

I have met a few genuinely lucky people in my life. They are among the few successful people I know who have found success without the simple "just do it" philosophy. Someone has to win the lottery, inherit millions, be at the proverbial right place at the right time, but for the rest of us, the will to dig in and "just do it" is almost always the key.

So, having this figured out, am I rich and successful as hell? Well, not necessarily rich, but not poor, either—unless, of course, this book becomes a bestseller—but most days, I feel pretty successful. Those who know me know that I am nothing if not decisive. I have been blessed all my life with the ability to make a decision and stick with it to a conclusion.

Now I guess I owe you some case studies to prove this point. "Dream, Plan, Do!," when done, actually works. If my only goal was to inspire, I could just point you to Bill Gates and his garage, or Apple's Steve Jobs, or the Google guys, or Jeff Bezos, or Elon Musk. Even before the cyber age, there were plenty of examples. The likes of Sam Walton, or before him, Henry Ford, Andrew Carnegie, or

John D. Rockefeller. The "Dream, Plan, Do!—just do it" premise is well supported and not just in business. Self-made men and women who would not take no for an answer is what America is all about.

This book is not about any of these folks, however. It is about me. Thus, I will digress into the eight businesses I have created over the years—a women's clothing store, an energy conservation company, a law firm, a bookstore, a real estate development company, a Vermont country inn, a Vermont products store, and finally, a charitable foundation. We need to see if I learned any lessons worth sharing, other than it never happens if you don't jump off and just Dream, Plan, Do!

Gazebo was a woman's clothing store in a central Pennsylvania college town. I started it with my then-girlfriend—later wife—in 1973, and it operated successfully until 1977. Lewisburg, Pennsylvania, home of Bucknell University, where Carol and I were undergraduates in the early seventies, and the less illustrious, but just as important to the town's economy, Lewisburg Federal Penitentiary. Lewisburg was then and still is a beautiful county seat in central Pennsylvania nestled along the Susquehanna River. It is equidistant from the urban centers of Philadelphia and Pittsburgh and sixty miles up the river from the state capital at Harrisburg.

Lewisburg, basically in the middle of nowhere, was a great place to go to college. I was less sure of this as an eighteen-year-old college applicant when I got stuck behind a coal delivery truck on a narrow downtown street when I came out from oh-so-hip northern New Jersey for a college interview. I told everyone I was headed for George Washington University, and only at the last minute opted for the small town and Bucknell, after a particularly compelling call from an alumnus.

During my first year of college, I lived in a dorm like everyone else. The second year I lived in a fraternity house, and by the third year, my plan was to share an apartment downtown with a fraternity buddy—which would facilitate frequent overnight visits by our respective girlfriends who happened to be sorority sisters.

The apartment was rented in June, and we moved in. We went

home for the summer. Midsummer of 1972, the Susquehanna River poured over its banks in what was called Hurricane Agnes, and, more relevantly, so did Bull Run Creek, a tributary that ran near the apartment. The result was two feet of water in the building. I didn't have much of value in those days, so I got the apartment fixed up pretty quickly, but the Main Street store in front of the apartment was damaged and then closed.

The waterlogged store was now for rent for $125 a month and it got my "Dream, Plan, Do!" juices flowing. "Gazebo—a young woman's boutique" was the result. I built a small eight-sided shingled example of the namesake in the middle of the store. We laid carpet, hung a ceiling, added dressing rooms, bought a cash register, and somehow purchased merchandise in the New York fashion market and opened for business on Valentine's Day 1973.

From the beginning, we had a few employees—a couple students and a college professor's wife—and made a little money. It was fun but never had sales much over $100,000, which was more then than now.

By 1977, we bought and owned the building. When Carol and I were ready to move on, no one wanted to buy the whole business, but some other dreamer couple had an idea for a new business, so we rented the store to them. Gazebo got renamed to Matters of Importance. This store hung in there for three or four more years.

Later, while I was in law school and running low on money, we sold the building to a husband and wife who wanted to change the store into a restaurant called Union Station. I should mention this downtown store began its life as an A & P when it was built in about 1900. To my knowledge, it also did time as a beauty shop, an antique store, and an apartment. Downtown stores usually have stories to tell. This one is no different.

My second "Dream, Plan, Do!" business was Central Pennsylvania Energy Savers located in, well, central Pennsylvania. This enterprise lasted about a year and a half, and by any measure, went bust. Jimmy Carter was president, and we were in the first energy crisis. We sold solar heat installations, extremely primitive by today's standards, did house insulation using cellulose and later-discredited urea formaldehyde, and sold woodstoves.

Carter, arguably our best ex-president, was not nearly so successful in office and, despite a majority Democratic congress, couldn't even get his pet energy bill through both houses into law. Lack of capital and no long-promised energy credit killed this company in no time flat. We avoided bankruptcy by paying all the bills the hard way.

A particularly expensive bill we had to pay captures the essence of this business. To be into solar heat in 1973, you had to be pretty forward thinking. There was no such thing as photovoltaics, so in those days, solar panels heated either air or water. The water systems used antifreeze pumped through roof panels and then pumped down to the basement where the solar-heated antifreeze would run through coils in the potable—read that "drinking"—water, thus heating it up, at least a little.

The alternative to this was a drain-down system. It pumped the potable water through the panel on the roof to heat it. Neither system heated the water all that well, and the water often needed to be further heated in a conventional water heater by electricity or gas, especially in the winter.

Winter and freezing temperatures were also the culprit of the drain-down system, when, if by some chance, the system did not drain down as instructed by a series of differential thermostats, certain freezing and a leak on the roof, or worse, in your attic, could result.

You absolutely do not want this to happen. This is the case if the family happens to be away for the weekend, like when the first of the two drain-down systems we installed failed. Water flows downward, of course, so a leak in the attic effectively puts water on every level, until it finally finds its way to the basement.

For years, I used the copper elbow joint that had the crack that leaked as my key chain fob to remind me to "stick with what you know"—which may be the flip side of "just do it."

After these two businesses, I had my only sustained period of paychecks from others, first in various law jobs while in law school, and then for two law firms—one really big with sixty lawyers, and a small one consisting of the principal and me. During this time, including the three years in law school, my paychecks lasted eight years. That's when I started my own law firm, which brings us to business number three and me back to "Dream, Plan, Do!"

I started my law practice with me and a secretary in 1986. By far my most successful venture, it still exists today as Wells, Jaworski & Liebman LLP and has thirteen lawyers and thirty-five staff. The first day was considerably less distinguished. As you learned earlier, in a huff, I had given my notice to the lawyer I was working for on a Saturday. For lots of reasons, including a personality that made me sure that quitting was a good idea, I was unemployed immediately. I had to open my own shop the following Monday. Dream—yes. Plan—not so much. Do—absolutely.

I was determined to do it my way: high-quality work, unpretentious and compassionate problem-solving, civic commitment, high ethics, and constant civility to all concerned, clients and adversaries. I opened for business at a borrowed desk in a borrowed office. Three weeks later, I had my own place and a secretary. Two months later, I hired an associate attorney and a second secretary.

After ten years, the law firm had already grown to roughly its present size. I was forty-four and ready for a change. You know from the "Living Your Dream" chapter I decamped to Vermont, or at least I thought I would. I tried to phase out of the New Jersey law practice. When it didn't happen, I enjoyed my status as a moving target, which, together with a rather national law practice, kept me on the road and in airplanes a lot. WJ&L will celebrate its fortieth anniversary in 2026.

The fourth business was a bookstore, Deerleap Books. As a kid, I read at the table and under the covers at night. I was a bit of a book nerd. I grew up loving bookstores, and when I saw one for sale in a small Vermont town in 1986, I just had to have it. Fortunately, as discussed elsewhere in this book, I am married to a saint and the plan was approved. The bookstore never made much money in the ten years we operated it, and that's why my retirement from the law practice didn't happen until much later.

Since I was a real estate and business lawyer, real estate is what I knew. If ever "Dream, Plan, Do!" applies, I thought it was this. Mostly in Vermont, I bought, rehabilitated, and then managed with Carol a half dozen real estate properties. This actually made us money, but also provided good tax benefits and prospects for retirement. Anyway, call this enterprise, Wells Mountain, LLC, business number five.

The real estate entity first included an apartment building that we slowly converted to a seven-room country inn, Bristol Suites, our version of Bob Newhart's Vermont country inn. Call this number six. Finally, in 2019, a Vermont products store, number seven. Both are quite successful, and we still own both, but as I write this, we have decided to list them for sale.

Wells Mountain Initiative (originally Wells Mountain Foundation) came into existence in 2005. Despite prominent use of the Wells name, it was not a private foundation as in Bill and Melinda Gates Foundation. Private foundations get more than 50 percent of their money from one individual or family. Mine doesn't. In fact, I fundraise most of its annual income, and one very generous client and friend was the real angel in the beginning. The foundation is the eighth business I created.

So, these are my personal examples of Dreaming, Planning, Doing. What have I learned from creating these eight businesses? First and foremost, each business could have died on the table if the fledgling entrepreneur took time to think about it—analysis paralysis, I like to call it. You could argue for Central Pennsylvania in this venture, but I gained valuable knowledge I later used to great advantage. Remember that principle: fail forward!

Eight businesses later, and those thirty-two other jobs I talked about earlier, I can honestly report I've enjoyed a well-lived life. Lots of fun, much learning, material success, and wonderful relationships. None of it would have happened without following the mantra, Dream, Plan, Do!

We All Have Something

"Is 'fat' really the worst thing a human being can be? Is 'fat' worse than 'vindictive,' 'jealous,' 'shallow,' 'vain,' 'boring,' or 'cruel?' Not to me."

—J. K. ROWLING

We all have something. I believe this. It is what I tell anybody who feels sorry for themself because of a calamity. For sure, some calamities are much worse than others: a bad diagnosis, a fatal one, your spouse just died, or, even worse, your child. However, much less significant stuff can be your something: a lost job, an injury, just a bad date, a terrible haircut, a bad cold sore prominently on your lip, or a person disappointing you.

I find the fastest way of talking myself off the cliff of sadness, and also of helping others when they hit their own wall, is to remind them of worse predicaments. Often, in the case of minor problems, it just takes a quick mental visit to all the much worse things that could be. Those like the first couple illustrations listed here. Compared with losing a child, nothing, even that fatal diagnosis, seems bad. A lost job pales to a health problem. A bad day, bad haircut, or the like diminish quickly in this analysis.

"Somethings" that are preventable seem like they are in a different category. A hangover, for example, the repercussions of underachieving clear ability, the effects on others of being mean or cruel, these all seem preventable. Just don't drink too much, study harder for the test, or be careful how you treat others. Easy enough. Well, often, not really. There is usually a much deeper cause for all self-destructive conduct.

How about the granddaddy of all preventable somethings, which is also one of my somethings? Being fat. I am not talking "a few pounds extra as you get older" fat. I am referring to "not looking good in clothes, looking unhealthy" fat. On the scale of preventable topics, this is probably at the top. In undertaking the research to write this book, I unearthed a journal entry from the year 2001. Written by me in an Amsterdam hotel room, it was the beginning of a vacation with Carol and all three girls that started in this city and included Antwerp and Paris. It was a unique and special trip. By the time we got to Paris, two Belgian boyfriends were along for the trip, and all of us were having a really magnificent time. Yet, in a quiet moment of writing, it was not the wonders of the cities I was visiting, nor the joy of being there with these folks. Instead, these were the words I felt compelled to write.

December 28, 2001, Amsterdam on vacation

Hey, my skin doesn't fit. Actually, it fits too well. It is just that it is stretched over too much body, and I don't like the shape of either. Fit is not a word that has ever been attached to me. Even college pictures, that I now look back to longingly, at least as to my waistline, hide a perpetually pudgy body. Lately however my sheer bulk, which fortunately for me my large 6'4" frame has generally helped me mask, has exploded to just plain fat. At almost 50, it is two weeks until my birthday, I am obese; frighteningly close to 300 pounds. It is sad to say that it is mostly only the last twenty or so pounds that historically has really bothered me. I have lost this last twenty, sometimes as much as thirty pounds many times over the years. Pathetically, I have gained back the lost pounds every single time usually within a year or six months. Back in fat clothes,

I would slowly layer on more pounds. In this manner my "fat weight" has slowly climbed from 225, when I was 20 years old and did my first crash diet, to 295 what I weigh now. It is early morning, and I am sitting in an Amsterdam hotel room. As I sit down to write this even my "fat clothes" feel tight and uncomfortable. I find myself out of breath almost all the time. Family photographs, unless I am standing at the back where I can make sure only my head and shoulders are visible, are mostly something I would rather not see. Something has to change, this is obvious. That I need to be thinner and in better shape is evident, but just as apparent is that I have to break the cycle once and for all.

The journal entry is kind of sad. What's worse, in the quarter of a century since I wrote it, not much has changed. Actually that is what being fat is for me: mostly kind of sad. Although, I have never really let it slow me down much. Nor, despite the fact I often do not feel like I look very good, do I ever really let on to this. I just press on.

Is there an excuse for being fat? In many cases, sure. Sometimes it may be a medical condition. It might be "in the genes;" we have all seen whole families of hefty-sized people. It could be cultural. I could make a good argument that, despite our worship of thin, especially for women, American culture and diet supports some level of obesity. We certainly have plenty of it. Processed foods seem to be a unique part of our culinary makeup.

I was always a little large. Luckily for me, when I was growing up, the slightly larger version of boys' clothes was called "husky." Girls had it much tougher; if they were a little oversized, they were "chubby." Nowadays, big little girls, like big moms, are "plus." Yup, nicer words.

Fortunately for me, I grew up to be very tall. Five foot seven by age eleven, two years later six foot one, and finally, in high school, I reached my full height of six foot four. Happily, during these fast-growth years, my tendency to eat the wrong stuff was swallowed up in all the growth. I have a picture of me on the beach with Carol at nineteen. I was by then 210 pounds. Because of my height, in this picture, I look about as good in my lifeguard trunks as she does in her bikini standing next to me. It was an amazing time. Of course, I did not appreciate it.

By the time Carol and I got married, two years later, I remember dieting from 225 back down to 212. From that day to now, I have lost and gained many hundreds of pounds. The base weight, what I was comfortable with, would creep up with each passing decade. Two-twenty, two-forty, and onward. I first crossed three hundred at about sixty years old and fought my way back down to 285 once, but continued to sneak ever upward, to the point that three hundred would now be considered a big victory.

I have had fat clothes and skinny clothes for as long as I can remember. The skinny clothes would always be kept in the hope they could be worn again. They practically never were. Eventually, I would purchase new, more comfortable clothes, and the then-fat clothes would become the skinny clothes for the next round.

Fortunately for me, I could afford to buy new clothes, so I tried not to add to my ever-advancing girth ill-fitting, too-tight clothes. It also helped that my fashion sense always favored khaki pants and polo shirts in the summer, and sweaters and button-downs for the rest of the year. I also like blue jeans. I would wear shorts all summer and suits for dress-up, and my much-loved blue blazer and gray flannel pants (or khakis in the summer) for whenever I could choose them. I kept it simple and continued buying clothes bigger and bigger. Since I like my shirts loose, these days they are 3X from the DXL Big + Tall store.

Lest we forget in all this opining about my being fat, technically my bigger "something" is more likely my long-term clinical depression, my good old nonspecific D. That is not how it feels, however. Honestly, if I told you being depressed sucks, as I did in an earlier chapter, then being fat sucks even more, at least for me. For depression, I take a pill. I don't like taking a pill, but I take it. I get better. Depression, especially under control, does not show. Being fat does. That this condition is arguably fixable simply by not eating as much is as maddening as it is simple.

I have yet another "something" I need to confess. It started simply about twenty-five years ago when I broke my leg in a ski accident. Actually, I compressed and smashed every bone—the tibia, fibula, and ankle—inside my right ski boot. Since all the smashing and bashing went on inside the boot, after two consults, I never had surgery. Instead, the boot was replaced with a foot-to-hip cast, followed by a wheelchair, crutches, and physical therapy over six months. The result was a leg a full inch shorter on my right side. Yup, I was then six foot three if I stood on one foot, my original six foot four on the other. I also had some nerve damage, so my right foot always felt a little numb.

Obviously not from the accident, over the years, my left foot got numb too, and the right foot even more so. I will skip all the medical stuff, but what I developed was neuropathy, a kind of slow death of the outer nerve membrane. My dad had this too in his last years, but to a lesser extent. For many who get this, neuropathy affects both feet and hands and is often intensely painful. Not for me, happily: I've got no hand numbness and no real pain. However, the numbness has kept progressing, eventually including my ankles, and these days, it makes my feet feel like I am walking on blocks.

For many years, this was all not a big deal. The shorter leg and increasing neuropathy meant running or even standing in one place for a long time were not easy, but little else. The combination of an occasional limp and walking on the ball of my foot got me through it. I would limp when I got really tired, but otherwise, you could not tell. I kept skiing with my ski buddies every year for a long time.

In the last couple years, it all got a bunch worse. No more skiing. The numbness increased and now basic balance has become an issue. I bet you didn't know balance comes from three places: your inner ear, the nerves in the feet connecting with the ground, and your vision. Apparently, the signals from my feet are basically gone. Now, if I close my eyes, as in the shower shampooing my head, I am downright wobbly. I had to install grab bars. It turns out operating with just one of the three sensors, in my case only the inner ear, is not enough.

I also occasionally use the wooden cane my dad had used in his latter years. Ironically, he got it from me. It's an extra-long model I purchased when I was first recovering from the ski accident. Occasional use of the cane has become more frequent in wintertime.

Then I fell and broke my leg, again! This fall had not been dramatic on a ski slope. Rather, I stupidly slipped on a wet floor in the bathroom. This time it was not a severe break; it was minor. The problem was, I could not really feel it. I walked around and even flew off to a meeting. It was only when my wife and daughter, concerned by all the swelling, talked me into an emergency room visit a few days after the accident happened that the broken tibia was discovered. Lots of swelling and no real feeling is, in the doctor's view, a very bad thing. Happily, nowadays they use air casts, not plaster. I got better quickly.

The result of all this was way too many X-rays to make sure I was progressing, a mandated visit to a neurologist, and a physical therapist for balance.

I confess this fall had a big effect on me. It scared me badly. I now really do not want to fall again. I need to avoid uneven ground and icy patches and use the cane almost all the time. I am adjusting to this new, old-man reality.

The cane, it turns out, has a major impact on many folks. Even women open doors for me. People offer to carry packages. I get sent to the head of lines and on a plane first. It is all embarrassing and still feels strange. On a recent trip, Carol ordered a wheelchair to take me across a very long trip between connecting gates. I groused that I did not need it, but actually I did. I now walk slowly. The poor girl has to downright shuffle not to leave me in the dust.

So, these are my somethings. I am overweight, can't really walk well anymore, and I am forever on medications for depression. I am telling you all this partly because I was told in writing a memoir it was important to share bad stuff too, even in what may otherwise be a very upbeat book. I was told readers will want to read my story more if I talk about my downs as well as my ups.

I am writing this book because I have had a very busy and very blessed life, and I want to share it and the importance of how giving back has impacted me. My somethings do not hold me back much. But they are indeed a part of me. And making sure they do not hold me back takes some effort.

The powerful message here is to deeply understand that everyone, and I mean absolutely everyone, has a something. The somethings are physical, mental, and emotional. They surround us, and they are often internal. Virtually no one has a path without obstacles. A man or woman born with beauty, an engaging personality, brains, and/or abundant common sense would seem to have it easier than someone missing any or all of these. But what if this person with the easy path lacks a moral compass, or good health, or anything else that makes it all work? If you look hard enough, you will find that everyone has their very own something or even somethings. To know this, to understand this, is the first key to never letting your something be any kind of excuse.

Lessons Learned

FAIR WARNING. I AM ABOUT TO GET DOWNRIGHT PHILOSOPH-ical and more than a bit wordy. By the end of this chapter, you will be introduced to the granddaddy of all my lists. Even a guy who believes in cute dollars and thought he was lost at sea when the wind died down and fog rolled in can have a theory about what life is all about. This is mine. It is my Lessons Learned.

I believe there are certain physical principles and natural laws, that all mankind—or should I say all people of the earth; no sexism of any kind is intended or wanted here—no matter where you are from, what your race or color of skin, how or where you were raised, the method or length of your studies, the deity you worship or have decided to ignore or not believe in, that you *must* nevertheless accept. These are universal principles, what I call *simple truths*.

The existence of the earth, for example, is such a simple truth. It is hard to pick a fight on this one. The earth's shape, more or less round, has also been universally accepted since the fifteenth century. Columbus did not sail off the end of the flat world. Admittedly, he did not reach India either, the pesky North and South American continents having gotten in his way. The fact that our little planet rotates around the sun, a concept first just a radical notion of guys like Nicolaus Copernicus and Galileo Galilei, grudgingly approved of by the Roman Catholic Church two hundred years later, can safely be added to the list of simple truths. While we still struggle with our planet's place in the universe, we accept the existence of the sun and its glowing presence in our sky. It is likewise tough to deny the existence of other suns, millions of them—more since we invented the telescope—and finally, as a logical extension, a universe of suns and planets.

We also accept gravity, again with clarifying help from Isaac Newton and others. We accept and respect, if not always completely understand, fire, the earth's rotation, water, air, agriculture, bodily functions, and that physical existence for all living things is finite and inevitably followed by nonexistence.

These are the simple truths, virtually undeniable. But, even some of these, it is important to note, we people of the earth have only recently come to know.

As we progress into the modern third millennium, roughly forty thousand years after our species, erect Homo sapiens, made its appearance on this earth, whether we identify more with the scientist or the priest, the prophet or the professor, we accept these *simple truths* as givens. Notice I did not write about climate change, which would seem to qualify, but for a handful of far-right politicians and followers who have yet to see the increasingly bright light on this one.

Using the simple truths then as an intellectual starting point, let's explore further. In a world where technology and science demand we move faster and faster, the simple truths are often layered with another layer of sometimes thoughtful, many times ridiculous, ideas of morality, science, governance, and matters spiritual that we cannot be as quick to accept.

The question for any thoughtful journey then becomes: What are the truths that are nonetheless critically important to all of us? Put another way, what have we people of the earth learned during our time here, beyond the simple truths? What in all the rest of our life existence is, if not undeniable, pretty clearly true, a Lesson Learned, if you will?

As I have made my personal journey on this earth, I think I have discovered a few things that seem to be *of the* simple truths, grown from them, and to me no less deniable. As my humble gift I here share with you these, my thoughts on life, on ways to grow, ways to live, roads to take, and those to avoid. These are my Lessons Learned—thirty-eight of them.

I get it. Thirty-eight principles? Who are you kidding? I told you, I like my lists. This list, like my life, is in process. As I grow, as I go forward, it will change. To write this list, I digested at least a hundred books and treatises, examined thousands of life lessons and self-help doctrines, and then winnowed down the teachings, more than once, to get to this number. I also lived these lessons, or at least most of them. My twelve principles given to WMI Scholars in Chapter 17 may be my best short list effort. This longer list says more. It started out at sixty and gradually came down to thirty-eight ideas.

I share my list with you along with a request that you improve it. Tell me what I missed. I also would love to hear which list you like better, or even if you like both.

1. **Time.** Time is precious. The lack of it or using it poorly can quickly become disabling. We should feel no guilt by taking time to be introspective.
2. **Tyranny of choices.** With so many good alternatives to occupy our time, we are often chronically overscheduled. Abe Lincoln read the few books he could borrow by candlelight because there was nothing else to do. No movies, videos, TV, magazines, net to surf, podcasts to watch, lectures to attend, classes to go to. With modern transportation and communication, the possibilities are endless, and the imprisonment by the tyranny of good choices can be overwhelming. Don't let it be.
3. **True self.** Seek always to reflect your true self through your actions. Actions, not words, are the best measure of a person. If your inner self is at peace, its reflection in actions will demonstrate it, and will likely be well received by others.

4. **Hypocrisy.** Hypocrisy, especially in the form of words that do not match actions, is one of the greatest ways to turn off your listener. Hypocrisy by those teaching young people, particularly parents, will almost always dull to meaninglessness the message of the speaker.
5. **Words.** We should aspire to talk less and say more, and if possible, only after listening long and well. Words can be so special, so moving, so motivating. They can educate; they can explain. Although they are only a part of our ability to communicate, they are the easiest and most accessible of our communication devices. Know, however, that with such accessibility comes a high potential for misuse. Because of this, credibility through honesty of the words and consistency of the words with actions is vital. Repetition of words, which would seem to make a point more emphatically, oftentimes has the opposite effect. To protest too much makes the listener suspicious. A speaker who speaks thoughtfully and to the point, after listening completely, is heard best. No matter how eloquent, words not consistent with the actions of the speaker inevitably ring hollow.
6. **Natural rhythms.** We must learn to love the natural rhythms of life: aging, seasons, months, weeks, days, and the nine months of pregnancy.
7. **Prayer.** Meditation, prayer, or just quiet contemplation and a conscious effort to be still, quiet, and centered is one of the best roads toward insight into who we are, our relationship to God, and to the people and world around us. Do not be afraid to also pray on the run. Both work.
8. **Golden rule.** Follow the golden rule of do unto others as you would have them do unto you. Go a step further: Make sure you tune into the other's needs, not just what *you* want to do to or for them. If you can meet the other's needs, do so joyfully; otherwise, move on. No matter what, do no harm to the person you espouse to help.
9. **Grace.** When being just comes into conflict with grace (forgive-

ness), try hard to choose grace. In the end, such a choice will almost always come out better. This is a hard one. Grace is forgiveness with no strings of any kind, no preconditions, no expectations. It is a province of God and only the very best of us at our very best moments can emulate it. To experience grace is to know love in its purest form.

10. **Forgive.** Forgiveness is seldom fair, but almost always right. The alternative is a never-ending cycle of retribution and vengeance in the name of justice.

11. **Love.** Love, no matter what anyone tells you, is the ultimate and most elemental emotion. To know joy, compassion, lust, fear, anger, envy, and grief is to live life, but all these emotions in the end lead to the primacy of love. Although it may take time, love almost always will beget love. If it does not, it makes no difference, as the true giving of love empowers the giver beyond anything that can be returned. To be "in love" is to give love completely honestly and with no expectation of its return. This is a high goal and one not easily achieved by men and women who usually need to feel love flowing toward them in order to give love.

12. **Romantic love.** Romantic love is something distinct and apart from love in its pure sense. Romantic love is at its essence a combination of feelings and thoughts that include aspects of physical attraction, intellectual compatibility, sentimentality, passion, and more. It is as inherently complex as love is simple. Although persons in romantic love can be in love, this is by no means automatic.

13. **Process.** Life is a process. Life lived fully is not likely to be smooth. We should not expect it to be. What we perceive as pitfalls and obstacles are often blessings, or simply lessons that need to be learned.

14. **Feeling good.** Feeling good is almost always good. Sadness imposed by other men and women, and elaborate rules and even ill-conceived laws beyond those of God, can represent man-made foolishness. Life will have its ups and downs. We should not work to create the downs or let others impose them on us. Pleasure, in

all its many forms, between truly consenting people, is almost never bad.

15. **Be aware.** Be aware of everything and everybody around you. Focus on the details. In these details is most of the beauty and virtually all of the meaning of life.

16. **Possessions.** The accumulation of physical possessions and comforts, and of more money than one needs to meet basic needs, is almost always as much a burden as it is a blessing. It is not a better path, just a different one. The simple path, the one traveled by a traveler lightly burdened, can be much easier to traverse than that of a traveler heavy laden. Both travelers can reach their destination; both can lose their way.

17. **New day.** Every day starts over. Leave behind your failings of the past day. Every day, attack the blank canvas of a new day. Paint your best picture. At the end of the day, take stock. The next day, start over and paint again.

18. **Win–win.** Whenever possible, look for a win–win strategy.

19. **Empower.** Empower others to be their best self. Don't worry if their best self is nothing like yours. Judge not, just love, empower, and support. If you can't do this, move away quickly.

20. **Children.** If you produce children, or if they come into your life through some other path, parent with passion, commitment, inspiration, patience, and zeal. Be a parent like both your life and the child's life depend upon your parenting. They do.

21. **Of the flesh.** Know that the truest and deepest feelings among men and women wishing to unite their spirits and bodies will come from a communion of compassionate acts, words, ideas, and emotions, and not just of the flesh. Know that fidelity can be as exciting as variety, and the moment after a sexual orgasm with someone you care little about can be as empty as you will ever know.

22. **Lies.** Know that lies can be of omission as well as of commission.

23. **Attitude.** Attitude is not everything, but it is the first and primal battlefront. It shapes the task. A positive attitude can take the most

mundane chore and make it sing, and thus provide the energy to attack what we really want to do. Expectations are often the key to attitude. Keep yours low.
24. **Trust.** Know that trust destroyed is not easily re-created.
25. **More.** Know that you can work harder, know more, understand better, persevere longer, sacrifice more, move faster, sit quieter, and be a better person than you think you can.
26. **Anger.** Know that while anger is a part of life, cruelty and violence should not be.
27. **Wisdom.** Know that wisdom is often simply having lived through a lesson before.
28. **Government.** Know that the form of government by which we govern ourselves ultimately makes less difference than the genuine intentions of those who lead. No governing concept is more beautiful than the "sharing" at the heart of communism, the "free will" at the heart of democracy, or the "love" of a truly benevolent dictator. However, nothing can be more oppressive or obscene than the way men and women govern themselves. The only rule that must be universal in the affairs of men and women is the fundamental equality of all who govern and are governed—the simply stated Golden Rule, "Do unto others as you would have them do unto you."
29. **Sunshine.** Everything looks better in bright sunlight, worse in its absence. Sunshine feels to me like God's smile.
30. **Not sure.** People who are very sure of themselves usually are not.
31. **Everything is attainable.** Everything you really need to be fulfilled is within you or is readily attainable.
32. **Urgent or important.** Learning the difference between urgent and important is difficult but necessary. Much of what we do every day is urgent but NOT necessarily important. Putting together a plan for your life and sticking to it, or at least mentally consulting it, will almost always help.
33. **Sadness.** We can no longer know happiness without sadness as we could know light without dark, cold without hot, or busyness without boredom.

34. **Too much.** Often our biggest problems stem from too much—too much to eat, too much to do, too much information to process, too many of us. When Christ was here two thousand years ago, there were 130 million people on the whole earth. Today, there are eight billion of us. We in the developed world live in abundance unknown to even royalty a century ago. In the developed world, we are often well fed, well clothed, well traveled, and many of us well educated. Many of us have nice houses and cars, in America far larger than anywhere else in the world. How to simplify in an age of plenty may be the ultimate paradox of our time.
35. **Responsibility.** Learn to take responsibility completely, forthrightly, and without excuses. This is very hard to do. How many of us blame our circumstances on others or just the ways of the world? If we truly make our own breaks, then we make our own failures too. Plan to succeed. Work to succeed. If you believe in God or a higher power, ask Him or Her to help you succeed. If after all this, you do not succeed, blame no one but yourself and reexamine the success you desire. If the goal still seems worthy, then try again. Repeat this process indefinitely.
36. **Mystery.** Mystery is good. For spiritual matters, we often try to understand too much. To understand is a worthy goal and helps us grow. However, sometimes it is even more worthy to surrender to the ecstasy of just believing.
37. **Death.** Death is not bad.
38. **Life.** Life, every day of it, is a magnificent blessing.

Middle of the Road

I seldom find myself without a definite opinion. I care a great deal about a great many things. I don't just mean the obvious stuff, like how much I enjoy a good chocolate chip cookie, how much I like macaroni and cheese, or that I react well to folks with good manners. On a whole range of subjects that we all carefully avoid in mixed company as just too controversial to discuss, like religion, politics, or even sex, I have downright strong opinions. No less so as to weighty issues like climate change, the value of education, health and diet, political correctness, media, money and wealth, agriculture, the oceans, water, fossil fuels, capitalism versus communism, and even death. I also have collected my thoughts on lots of more mundane topics, like clothes I like and those I do not, TV commercials, celebrities, leisure time, and what to read.

Here is the thing. Although I have strongly held views, they are not generally the views that seem to get all the airplay these days. My views don't land me in any of the extreme ends of our society. They are not the views that populate our seemingly endless appetite for point–counterpoint argument and increasingly strident litmus tests for the groups we divide ourselves into these days. For better or worse, I usually find that I am hopelessly middle of the road.

I find myself in this thoughtful middle spot, and this is an important point for me, not because I am intellectually lazy, passionless, tired, or just don't care. To the contrary, I am very thoughtful, almost annoyingly so, and I care a lot. I just think moderation in most things, compromise between the extremes, is usually the right answer. Not the easy answer, the right answer.

The 2016 election was shocking for me in many respects; no less so 2024. As usual, for both elections, we were told by commentators that the election would be the most important one in [fill in the blank]. In neither case was it really the issues that were so extraordinary, however. What was shocking was, both years, large swaths of American citizens, often folks who may have not even voted before, were finding voice in a nonpolitician, Donald Trump, and resonating with some extreme ideas. Extreme authenticity, extreme outrageousness, extreme negativity were having their day at the expense of anything that seemed to represent the status quo. The American people in large numbers had completely lost their collective patience with American politicians. No matter how it came out, the winds of discontent were hard to ignore. They were blowing very strongly. For the most part, these winds have not stopped blowing since.

As the years passed and elections themselves began to be questioned by Republicans who did not like the results, all measure of democratic and leadership norms have fallen away. What began in 2016 erupted into something much bigger. The MAGA movement was anchored in deep discontent but largely divorced of any real truths or clear paths to success. I will make clear elsewhere just how negatively I feel about Donald Trump, who has led us into all this.

I decided to write about this because I think a tipping point may have been reached. Not the obvious one that we have become completely fed up about all this. Something different: The American people in large numbers, perhaps even the majority, were now so crazy discouraged, so convinced their values were not being represented, that they sought risky change in the form of candidates from the extremes.

Admittedly we have been here before, Ralph Nader, Ross Perot, and George Wallace being only the most recent examples of good-sized alternative movements in the political arena. Even extreme populism—think Andrew Jackson. We actually have a system that nourishes and supports all this. Free press, our touchstone bedrock, always has; our modern, often sensationalist media, even more so. The tipping point this time, what makes this time unique, is the sheer numbers. Beginning in 2016 and since, the lunatics actually looked like they might outnumber the sane, and thus threaten the asylum. Those numbers, always a scary minority, seem to grow, and now, with Trump's reelection, will have their chance to lead. I profoundly believe this will not work and that I would be lying if I did not say I am deeply worried.

My premise has always been that the real power base is not at the fringes; it is the arguably boring, underreported, often overly passive middle. It is not the crazies on the right nor the left or those who want to change faster or not at all, or even the very rich or the very poor, who are the unalterable key to the future. These folks are all important, but they should not get to drive the boat. It is the vast middle-of-the-road folks who need to get a grip and speak out. And because the tipping point has been reached, or soon will be, the middle needs to pay attention right now, or the opportunity may not come again for a long time.

Since I, like everyone, have my own biases, my center won't be the same as everyone's. Middle of the road is not actually the line down the middle of a road, as the label would imply. Rather, it is the entire region of potential compromise between the extremes. It's the whole road width rather than the double line if you want to stick with the road metaphor. A nice wide road where solutions are possible, if rarely easy.

My support for the middle of the road has another exciting component. It is not just a thoughtful region of policy and process between the extreme views. It is a philosophy of compromise and pragmatism. It allows its proponents to take one from column A and one from column B or even ignore both and propose column C, all in the interest of pleasing the most folks. It is a philosophy that total inaction serves no one, and everyone (or most everyone; you will never please the extremes) is better off with some of the pie even if it is not the exact flavor they would have chosen. My philosophy rejects grandstanding and intransigence and rewards compromise. It believes half a loaf is better than no loaf.

Behind all this is something more than just respect for the value of compromise; it is a philosophy that has its core respect for, if not agreement with, folks who see things differently. It does not turn those who disagree into villains or worse just because they wanted a different flavor pie or different wheat in the loaf, or more to the actual point, more government or freer markets.

In my middle-of-the-road world, the enemy is not the guy who sees it differently from me. It is the guy or girl who refuses any dialogue and who is unwilling to work hard for win–win solutions and, when those can't be found, who lets both sides win some and lose some. The ultimate enemy in this world is being flat-out stuck, arms crossed and glaring, having lost all sight that the other side has a point too. In my not-so-humble view, thoughtful, truth-respecting compromise is the best way to get things done in a pluralistic society.

Fifties Values

At the beginning of the 1950s, the very dominant view was that a woman's place was in the home caring for children. It was thought then, by most everyone, that when a woman worked outside the home, she did not need to make as much money as a man because the man was properly the breadwinner of the family. Working so hard outside the home, the man should be cared for by the woman in the home. Marriage was very much between a man and a woman and only within a single race. If you thought you were more comfortable in a relationship with someone of your own sex or, God forbid, you were of the gender other than to which you were born, get over it.

I grew up in the 1950s, and I thought marriages had a senior partner, the father, that mothers appropriately did not work outside the home, and what we then called child-rearing, now parenting, was primarily the mother's job. Most of this I let go of by the time I met and married my wife in the early 1970s, although I briefly thought a 60/40 relationship might be a reasonable compromise.

This all feels gone for almost everyone nowadays. I notice at the country club we belong to that there still is such a thing as a housewife who enjoys golf, bridge, fashion shows, and hanging out with other rich—and, for some reason, all amazingly good looking—women married to guys whose success is not complete without having a wife who does all of the above. These women, from all appearances, have the education and skills to do more; they just buy into this. Throwbacks, or perhaps just the benefits of wealth?

Don't get me wrong; the parenting part of this is vitally important, and when our modern lifestyle could not be supported without two working parents, something was lost. This happened, however, and quite some time ago, so those country club wives seemed stuck in another time. Less so mothers of big families who homeschool while the father does the extreme breadwinner routine, but this also strikes me as anachronistic, starting with the large brood.

Kids need a mother and father, and my middle-ground view says both should work enough to keep the family prosperous, but not necessarily rolling in dough. Both should share in parenting, and for that matter, the whole range of other tasks that keep a home and family running. I think it is best if we do what we are good at. Whoever cooks best, cooks. The one who can fix things, fixes them. Women's work or men's work stereotypes can be ignored or followed as logic dictates.

The bottom line is to share the family responsibilities and the work. No one gets to live on the couch when the partner toils into the night. As to careers, be reasonable and do what works. If one spouse has a career outside the home, maybe the other doesn't. Likewise, if one parent makes lots of money and the other doesn't, just figure it out, and most of all, be fair. If both have very big lives outside the home, be prepared to pay and delegate stuff you prefer and really should do to others, or don't have kids. Not great choices, but if they come to you, do the best you can.

There was a time when women were not a big part of the workforce. They are now, and they are not paid the same for the same work. This, pardon the French, is total bullshit and should be just plain illegal. Making it illegal leads to a later chapter: How much government is the right amount? Not to jump ahead, but if the illegal part bothers you, let's go with "just plain stop now!"

It does not seem possible now, but the laws of most states once made it illegal for a man and woman of different races to marry. It was called miscegenation. Before *Brown v Board of Education*, we had segregated schools, and before the 1964 Civil Rights Act, which struck down many forms of discrimination, often called "Jim Crow," that had been actively practiced until then. All ancient history now, right? After all, we had a black president of the United States born of a mixed-race couple just a few years ago. When he was elected, many of us thought all the blatant racial stuff was gone for good, and our laws cleaned up, or soon would be. Instead, this watershed moment sent many hurtling backward.

Another thing us 1950s kids did not come prepared for was gays out of the closet, and certainly not transgendered folks. Later, we learned that homosexuality has been around forever, if hushed up and decried by many. I certainly remember a time when the idea of a gay or lesbian couple was beyond the pale for me and well outside my comfort zone. This is now long gone for me, as with so many Americans.

The logic of revising all our views on homosexuality came initially based on the sheer numbers as much as logic. To me, there were just too many homosexuals for this disposition to be anything but a different part of God's plan. God, or if you don't believe in God, nature just doesn't make that many mistakes. The rest just falls into place. Loving couples first together and later married just makes sense. Discrimination of such folks makes none. The vast majority of Americans now get this. To the rest I say get over it.

Not treating transgendered folks in a discriminatory way follows, and for me more because they are doing no harm, and I see no state interest in interfering. However, unlike the millions of homosexuals who come naturally to a different sexual orientation, these folks need surgery and often strong drugs to get to where they say they belong. I confess I am not yet completely comfortable with this.

The fifties when I grew up are gone for good, but then so are the sixties, the seventies, etc. Time marches on. I say, adapt, compromise, grow with it. Hold unto the truly important stuff, and let the rest go.

Death and Dying

HAVE YOU EVER SEEN A TODDLER FIGHTING OFF SLEEP, TRYING to squeeze every last minute of play in before literally crashing down in exhaustion? To me, many people live their lives like this. Others adopt a more relaxed pace but are no less fearful of the crash—as in, the end of their life.

I totally get that losing a loved one, especially if too soon in terms of earthly years, really sucks. For many, it brings on the saddest moments of their life. However, I do not understand unrestrained horror and grief for imminent departure from what we know as life. Death is never completely an accident. From the moment we are born, we have begun a natural journey toward our death. Like everything in nature, we have a beginning and an end. Like all nature, the end often does not come in any preordained, predictable manner.

Why do we fight death so hard? What is with a prayer vigil for the sick or injured? If it is for those who will miss the stricken individual, it works for me. But honestly, that is not how we bill it. We are actively imploring God to stave off the natural result of life: death.

I know I am a little weird on this subject. I will freely admit some of my non-fear of death, at least in part, comes from my Christian belief of going home to a creator God. Like everyone else, I have no idea what this really means or what it will be like, but I accept the idea of something as opposed to nothing when my heart stops beating, and my brain goes completely and permanently to sleep. Rejoining already passed relatives seems particularly cool, but you can't dwell on such ideas too much because really, who knows?

A few years back, in our little country church in Vermont, four of our patriarchs, all well into their eighties, passed in a single winter. Shocking and saddening, you think? Not so much. A loss for their close family and loved ones for sure, but they, as all the rest of us in our tiny church family, were taken to school by these four old men. These men had for so many exemplified how to live: kindly, compassionately, sometimes joyfully—but not too much. They were Vermonters, after all. What they showed us was life lived not perfectly, but well. Now, to a man facing the end of his years, they taught us how to die: kindly, compassionately, joyfully, not perfectly, but well. It was a very special gift to all those left behind.

My philosophy on life being fleeting, and death certain and not to be feared, is much more rooted in the oh-so-obvious fact that this is the natural order. I like the notion of mid-century Swiss-born psychiatrist Elisabeth Kübler-Ross. That's right, the lady who came up with the five stages of grief—brilliant lady—when she said, "Watching a peaceful death of a human being reminds us of a falling star; one of a million lights in a vast sky that flares up for a brief moment only to disappear into the endless night forever." I would argue the stars in the sky metaphor is no less accurate if the death is not so peaceful. Sigmund Freud said, "The goal of all life is death."

I should stop quoting long-dead, if brilliant, folks. I believe, however, that one life, no matter how much it will be missed, whether the most successful of people or the least, is just a brief flare in the night sky. Its demise is as certain as the existence and end of the star, just as the beginning and end of every natural thing, be it plant or animal.

The much-quoted verses from Ecclesiastes tell us, "To everything there is a season, and a time to every purpose under heaven: a time to be born, and a time to die; a time to plant, and a time to pluck up that which is planted." The real gift is to just let it happen.

Coincidents

MY DAUGHTER JORDYN AND I ARE BOTH READERS. WE ALSO both like literary authors, particularly those with their social conscience readily apparent in their writing. It was no surprise, then, when one year a birthday gift from my daughter was an invitation to a joint reading by two such authors: one Haitian, Edwidge Danticat, and one Native American, Sherman Alexie. Her gift also included copies of the most recent book by each author. I read both books. I had read Edwidge before and have made more than twenty trips to Haiti actively working on projects there, so while enjoyable, her stories were not new to me, at least not as to subject matter.

Sherman Alexie, however, while I had heard of him, was new to me. In every way, he was a firehose in the face when I read his collection of short stories, *Blasphemy*. His gritty, very modern stories of life on and off, but never too far from, the "rez" were eye-opening. Like many, especially those of us from the northeast, my experience with Native Americans is secondhand and mostly from schoolbook history: Custer and the like, pilgrims and Thanksgiving, Jamestown and Pocahontas. More fable than real.

Other than a vague awareness of what seemed like a lot of Indian casinos as I traveled, and a passing amusement at PC efforts to rename teams like the Washington Redskins and the Cleveland Indians, not much was getting through to me on the subject of these people, more correctly the descendants of the people who were here first, and from whom my ancestors essentially stole the country.

Sherman's stories hit me hard, fast, and intensely. No less so when the day came to hear him speak. He woke me up to the subject, big time. I needed to know more. Before I went to bed that night, I did a dozen Google searches.

A jam-packed week later, having let life interfere with my night of compassionate interest, I found myself on a two-day trip to Minnesota. For the last couple years, I have been serving as a trustee for a trust that owned more than forty properties, mostly industrial and retail, all over the country. A longtime client and friend who had acquired all these properties was now elderly. The properties were managed by me as his lawyer and now trustee, together with his very capable son, who handled all day-to-day stuff. Slowly, I tried to lay eyes on each property in the trust that I was charged to oversee.

On this day, we were off to see a plant the trust owned in Woodbury, Minnesota, not far from Minneapolis–St. Paul. It was about two hundred thousand square feet of office space and one hundred thousand of manufacturing space. Originally used to build railroad tank cars, for many years, the plant and office had been the home of a very successful national company that builds and sells water softeners. We were visiting because the lease would be renewed in just a few years and the tenant had made some noise about maybe picking up the whole operation and moving it south to Mississippi where costs—yes, that means wages—were lower.

As it turned out, the facility was great, well maintained, and still well located after forty years. Both are often not the case, as many long-term tenants do not take good care of their leased homes. With the passage of time, a popular, well-located area sometimes becomes neither. Not so here. All good. And happily, our folks had resolved their brief inkling to move in favor of staying put in "Minnesota nice."

Having made the trip, I wanted to visit the other trust property in the state of Minnesota while I was there. This involved a four-and-one-half-hour drive north to a town on a lake, both named Bemidji. This town was the legendary birthplace of Paul Bunyan and featured oversized statues of both Paul and his blue ox, Babe. I missed getting a picture with them, which most visitors apparently do. The town is also close, only one lake away from the headwaters of the Mississippi River.

In years gone by, the trust had financed, built, and rented large stores to a successful retail chain, Pamida. Pamida was later absorbed into Shopko and, alas—remember what I told you about popular and well-located areas becoming neither? The downtown Bemidji store fit this description. Successful for more than forty years, it was now abandoned. A new, hot retail area outside downtown and the killer competitor, Walmart, had "done in" this otherwise nice forty-thousand-square-foot building. For laymen, for forty thousand square feet, think two football fields side by side; that gets you 75 percent of the way there. You get the idea. It was a big empty building.

Fortunately for us, a lease is a lease, and although they would be glad to negotiate a departure, for a couple more years Shopko was obligated to pay the rent, even though they had given up the store. We had thrown out some feelers for possible new tenants or buyers but no bites, so it was time to take a look.

We were met by our local broker after looking over the town, very pleasantly surprised to find it thriving, with three new hotels, few vacancies, and clever reuse of older buildings. Despite the aforementioned sprawl of discount retail on the highway outside of the downtown—not just the Walmart, but Home Depot, Lowe's, the whole big-box crowd—the historic downtown was doing fine. That is, except for our rather large vacant building sitting right in the middle of all the prosperity. We had subdivided a piece of our too-big parking lot a half dozen years ago, and now a successful Subway establishment and a little retail-oriented chiropractic office occupied that space.

We had a few more years with rent coming in and needed to repurpose the existing building. This would likely mean a cluster of smaller tenants because, as I said, the big-box crowd had fled to other pastures, and as they like to stick together, the chances of one of the same liking our site was not good.

The other alternative was to tear the place down and perhaps build another hotel. You may have noticed those folks like to hang together too. So, if three are doing well, you can assume there will soon be a fourth. The broker confirmed he had had interest from a hotel developer.

Not so fast. Here is where I finally reconnect with the beginning of this chapter. Minnesota is not only the land of ten thousand lakes, but also the home of the Anishinaabe and Dakota (often known as Sioux) tribes, spread out nowadays over eleven reservations. Who knew?

Well, our building is not on or in an Indian reservation. However, apparently not discovered until the mid-1980s, when an addition was put on the original building, the whole site, or at least a good chunk of it, is squarely on top of Native American burial grounds—you got it, as in human remains.

It was just the right location between the lake and the village, so that in the 1600s for the Dakota Indians who lived nearby, this was often their final resting place. Sacred ground for sure, and under Minnesota law, and federal law for that matter, it was "protected" and put under the jurisdiction of the Minnesota Indian Affairs Council.

The bottom line was simple enough: If staggering in its potential for roadblocks to redevelopment of this property, anything we wanted to do to redevelop the property would need the full concurrence of the Minnesota Indian Affairs office and the support of the elders of the four surviving Dakota Indian tribes spread around the state of Minnesota. Without it, forget about ever disturbing even one shovelful of this ground, ever again.

If nothing is not for a reason, then surely my recent interest in Native Americans, just weeks old, had found its "coincident." The next step was to meet with the chiefs (nowadays called the chairmen!) of the four tribes.

Real Americans

We are a country of immigrants. Except for the comparatively few Native Americans—at last count just under ten million or 3 percent of the US population—among us, we are all newcomers.

I can't think of anything ever said by an American political figure—and there have been many stupid, inflammatory, and untruthful things said; think Donald Trump—that got under my skin as much as Sarah Palin's initial exhortations on behalf of what she called "Real Americans." Jeez! It is hard to pin down exactly who she included and excluded from her club, but it became clear enough that her Real Americans were probably mostly evangelical Christian, conservative rural folks, virtually all of European descent, presumably mostly working class. Although never explicitly excluded, folks of color, any color; anybody with too much education; immigrants of all stripes; I guess even the Native-Americans; and anybody whose religion might be a bit exotic were by implication not "real." I am a white male, a Christian, and live in a rural state, so maybe I could get in.

Even if they would have me, however, this is a club I don't want to join. It is not a membership to be coveted. Sarah, and to a large extent the core, as I understand it, of Donald Trump's base of support, the MAGA crowd, as well as Donald himself, misses the point badly.

They seem to have missed an important segment of their elementary school American history education—the part when we learned about the whole melting pot concept, the diversity that America was built on and made it great.

This Real Americans' narrative ignores our roots. Not only our continent's indigenous peoples, but wave after wave of immigrants: Dutch; English; German; Irish; Italian; Norwegian; Japanese; Korean; Chinese; Indian; Arab; Hispanic from all over; African, most brought to our shores involuntarily. Virtually every country and race you can think of is represented, and to my view, every single one of these people are Americans—very much of the "real" variety. In my big melting pot, even Sarah and her select group are welcome. This is who we are, or at least should be!

I grew up in northern New Jersey and created and maintained my law office there for more than thirty years. I have had homes in Vermont, Pennsylvania, Ohio, New Jersey, New York City, and St. Thomas in the Virgin Islands. I have been on boards of businesses in Oregon, Texas, and in Florida. These days, I am lucky enough to live in Vermont most of the year and St. Thomas in the worst of winter. With many friends and business interests in rural Vermont, the greater New York City area, and a Caribbean island that happens to be a US territory, I live, firsthand, the diversity that our country offers. In St. Thomas, I drive on the left side of the road, usually slowly and courteously. In New York and New Jersey, I am back on the right side of the road, and I drive with passion, fighting for a gap in traffic to enter the road, aggressively change lanes, and with others squeeze out the last bit of yellow at a stop light. When I am driving, I wave to no one—well, maybe a relative or close friend. In Vermont, first I ditch my lawyer car in favor of my considerably older pickup truck. Then I drive slowly and courteously again. I yield to pedestrians, and I wave and acknowledge absolutely everyone.

And so it goes. It's all part of the America I love. Walking down Broadway in New York City is nothing like sitting by the river in my little Vermont town, nor is it like the high desert of central Oregon.

Both sunrises off the East Coast and sunsets out west are special. It's all special, every bit of it: New England clam chowder, Texas barbeque, salmon from the northwest, Chicago pizza, Kansas pork chops, New York strip steak, corn on the cob, grits, and Ben and Jerry's ice cream. All those Little Italys and Chinatowns; those cool-talking North Dakotans; Southerners, oh, those Southerners; rock-ribbed New Englanders; and Southern California beach dudes, cowboys, ballerinas, auto workers, concert violinists, fisherman, farmers, and college professors…it goes on and on. It is the sheer diversity of locales, cultures, cuisines, and people that makes America hum. For many of us, me for sure, this is the very essence of our country.

Even before my multilocation existence, which came gradually in recent years, growing up in northern New Jersey I quickly realized all Americans did not look alike or often even similar to, say, someone from a less racially diverse place like Japan or a Scandinavian country.

My suburban town had two dominant population groups: Italians and Jews. There were a few of us token WASPs (white Anglo-Saxon Protestants) as well. I played on the football team, not so well, with the Italians, and did all the advanced classes and the yearbook with the Jews. I learned from both. Although these groups had some degree of cohesion—a clique, I guess—I never really felt excluded. It was a great way to grow up. If I have a regret, it is that I knew very little racial diversity during these early years. I believe I would be far better off if I had.

It is so much easier to understand people you actually know. Whatever the differences, especially those of race, religion, class, culture, education, and talents, and certainly as to sexual preference or gender, we share much more, a common humanity. We all bleed. Soldiers who have fought alongside someone very different have told us this.

We all experience joy, sadness, and ambition. We all get to know anxiety, most of us grief. We were all born of a mother and a father, and we will all die. Sometimes it takes only breaking bread together to know and appreciate this connection. For others, it is a much harder lesson to learn. For some, it is their life's work. I so much wish this simple lesson could be utterly and completely known by everyone.

In my middle-of-the-road world, we are all real Americans. Compromise is encouraged, and giving back is the rule. What follows naturally is universal application of the Golden Rule of doing unto others as we would have them do unto us. That diversity is to be cherished, not ridiculed, and that comes very natural to me. I don't find this at all hard and wonder deeply why so many do. We are all way more alike than we are different.

Separation of Church and State

A SIGNIFICANT GROUP OF AMERICANS SEEMS TO BELIEVE OUR founding fathers were all deeply religious men who wanted Christian values built into the Constitution and upheld in our country. This is just not true. Like folks today, our founding fathers held a myriad of views, from deeply religious to decidedly not so. The leaders among them were mostly Deists, believing in a supreme being creator, but much more in ethical conduct and natural laws than dogma or interaction between the deity and humankind. It was not so much Bible-based theology, but broader-based concerns about religious persecution that brought many to a new life in America. Our founding documents firmly entrenched this latter concern with a profound and pronounced separation of church and state. No state religion! Freedom to worship as you choose!

"In God We Trust" on currency, and "under God" in the pledge of allegiance, and mandatory prayer in school all date to the anticommunist mid-1950s. The founding fathers gave us instead the Establishment Clause of the First Amendment. The first immigrant Americans, a melting pot of Europeans, who basically wiped out the indigenous Native American population and their more earth-centered beliefs, when they arrived, started us down this road.

As the United States population grew and diversified, we as people remained pretty religious and dominantly Christian, at least as compared to where we came from. Today, roughly 60 percent of Americans say religion (or at least some sense of spirituality) is important to them, as compared to 33 percent in Great Britain, 27 percent in Italy, 21 percent in Germany, 12 percent in Japan, and only 11 percent in France.

We are indeed, even today, mostly a Christian nation with adherents (although, as we see above, often not very religious ones) making up by most counts approximately 50 percent of the population with about 7 percent spread among Jews, Muslim, Buddhists, and Mormons, and the rest, call it 40 percent of Americans, declaring themselves basically nonreligious. Even adherence takes many forms, of course, from life-guiding everyday worship and conduct to oh-so-much less.

Except for those countries, mostly in the Middle East, where religion is not optional, Americans stand out as a religious people. Among truly free people, we are by far the most religious. This said, active practice of religion is not a dominant aspect of our culture (unless you count Christmas) and, to my point here, religion has never been a part of our government. This has worked well for us.

Now, as when it was written into the Constitution, the separation of church and state was sheer brilliance by our founding fathers. The First Amendment could not be clearer: "Congress shall make no law respecting the establishment of religion or prohibiting the free exercise thereof."

As I reread my last couple paragraphs, I wonder if my use of the word "religious" is right. I once heard a wise Christian minister begin an ecumenical service stating straightforwardly "religions divide, spirituality unites." Especially since we know Americans are more likely to state the importance of their beliefs than to attend religious services, perhaps the idea of people being spiritual might define it better for many, if certainly not all, Americans.

I am a Christian, always have been, and I am very proud of and strong in my beliefs. However, when others try to remake the United States into a Christian nation, they do so without historical support and at considerable peril. Christ himself understood this when answering a question designed to pull him into the politics of his time, when he responded, "Render unto Caesar what is Caesar's and unto God what is God's." (Matthew 22:21)

My faith beliefs have always been largely private except, I hope, as they could be discerned by my actions. I think our beliefs should inform how we treat others around us. As they say, it is more how we walk the walk than how we talk the talk. I believe my middle-of-the-road position actually works well with a belief in God or other deity, or for that matter any belief system that keeps such a walk moral and fundamentally fair. I don't think this process can be imposed on mankind by the state. Nor am I fond of how we judge fellow adherents of a common faith. Judging—holding accountable, if you will—a person's beliefs and actions is best left to a higher and smarter power than our fellow men. For me, that's God's job, or at least one of them.

There is a complication of sorts that is glossed over by my simple pronouncements as to separation. The civil laws of a society are of necessity informed by the moral beliefs of its citizens. Here purity has to give way to majority rule. Thus, on the restrictions on conduct on which there is broad agreement, put it in the civil law. Easy enough to agree on murder, rape, theft, and the like, and even more mundane stuff like speeding or the drinking age. Not so easy on big issues on which we do not agree, like same-sex marriage, transgender laws, and, for most of my adult life, abortion.

I believe we should all live life in accordance with our own moral and religious code and get along with others by enforcing on all of society only what the majority can agree on. This is not perfect, but it works, and it is also profoundly wise.

Evangelicals

I HAVE SEVERAL BIG PROBLEMS WITH "EVANGELICALS." WHEN I use this expression, I am talking about zealous believers of all stripes, but as I am most familiar with the Christian sort, they are my primary focus. My concerns come from my perch, not as an atheist or proponent of other beliefs, but as a thoughtful lifelong Christian who admittedly has always been more about the walk than the talk.

My problems with evangelicals are these: They talk too much, judge too much, and oversimplify. Most of all, and here is where I get rather strident, I think often they shame God.

Before I go down this road too far, let me start by saying that, as I already shared, I don't like judging by or of my fellows, and I am about to do just that here. So, I want to be clear that by evangelicals I do not mean all folks who might identify as such. As Tim Alberta, in his recent insightful book, *The Kingdom, the Power, and the Glory*, made clear, all Christian evangelicals are not alike.

I have in my sights those who loudly and proudly express the behaviors I will describe. The folks who march off to war in a way that has no meaningful connection to the values I have always understood at the heart of Christianity and being a Christian: a creator God with eternal grace, and the message of His son to do unto others as we would have them do unto us. The ones who have lost sight of the humble, egalitarian, compassionate message and ministry of Jesus, and instead cherish and support selfish concerns, toughness, and vitriolic take-no-prisoners speech.

The "talk too much" concern is not just things we hear these brethren say. It is the actions that are deeply out of sync with my straightforward beliefs. Even couched in thoughtful beliefs, violence of any kind, exclusivity, superiority, racism, and discrimination against the poor, immigrants, or folks with different sexual preferences or gender goals to me just has no role in the world created by God. To those born-again folks, proclaiming their personal relationship with Jesus Christ, I ask, "How does any of this pass the simple 'What would Jesus do' test?"

Christian evangelicalism is complicated, but I believe it can be reduced to a few widely accepted concepts. Evangelicals believe the Bible is the supreme ultimate authority, that it is inerrant. They believe that to be a Christian you must be "born again"; you should give public testimony to your faith; and you must have a personal relationship with Christ and accept that belief in His crucifixion, death, and resurrection is the key to salvation.

Lately in America, as they had a few times earlier, most recently in the 1930s, evangelicals seem to be leading us down a road of what is loosely called Christian Nationalism. I understand their arguments; I just do not agree with them. First, as I said earlier in the last chapter, the United States is not a Christian nation; rather, we are a nation born on the tenets of religious independence, freedom to worship in any way we wish, and separation of church and state. This does not mean that Christians, like those of all other religions, should not be respected, and the common threads of virtually all the religions are incorporated into our civil laws. Christians just do not get to impose Christianity on all Americans. As a Christian, I am good with this. As an American, I am great with this.

I know I am not an evangelical, not just because I do not like the actions and words that profess that they are, but because I do not do too well on their basic requirements. We can start with the Bible. I have read it cover to cover and reread many parts, in particular the New Testament gospels, many, many times. I love so many things it tells me. I do not, however, believe it is the "definitive word of God."

I know the Bible's history, the selection of certain books, the elimination of others in the three hundred or so years after Christ's death. Whether you believe the "final cut" was made by the Council of Nicaea in AD 325 or not, it is clear the early Roman Catholic Church, not God, did the initial selection and later made the changes. The modern Protestant Bible has sixty-six books, the Roman Catholic version has seventy-one, and some orthodox versions have as many as eighty-one. Then there are all the books, often referred to as the Apocrypha, that were left out. I have read many of them as well, and particularly focused on the Gospel of Thomas—and not just because of the shared name.

This history and the thousands of internal contradictions in a book written by so many people over a thousand-year period makes me comfortable concluding that while the Bible is deeply instructive, it is not the inerrant word of God. Of even less authority is the often-cherry-picked scripture from the mouth of someone who, except for the fact he or she is quoting scripture, does not at all seem to me to be of God.

I have said elsewhere that I am not born again. I say this because my long-held beliefs of the primacy of the Golden Rule, my committed relationship with a grace-filled creator God, and my love of giving back have been with me from my earliest childhood. I did not come to these as part of a cataclysmic event. I just can't think of a time when I did not stridently believe all this.

The elephant in the room is whether I believe in Jesus Christ. To this, I answer, "Of course, I do." However, on this question I think I fall in with Thomas Jefferson, author of the Declaration of Independence and our third president, who wrote his own version of the Gospels called the Jefferson Bible. When Jefferson wrote this, he took only Christ's words for his Bible and left out all the myth-like storytelling around them. I find Christ's words and life model way more compelling than some of the rest. I try to model much of how I live my life on His teachings. However, I do not deep in my heart truly understand whether miracles and other stories about or attributed to Him are myth or truth. Nor frankly do I care one way or the other. Whether Christ was "the" son of God or "a" son of God is not important to me. His teachings on how to live and treat each other are to me unassailable and holy. In this sense, He is my personal savior.

Starting with Paul, and most of the New Testament beyond the Gospels, and leading right up to organized church today, what we have all done with Christ's teachings is at best imperfect. Often well meaning, at least at the start, Christians made rules for each other and defined sin in ways that often overreach Christ's basic teachings. Especially when these believers judge each other and damn those who do not agree with them to all manner of punishment from exclusion to eternal hell, I think they have gone astray.

My God just isn't that God. My God understands, He or She forgives, He or She has grace. He or She helps me every day be my best self. He or She is open to letting everyone, absolutely everyone, into His or Her kingdom. If He or She does judge me, it is on how I live: on my walk, less so on my words.

9/11

IN THE YEAR 2001, MY RATHER STRONG FEELINGS ABOUT world peace bubbled to the surface again. They had been largely dormant since my fervent anti-Vietnam days and tempered by the passage of thirty years of hanging out with businesspeople and professionals, who, much like me, were committed more than anything to consumptive and increasingly comfortable lifestyles. When a friend wrote a book called *The Peace Book*, a how-to guide for seeking peaceful approaches at every level, it pricked my conscience. She looked for sponsors to underwrite the publication costs, so I signed up.

The book was a little "new age" for my personal taste and certainly for my public path. I did not love the book, but I thought it was saying something that needed saying and needed more focus and attention. It would not be a comfortable read for many of the folks I hang out with these days, so it was a little "out there" for me to send it out, which I ultimately did.

I was not the only one with no real concern about far-off wars and turmoil. Besides, there was nothing like the lack of any real threat for decades to America and our privileged lifestyle to cool one's jets on the lack of front-and-center importance of world peace. Hitler and Pearl Harbor, real threats for our parents' generation, were just school-book history subjects for us, and Vietnam seemed like just a big mistake. Faraway conflicts just did not seem all that real or relevant. Even with ongoing tension in the Middle East, we had begun to accept it as a permanent background on the world stage. Finally, even the words "world peace" and all that it implied, seemed best relegated to a convenient platitude left for staged interviews of beauty queens and for presidential candidates on the stump every fourth year.

Then came 9/11, September 11, 2001. The jets that crashed into the World Trade Center and the Pentagon that morning were nothing short of once-in-a-generation shocking. The fire and explosions that tumbled these icons to the ground and then raged across America completely reawakened many dulled psyches, including my own.

Now *The Peace Book* and Carol and my underwriting of its publication seemed to make lots of sense. After September 11, and at least for a while, everything felt fundamentally changed. A week or two after the event, while Carol and I were still processing this monumental tragedy, the 150 copies of the book I received for being an underwriter arrived in two big cardboard boxes. The timing seemed planned, certainly not a coincidence. We were looking for a way to somehow make sense of the tragedy and do something constructive in its wake. I decided to send the book to friends and family. I composed a letter from Carol and me and sent out all 150 copies.

Here is what my letter said:

Dear Friends,

Recent world events made each of us stop in our tracks and think about our futures, and that of our country and the world. The oft-repeated phrase "things will never be the same" seems undoubtedly true. We believe this thoughtful time represents a challenge to shape this change for the better. We also believe we all need to examine what role we can and should play in this change.

It is our hope and prayer that we Americans, through our government, together with like-minded people and governments throughout the world, will be able to make terrorism unacceptable anywhere. We also believe, however, that the attack on our country, and now our attack on terrorism, must also serve as a wake-up call as to the broad and pervasive inequities and cultural differences that demand expansive, thoughtful, caring solutions.

There is work for all of us to do. Our first thought, like that of so many others, was to make a financial contribution to the families of the firefighters and police, and others who lost their lives in the World Trade Center tragedy. We felt privileged to be able to do this. Tom and his partners at the law firm will forego holiday gifts to clients this year and make an even bigger contribution. Writing checks, however, is not enough.

More is necessary. We Americans tend to have a short attention span and our tendency toward isolationism is legion. Hopefully, not this time. It is our hope each of us will use the tragedy of September 11 and its aftermath as fuel to create meaningful change. We recognize that world peace and more equitable conditions for all are huge mountains to climb. So, think globally but act locally. Start in your own town to bridge gaps, build community, and effect change. We have done this for years through the parent organizations at our children's schools, our church, Rotary, arts organizations, youth sports, merchants councils, creation of affordable housing, and our community center of a bookstore. Take our word for it: in the end, all this activity allows us to receive far more than we give.

You can act globally as well. There are many opportunities to make a difference in organizations that have worldwide reach. We have sought to effect such change with Tom's work with YMCA World Service projects in Kenya and Senegal, and Tom and Jordyn's efforts with an adolescent reproductive health program in Ghana. As you read this letter, Tom is with Rotary working on renovating an orphanage in Haiti. If all this sounds overwhelming and you think you do not have the time, trust us, you do. It is critical we all find time to make a difference. Please do not wait for someone else to do what needs to be done.

There is one more thing we can do, and hence the purpose of this letter. We have joined with others to sponsor the publication of a special and oh-so-timely book called *The Peace Book: 108 Ways to Create a More Peaceful World*. This book was written by Louise Diamond, a friend of ours who is an internationally known peace expert. She has spent years working to bridge the gap of ethnic and religious conflict in the Middle East and throughout the world. *The Peace Book* offers practical suggestions on how each of us can do our part to start and sustain a peace revolution. People are ready to hear this message. Last weekend, Louise spoke to a standing-room-only crowd in our bookstore.

In this challenging time, this book is our gift to you. We hope it will inspire and challenge you to make a difference.

I wish I could say the response was overwhelming. A couple recipients offered mumbled thanks. For most, the book likely went where most books that people give me go—in a pile somewhere with the best of intentions to read it someday. I received a great email from an old friend, a lawyer and Sierra Club activist in Columbus, Ohio, who opined that America leaves very big footprints around the world, and he seemed to appreciate my implied comment of the interconnectedness that made the problems brought on by September 11 more complex than some might think.

My biggest response came from two of my sisters, one with a thoughtful card, the other with a long, heartfelt letter. For both, I was preaching a "counterfeit peace," the only real peace being when all of the world accepts Jesus Christ as a personal savior. Whoa!

My rather inclusive, and decidedly nonevangelical brand of Christianity was on the firing line. In the past, when this happened, I just ducked for cover. This time, however, my juices were flowing. I felt the desire to shoot back. I know, not a very peaceful response. But how could I ignore all this piety aimed at me from true believers who thought the peaceful teachings of Christ Himself were off the point. After all, I was a true believer too; I just did not believe what my sisters did.

When I got the letters, though I was a bit agitated, I stewed for a while rather than taking action. However, my side of this argument kept running through my head. After a couple days, I sat down at the keyboard and pounded out a tirade, nothing very polished, really just an outpouring of my thoughts. I let it cool. It needed cooling. The written diatribe needed much more than that. I did a little internet research. I studied the Bible, carefully reading or rereading all the verses to which I had been directed.

I was then ready to write again. When I was finished this time, I gave the letter, for that is what my efforts had become, to Carol to edit and comment upon. I then went through a couple more drafts, and as I do on strong letters, at one point, I put it aside for a couple days to cool off again. Then I edited it again, specifically looking for nicer ways to get my point across instead of letting my language wander toward stridency. Finally, I took the letter to a minister friend, Randy Rice, who I respected deeply. I told him the story and asked him to read the letter. He questioned my motives. What did I intend to accomplish with the letter? Seemingly satisfied with my response, he suggested only that I change my reference to "fundamentalists" to "evangelicals" and pronounced, "I would send it."

I did. This is what I said:

> "Oh God open all doors for me…God I lay my life in your hands." These could be my words. I have prayed this prayer or something very much like it many times. I suspect you have too. This humble prayer, however, was not mine. It was found as part of a checklist of terrorism left behind by one of the suicide bombers who, in his view, gave up his life on September 11 to do his part to rid the world of infidels in the name of and as the ultimate sacrifice to his God. His God is our God. That bothers me a great deal. I profoundly believe it also bothers God.

To me, there is only one God! Two billion Christians, 1.3 billion worshipers of Islam, and 14 million Jews acknowledge the God of Abraham as their God. In my view, God is bigger still. He is the God of the universe known and unknown. He is the God of the new agers and the indigenous peoples, the Mormons, the Rastafarians, and of those whose worship leads them to reject monotheism like the Buddhists and Hindus. He is the God of the Agnostics and the Atheists. He is really big.

I believe that God is not only really big, he (or she or it, does it really matter?) is universal, is endlessly patient and forgiving, and understanding beyond all relevant meanings of this word. I believe he even has a sense of humor. How else could he endure the foolishness and futility of human endeavor by both his believers and those who are not? I profoundly believe that the reality of God is too big for human understanding. Because of this, I confess I have a bit of trouble with those, believers mostly, who claim to know the heart of God and even to speak for him with a sense of absolute authority.

Underlying your letters to me over the years, and certainly your strongly worded response to *The Peace Book* and our letter circulating same, is your witness to a heartfelt conviction of evangelical Christian doctrine. I am very okay with this. In fact, I am more than okay with it. Your views and how you have acted out your life as a result of them makes my heart smile. The big God I love and have dedicated my life to serving, who as I admitted above, I don't presume to speak for, I do believe has many rooms in his house for such believers.

Where you and I differ is that I believe God has rooms in his house for others as well. I find it very upsetting when God's children, even those well-versed in scripture, perhaps particularly those well-versed in scripture, take upon themselves a job that should be left to God, that of being the ultimate judge of who and what pleases God, and who and what doesn't. Countless historical texts, both scriptural and political, tell the story over and over again of man's attempts to take on God's job.

Almost every serious war among men has been fought in God's name and man's flawed sense of judgment of each other. You quote Ecclesiastes in support of a time of war. I am very fond of Ecclesiastes 3. However, when we men and women fight in God's name, I can't help thinking of a cartoon that was drawn at the time of President John Kennedy's assassination showing Abraham Lincoln who, as we know, in reality permanently sits proudly erect in his chair in the Lincoln Memorial, at this tragic event sitting instead with his head down and in his hands. To me, even our endlessly patient God must put his head in his hands when we fight in his name.

Candidly, I am no more comfortable with your implied enthusiasm for a just war in the name of Christ than I am in Osama Bin Laden's desire to rid the world of Christians and Jews. Killing to further one's religious (or political) views, especially in God's name is, to me, wrong. If we must kill, it should be only in defense of God's most basic laws, those accepted by all civilized peoples. For this reason, I believe that terrorism should be stopped, whether it be that of radical Muslims or Christian Timothy McVeighs who, I believe, was justifiably executed. Beyond that, I believe we should bridge our gaps, exercise tolerance for each other, and respect our differences: in short, follow Christ's golden rule.

By now you think I am a lost soul, or worse, Satan's messenger. I am neither. I am a very thoughtful child of God, who has sinned and enjoyed God's grace, who believes very deeply that my salvation is dependent on my relationship, love, and devotion to God. I thank God and Jesus every day for their influence in my life and pray for their guidance and support as I finish my time on this earth. I look forward to the time when I can be with them. Because of this conviction, not despite it, as you might suggest, I am profoundly unwilling to judge others who have found another path to God. I leave this judging to God. I do, however, pray that God will judge those who have found their way to him by another path with the same grace that we hopelessly flawed Christians will need.

Lest you be tempted to quote to me scripture which supports the need of men holding each other accountable to their perceived requirements of God, please know that I have carefully read the same and prayed about this for years and asked for God's help in understanding what the Bible says on this and most every subject. However, I should admit to you that my belief and faith in scripture is not in the same league with my unshakable belief in the living God. Here I am forced to recognize the fallibility of the men who wrote the books of our Bible, those who translated it from ancient languages, those who selected the books and passages that make up our modern versions, and those who profess certainty in interpreting its frequently contradictory passages. I feel the same way, at least as to the interpretations, about the Koran.

There are unfortunately many traps to fall into when men try to interpret the heart of God. Jesus, by his living example and his fundamental message, as reported in the scriptures, has helped me a great deal, if not so every word which men attribute to him. I prefer to steer out of the way of those who want to follow the Bible literally, as I do those who wish to reinterpret its every word using a modern cultural filter. Quite frankly, neither camp speaks loudly to me in my relationship with God. Instead, I always seek to understand God's plan for me, and to a lesser extent for those around me and the world, through my own study and prayer. Although a crystal-clear understanding of God's plan eludes me, as it does all of us, happily I have come to revel in this more than I let it torment me, usually ultimately surrendering to the ecstasy of just believing, and recognizing that God's plan is likely just too big, too complex, or too magnificent (or for that matter, too simple) for me to understand. The next day, of course, I start all over again trying to figure it all out. At the same time I take some comfort in the fact that if God is not willing to just tell us his plan, I believe if we allow ourselves to observe very closely the world and God's creatures, empower both through actions taken in love, and stay very close to God, once in a while God does, right here on earth, show us his plan and his glory. I try to stay alert for his message.

As to God's plan for our country, only he knows what it is. I believe we are a blessed nation. I believe this is so not only because of our reverence of God but also because of our reverence of freedom, tolerance, and our acceptance of diversity. As one of the few great nations to apply Jesus' invocation to "Render unto Caesar what is Caesar's and unto God what is God's" by separating church and state, we have prospered. I know many Christians bemoan a seeming lessening of general moral standards, as do I, and as we all should. It seems to me, however, that we should look into our own lives, homes, families, and churches rather than to our government on these issues. What we should not do is seek to mix government and religion. History tells us that this has never worked. This is why the Islamic state of Turkey prospers and the Taliban-controlled Afghanistan did not. Religious leaders like Jerry Falwell and Pat Robertson who try to reshape us into a church-state and worse on national television declare the terrorist killing of thousands of innocent civilians as God's retribution on our country for homosexuality, abortion, and the ACLU discredit themselves and all Christians. Christian zealotry like Islamic zealotry when it takes the form of intolerance, and a lack of grace is to me profoundly upsetting. I fear faith that manifests itself in such stridency strains even God's sense of understanding. I know that here, too, you and I differ deeply in our views.

I have not felt the need to communicate to you my views on all this until now. First, I am not much of a witness. Although I have studied, prayed, and journaled on these subjects for years, I am mostly content to keep my views to myself, of course, venting once in a while to Carol or to my Monday morning men's group. While you, sometimes Mom, have witnessed to me a more evangelical perspective, I have remained mum except to Mom. I have long felt there was no reason for debating these issues and certainly did not want to judge any of you or those of your beliefs that I do not agree with but that are certainly acceptable in the sight of God. Perhaps your letter with its harsher tone has awoken a need to speak out. Maybe that awakening is God's plan, if not your intention.

Please indulge me with the right to criticize back, just a little. Your comment as to Carol and I being loving, kind, and good people is sincerely appreciated. What follows the comment, a passage instructing us the way to salvation being through belief, not works, and your follow-up letter on this same subject were both rather condescending in their implication. I can, of course, let that go. Yes, I have read Isaiah. I have always appreciated your prayers and concern for me, even when I thought they were misdirected. I do want to say, however, that to me, works are not the key to salvation. They are a demonstration of our love for God. I cannot imagine professing love for God and not doing everything possible to make his world a better place and trying to love all of his creatures. While I leave all judging to God, in his, not my, time, I think one of the things that men should fear most is that God will judge them a hypocrite.

Finally, why *The Peace Book*? You have judged it harshly because of the author's very inclusive approach. To me, it is a book about bridging gaps, finding common ground among a variety of cultures and religious beliefs prevalent in today's world. Candidly, I don't find the book itself all that compelling, nor do I even begin to agree with everything in it, as you seem to assume I do. I am much more impressed by this book's intent than its content, which I find somewhat simplistic and certainly redundant. However, I think you confuse personal peace, found only in a relationship with God, and for you with a God reached only through Jesus Christ, and world peace which on this earth, I believe can be found only in our tolerance of each other and in finding common ground. (Yes, I have read all of the Left Behind series and Revelation on which they are based, which I confess I find difficult. I just don't agree with Jenkins and LaHaye or believe that God is bound to their script.) You seem to be willing to sacrifice world peace, believing that God's Kingdom plan is for your view, that there can be no world peace until the whole world believes in Christ, to prevail no matter what. I hope you are humbled, at least a little bit, by the fact that billions of deeply religious and devout people throughout the world are praying to the same God and not coming up with the same conclusion. I am.

I confess I have written this letter to you as much for me as for you. I have no plan to bring you around to my point of view on these matters. I do not need this affirmation. My convictions are deeply held, although admittedly perpetually "in process," and until now for the most part between me and God as I believe, in the end, we should all hold our inner council. Because my God is a big, magnanimous, endlessly understanding, inclusive, and all-powerful one, he does not need me to speak out in his defense.

My personal need to write back is thus borne more of my need to let you, and others in the family with whom I understand you share your concerns about me, know from where I come, and that my views are not the sloppy thinking of someone who just does not want to face the reality of a complex world or that of a demanding (yet, I would argue endlessly understanding) God, but the carefully considered and studied views of a man in the midst of a fascinating and wonderful journey through life in partnership with a wonderful, loving God—who happens to have a different world view than you.

I will pray for you. Please continue to pray for me. God needs to hear from both of us.

Life on this earth is a journey. To be one with God is our destination.

I signed the letter, "With much love," which is what I felt.

Damn Good Country

THE UNITED STATES IS, IN MY HUMBLE VIEW, A GREAT COUNtry; actually, a damn good country. I know some think our golden days are behind us. The middle class, on which our society is built, has been marginalized. We are on our way to becoming like a third-world nation with a small, very wealthy class, the top 1 percent, and everyone else poor. Others feel we have way too much government. We are becoming a socialist nation, rife with high taxes, too much government regulation, and fewer and fewer personal freedoms. Don't even get me started on race or cultural issues that more divide than unify us these days.

Maybe the US is not quite the shining city on the hill first alluded to by Christ as reported in Matthew 5:14–16 and later resurrected and claimed by Ronald Regan, but I ask you: Who does it better? Who even comes close? Our mix of copious amounts of freedom, an economy and lack of class structure that lets anyone who is willing to work hard succeed, and enough free market to allow for all that entrepreneurship but enough government to curb the excesses works very well. Throw in abundant natural resources, great climate, coast-to-coast scenic beauty, and an amazingly diverse and inherently generous and caring population, and we are rightly the envy of the world.

For sure, we could do better on every one of these scores; more or less government needed, depending on your politics; better care of all that natural beauty and our resources. But, who comes closer; who does it better? Democracy, as in rule by the people, is messy. Don't let anybody tell you differently. This will sound crazy but, if we are honest, a benevolent dictatorship is far better. One leader who cares deeply and does the very best for the people, now that could work. This assumes this leader is truly "benevolent." History tells us this does not happen. Even those who start out with good intentions in the crucible of tough choices inevitably make bad ones. Benevolent seems, in reality, to become fascist.

But what about the freedom we want and cherish as our right? With freedom comes choice, and with choice comes the possibility of disagreement. Even the benevolent leader scenario breaks down quickly unless that leader is also authoritarian and takes away free will. Once the people have free will, then who's to say what is best for the people? The leader the people elected? Maybe the courts, or a legislature—are they also elected? Oh, yes, that brings it back to democracy being messy.

The mess that comes with majority rule is one thing, but we have made messy even messier. Compromise, which is the grease that lets factions that do not agree forge ahead, is in short supply. My middle-of-the-road approach is this has to go. Absolute intransigence around a principle is a strategy that could take the whole messy democracy thing down. We have to find our way out of this.

If it doesn't, we may be in trouble. Starting with Newt Gingrich, politicians on his side of the aisle declared the other side more than wrong. They painted the other side as evil. This vilification reached alarming new heights in 2016, and in the presidency and campaigns of Donald Trump. Dividing the American people into camps became the goal. Say awful things about each other, more recently with no regard to whether the awful things were true. Create an "other" to blame all problems on. For Hitler, this was Jews; for Trump, it's immigrants, liberals, and even RINO Republicans. Then use your most loyal and friendly media to create a closed loop of slanted information and support. This last element of the fascist playbook is important to ignore objective truth completely, and attack basic societal elements like elections, the courts, and, for the emboldened MAGA folks, basically anything that does not fit their distinct worldview.

Democracy is difficult. It is getting harder. I believe for the United States, the key is for the majority in the middle to take control and respect but control the extremes. The extremes, left or right, can never gain veto power over the whole process. If this happens, our democracy fails.

As I write this, the election of 2024 came and was decided. The usual election year proclamations that this was an unprecedented election and even that it was existential for our democracy seemed, this year, actually accurate. I, and basically half the country, was hoping American voters would turn us back away from MAGA. It did not happen. I remain convinced that the solution for America is not careening right as we are now nor even all the way left, rather finding its natural middle, so we can remain the damn good country I have declared us, or at least the best there is.

The First Amendment

THE FIRST AMENDMENT STATES IN ITS ENTIRETY, "CONGRESS shall make no law respecting an establishment of religion, or prohibiting the free exercise thereof; or abridging the freedom of speech, or of the press; or the right of the people peaceably to assemble, and to petition the Government for a redress of grievances." All three rights have had some clarification and elaboration over the years, but all have stood on a strong bedrock at the core of Americanism. I discuss elsewhere the emerging view that seems to ignore our founders' strong intention not to establish a state religion. My focus here is the other part of this vital precept, free speech.

Purists believe that free speech cannot be abridged. No matter how outrageous, dishonest, vile, or designed to misinform, we should defend free speech. In recent years, this camp convinced the Supreme Court to include giving money and to be loose on disclosure of just who is speaking or giving freely. Coming the other way, many, including me, have wondered whether all this freedom does not need some control to preserve the greater good.

Controlling free speech is not without precedent. We have all heard it is illegal to yell fire in a theater. Laws vary from state to state, but limits have popped up for true threats, harassment, libel, slander, and obscenity. In 1969, the Supreme Court said speech intended to create inherent lawless action was not constitutional. Free speech is a hallmark of democracies, and it is one area where the contrast with authoritarian governments is so clear. Many democracies have tightened the limits. In France and Germany, for example, it is not legal to deny the Holocaust.

We could not be the great country we are without First Amendment free speech, but lately it seems its most visible manifestation, modern media, may kill us. Donald Trump, in his campaigns and presidencies, has consistent barn-burning success when he declares from the stage that the attendant media is the enemy. He quite literally uses the press gaggle of print and TV journalists roped off within the crowd as a prop. It works every time. His ridicule gets him wild applause and approval. Part of the reason this works so well is Trump is not wrong, at least not completely. However, in the most ironic of twists, as only a master manipulator could pull off, Donald scored this point at the same time he demonstrated one thing that is most wrong with the media—it supports, glorifies, and makes household names of the likes of Donald Trump.

The airtime Trump received from the very beginning of his first presidential campaign and ever since, and his ability to, especially with cable and social media, air his daily rants, is nothing short of, to use one of his favorite words, "disgusting." Objective truth, which many would argue is the goal of free speech, gets completely lost. The bigger the lie seems almost the goal. Trump, who lives by polls and ratings, understands it is ratings, not newsworthiness, that dictates what is on the airwaves. He dominates almost every news cycle, simply by being more outrageous than anyone or anything else. It is reality TV writ large, and it is very out of control.

I wish I knew the solution to this. I do not. Free speech is free speech. Once we say only reasonable speech should be free, some of our freedom will be lost. To defend free speech, we have to be just as willing to defend speech we consider unreasonable, or for that matter, inappropriate, inflammatory, provocative, and worse.

If we dare not touch the basic freedom, then I believe we have to at least move the dial on public taste and gullibility. In a very real sense, we get what we ask for when it comes to unreasonable and inappropriate speech. It is all too apparent that Trump is successful because he understands that ratings are everything for those who make money on his version of free speech. It is no coincidence this master showman, who honed his media skills in the hallowed halls of reality TV, could now cross over into politics. He provides the show that large swaths of the American people want to see.

A measure we could take that seems easy to me, but significant, would be to require full disclosure. Much of the free speech that seems the most offensive is frequently anonymous or disguised. I do not think it at all offends the constitutional right to make full disclosure of who said what transparent. I think it is obvious that social media and political giving (read that as super PACs) have to be fixed to tell us exactly who is enjoying this sacred right.

The beauty of all our freedom is that WrestleMania is no less valuable than *Masterpiece Theatre*. That housewives of everywhere (the more outrageous the better) can exist and enjoy a following alongside the Sunday *New York Times* book review. Likewise, the visuals, both still and moving, from a photo of breathtaking natural beauty or a newborn infant to the most graphic pornography.

With all our freedom comes some obligation, however. The collective we, this means all of us, can and should decide what is appropriate and where. We can decide what we want from our elected officials, our teachers, our business leaders, our scientists and academics, our spiritual leaders, and all those who, up until now, have been on the serious side of the ledger. If we want them to be indistinguishable from hero-worshiped celebrities and reality TV characters, we have only ourselves to blame. If we let ourselves believe obvious lies, if we watch and then parrot deeply slanted media, if we do not seek to know who said what and who gave the money, same thing.

Having flirted with the extremes of free speech lately, let's find our way back. If not a law restricting free speech, our collective market pressure must fix this. Let's use our right of free speech to foster free debate and expression. We need also to work hard to make objective truth easier to discern. It won't be easy, but limits on free speech to achieve this are a worthy goal.

Who Will Buy the Yearbook Ads?

Recently, I was talking with a local contractor friend. We were standing next to his truck, jam-packed with tools and materials, the lifeblood of his business. He told me he was thinking of buying a new vehicle. We talked about the latest features. "The new ones do everything but cook breakfast," he said. Our conversation turned to the price of a new truck that will do everything. It would cost a mountain of cash.

"I am shopping around though," he told me. Even though my friend had bought all his trucks for years from a local dealer, he was now using his computer to shop for his new one over the internet. "I am getting a good deal from some guy in Delaware," he boasted.

"Yeah," I said, "but who will buy the yearbook ads?" My friend looked at me puzzled, as if to say, "What do yearbook ads have to do with buying a new truck?"

What my contractor friend doesn't realize *yet* is that it's all connected, much more than we would like to admit. I read last week that experts believe e-commerce—shopping on the internet—will grow past five trillion dollars worldwide in the next several years. While brick-and-mortar stores are still 80 percent of all retailing, digital shopping is a big deal and getting bigger.

Don't get me wrong, I believe in progress. The digital age and an increasingly robust "cyberworld" are here to stay. The question is, "Should we let this phenomenon dominate us, literally overrun the local landscape?" An internet-based retail world could easily leave us isolated in our homes with our pulsing screens, our main streets boarded up, with an army of UPS and FedEx trucks everywhere.

Putting aside the very valid quality of life issues of interacting with real people in pleasant stores, let's look at the economics of shopping locally. Why does the local car dealer seem to charge more? First, often he does not. If he does, one reason may be because he employs local people, and because he buys a yearbook ad, sponsors a local team, and makes donations to local charities. Not to mention he sends dollars to local utilities, employs local service people, advertises in the local paper, uses the local printer, and if anything is left over, puts money in the collection plate at the local church. All this creates overhead.

Here is the scary part. Eventually, if enough folks choose e-commerce over the local guy, the yearbook ad and all the rest of the donations and dollars that now flow back into the local community will simply go away. Assuming the yearbook can still be published without the local ads, it will cost more. So where is the savings? In the end, if there ever were any, they certainly won't end up in my contractor friend's pocket. And of course, if not just a truck, but say everything else is also purchased over the internet, he will no longer find work locally, because no one will be able to afford him.

So, what to do? Embrace all the wonderful things the digital age brings us. But also stay focused on all the other things that are important to us: real people, real downtowns…in short, the local community. This will not be easy.

Going Green

The concept that the earth is precious and vital has never been the least bit difficult for me to grasp and fully support. I totally get it. If I ever littered, I stopped as a kid and made myself a personal pledge never to do it again. I am almost perverse about this. Too bad I cannot be as diligent about what I put into my body. But that is another story. I have owned first hybrid, then electric, cars since they came out. I live in a house off the grid and use solar and geothermal as much as possible to keep us comfortable.

I really think we humans have screwed up the planet, big time, and the climate crisis is very real and happening now. If there is any saving grace at all it will be that we are resourceful, and we may invent our way out of this mess if we are very lucky. By far, luckier than we deserve to be.

I am no environmental saint. I fly around in airplanes all the time because they take me to lots of places I really want to go. I also burn stuff, logs mostly in our fireplaces at Camp Carol, and sometimes pesky piles of cardboard I just don't feel like recycling. I drink from way too many plastic bottles of water.

It would be convenient to blame many of these weaknesses on some brain damage from my all-time worst interplay with toxic chemicals. When I was about twelve years old, I would, along with my friends, ride around on my bicycle behind a truck we called "stink bomb," for hours. This truck and the giant device connected to the back of it was dispatched to rid the shore community we lived in of summer mosquitos by dispersing a massive cloud of DDT. It was so much fun, and I loved the smell.

I realize environmental enlightenment is a process that does not come as easy for some as others. Choices must be made, compromises embraced.

Humankind's serious impact on the planet did not begin until the Industrial Revolution, which is dated from 1740 to 1850. It is right about the 1850 date that experts tell us we started having a measurable effect, mostly from burning carbon-based fuels.

The time from then to now is an almost immeasurably short period when recollecting that the earth is 4.5 billion years old and that 25,000 years ago was the end of the last ice age. Humans in our erect form (Homo erectus) have only been around for a couple million years, gradually evolving but not to the point of rudimentary language until about 50,000 years ago. Humans did not replace nomadic hunter gathering with agriculture on any real scale until 12,000 years ago. The world population was then just about one million. We are talking about the whole world with about as many people as Jacksonville, Florida, or Columbus, Ohio.

By the time of Christ, 2000 years ago, the world population had reached only 275 million. We are at about eight billion people today, heading to 9.7 billion by 2050. Despite this population growth, the growth rate, has dropped dramatically from 1.86 in the late 1980s to just 1.05 today. If these numbers don't stupefy you, they do me. Does this tell you we had better worry about our little planet? It does me.

How to feed and provide drinking water for all these people is the subject of a virtual rabbit hole of scary stuff and conjecture. Sticking just with our environment and climate change, we have been growing big time since we started all the polluting.

Even assuming humankind's fantastic capacity to innovate, we need to be all in on this. Okay, I will stop burning boxes. Seems inconsequential, I know, but as I am an absolute believer that small actions by many many people can make a gigantic difference, find your own little piece of this attackable problem and take a bite. It might not taste that bad.

Me and the Donald

ANYBODY WHO KNOWS ME AT ALL KNOWS I AM NO FAN OF Donald Trump. This is despite the fact I was hired by him as a lawyer on a really big project, way back when I was thirty-five and he was forty-one years old. In many ways, this representation kicked off years of a successful career for me. I met him long before his name became a household word, or he even thought of becoming the president. However, he was then, as he is now, larger than life. This was especially in his own mind. He believed it. He lived it. As a result, even then, Donald was not at all pleasant to work for.

Trump's larger-than-life persona and P. T. Barnum sense of showmanship was, to my way of thinking, always his "secret sauce." It was the power of positive thinking, learned from family preacher Norman Vincent Peale, but with him on steroids and unmoored from any meaningful moral constraints or eventually even objective truth.

Later, people would widely label Trump as a narcissist, but at this early point, it came across more as focused ambition. It worked for him. What he wanted, what he believed, his reality, more often than not, became the reality for all those around him, certainly for those who worked for him. Even setbacks and failures, when they came, were rebranded as success for this very ambitious young man.

It was not all pretty, though. Trump always had his detractors. Long before he took his schtick national with reality TV, many, dare I say, most, of his fellow New Yorkers found him rather classless and garish. I am embarrassed to say my thirty-five-year-old self was not among this group. Instead, I was rather impressed with all the trappings: casinos, an airline, a very big boat. I was thrilled to have been hired by him. This said, I found Trump shallow and remarkably crude behind the curtain. Sadly, "crude" was a little bit in fashion in the eighties, especially for the young and ambitious.

After working for Trump for a while, I suspected the truth and know now that Donald Trump's business success was largely a myth. At his peak, he was no more than the fourteenth largest real estate developer in New York City. He owned three casinos—but all went bankrupt. He owned the West Side Rail Yards in Manhattan, the Plaza Hotel, and that airline—all taken back by the banks. The big boat came and went. Actually, most of Trump's successes were those self-described as such, or the product of his prodigious public relations man, "John Barron." Oh yeah, that guy turned out to be him.

Many of the pretty toys were real enough: Trump's Mar-a-Lago, bought as a home and turned into a club; Trump Tower; later a whole lot of golf courses; and, of course, all those licensing deals. However, Trump was not a real builder or developer after the early 1980s. Selling his name to add to a project, as a moniker for luxury, was how he made most of his money. That and TV. But then, there were the mortgages and other loans. Leverage is how many rich people get that way. However, too much leverage, especially if the value of the asset drops, or perhaps was never there, will kill you every time.

Trump's desire to get on the *Forbes* list, to need to look rich at all costs, and fights to keep his tax returns and any other real evidence of the actual reality of his finances out of the public eye are now well known. Just as myth busting is the $400 million, plus or minus, it turns out he inherited from his father or chiseled away from other relatives. The reality is that his actual net worth today is likely less than that inherited wealth invested conservatively. All smoke and mirrors.

So what we have is essentially a seventy-eight-year-long lie. Donald Trump is a trust fund kid, full of bluster, narcissistic in the extreme, basically a world-class bullshitter. There was more, however. Those who have spent time with Trump, as I have, and as many books have told us, find Trump to be intellectually challenged, amazingly undisciplined, almost always unprepared, and extremely prone to tangents, the more irrelevant the better. Then there is the temper, notorious for its regular appearances, unfairness, and irrationality.

So flash ahead to 2016 and my erstwhile client is running for president. At first it didn't seem at all real. He seemed like more of a joke. Knowing him, I was sure, as it later turned out, the initial effort was more about brand building than serious. Then all of a sudden, it was—serious, that is.

I felt like I had to do something. I sat down to put my thoughts in writing. I wasn't sure what I would do with what I wrote but I started anyway. I wanted to list my reasons why Donald Trump would not be a good president. On my first pass, I had five then quickly the list grew. Eventually, I had twenty reasons. I sent the list to the local newspaper, and at the suggestion of a client's sister, who happened to be a good friend of Hillary Clinton, to the *Huffington Post*.

The *Huff Post* gave my treatise a new title and added some stock photos. They called my effort "Donald Trump Hired Me as an Attorney…Please Don't Support Him for President" and published it, and off I went on what would be a wild ride. The article went viral and would eventually have tens of millions of views when I stopped checking. Early on, there were something like 39,000 shares and 122,000 likes on the *Huff Post* alone, and many, many more of both at all the other sites that picked it up. I was absolutely shocked. Then media invitations came in. I gave it some thought, then politely turned them down. I believed the story should be all about the substance of the article, and I really did not want it to be about me.

I was also concerned because while most of the thousands of emails I received were overwhelmingly positive, the few negative comments were not on the substance but pointing toward the issue of a lawyer talking about his client. To these, I mostly did not respond but, to the few I did. I told them there are a whole host of reasons why there was no ethical breach. The conversations referenced were not about legal matters and no legal advice was sought or given. There were third parties present for the conversations, and technically, I represented not Donald or his Trump Organization but a New York department store chain, of which for a while he had a substantial stock interest and development control.

This said, I understood the basis of the criticism. I had talked about sensitive stuff, said to me with at least some expectation of privacy. Thus, even if there was no technical breach of ethics, I did something that would make many lawyers feel uncomfortable, including me. To this I could only reply that I could conceive of no other situation in which I would be inclined to talk about someone I knew, client or not, as I did in the article, even with respect to matters that happened thirty years ago, were it not for the grave consequences should this man be elected president.

Although obviously my efforts were for naught. Trump got elected, but here is what I said in August 2016 as printed in the *Huffington Post*:

DONALD TRUMP HIRED ME AS AN ATTORNEY... PLEASE DON'T SUPPORT HIM FOR PRESIDENT

I like authenticity, especially as compared to survey-tested or heavily spun. I am prepared to let a candidate say something that I don't completely agree with and still support him or her. I think the need to be politically correct has gone too far. I also think the media often hypes and slants stories to the point of being untruthful. I think a prosperous middle class is the key to the American success story, both economically and politically and that lobbyists have way too much sway. I am very much a pragmatist, so much so that I like compromise, more than I like ideology. I like deals, especially those that are win, win. So Donald Trump is my candidate, right? He is NOT!

In 1987, when I was 35 years old and he was 41, Donald Trump hired me to be his attorney on a major northern New Jersey project, a shopping center, which like everything else, was to bear his name, Trump Centre. It was a big deal that he picked me and a high honor for me just a couple of years after I started my law firm, which is now over 30 years old. This was at a time when Trump still built things, having recently finished Trump Tower. He seemed smart, business savvy, and decisive. He had a very impressive office, a fancy, very big boat, an airline, a helicopter shuttle and several casinos. Within a few years, virtually all of this would be lost because of bad business decisions. Lots of lawyers have worked for Donald Trump; lots and lots. I am no Roy Cohn, neither as aggressive, nor, hopefully, nearly as ethically challenged, but I did know well how to get very tough land use matters through an always challenging application process in New Jersey. I was thrilled when he hired me.

After the initial interview, my client contact with Donald was actually not very much. One low point I do remember (actually will never forget) is a limousine ride to a meeting with the editorial board of a New Jersey newspaper in which my married client sought to regale me with the number and quality of eligible young women who in his words "want me." I was just plain shocked and embarrassed, but I kept smiling. I wanted and needed this client to be happy. While I was working for Donald, various press reports had Trump and his then wife Ivanna, living in a personal apartment in the Trump Tower of 8, 16, and even 20 or 30 rooms. Genuinely curious, I once asked him how many rooms the apartment actually had. I will never forget his response to me, "However many they will print." Donald Trump was then, as he is now, larger than life, particularly in his own eyes, and at the same time frighteningly small—with very little moral grounding. He was then, and still is, all ego and show.

I have thought about this a lot and I want to share my humble insights of why we cannot elect Donald Trump President of the United States. To me it is more about character than politics. Because of the lack of the former, the latter...the actual politics of Donald Trump... are not that easy to discern. Once I got going with my reasons why Donald would not be good for our country, it was hard to stop. I did stop, however, when I hit twenty, about 4000 words from here. Read on if you are interested.

1. **The man lies all the time.** Like the skilled liar he is, he does it with impunity. "I watched in Jersey City, NJ when thousands and thousands of people were cheering as the World Trade Center collapsed." "Last quarter the gross domestic product was less than zero." The number of illegal immigrants in the United States is 30 million, it could be 34 million." "The Mexican government forces bad people into our country." "The unemployment rate may be as high as 42 percent." All these things have been said by Donald, actually often yelled by him, and many times over and over in front of large crowds. How about the whopper "Crime statistics show blacks kill 81 percent of white homicide victims." One has to wonder why this lie would be conceived, much less told. Donald Trump says all of these things forcefully, so they must be true. But they are not! Unambiguously, they are what is described as "pants on fire" untruthful, as in, not a shred of truth. In passing, you have to ponder whether yet another of Donald Trump's oft made statements about the fervor of his Christianity and the Bible being his favorite book are also not grounded in truth. Clearly "thou shall not lie," is not his favorite of the Ten Commandments.

2. **It is actually not all about the candidate.** "It's amazing how often I am right?" "I alone can fix this." "I have a big brain." "I advise myself." "I am very, very rich." Donald really said all these things. His ego seems to know no bounds. When Donald feels insulted by someone, he obsesses without control. He fusses, he fumes, and he says unbelievably inappropriate things. He is in his glory when he can bully his way to a result he covets. Did you ever notice that those real people stories other candidates are always telling about someone they just met, struggling with a difficult problem, are just not in the Trump lexicon? He keeps telling us he is all about winners. I guess these folks don't qualify. Said another way, Donald Trump doesn't play well in

the sandbox with others. First, he has his own ideas as to who can be in the sandbox with him. He also wants to run the sandbox. He is the kid who gets his way or stomps off in a huff. What happens when he figures out, even our nation's highest office is not all about him? Do we want him with the codes to nuclear weapons?

3. **US Presidents are by design not kings.** The Constitution makes them share power. Donald Trump, who uses the "I" word more than anyone who has ever aspired to the job, has a brazenly authoritarian bent. He wants to be a "strongman," not a President. One has to wonder what would happen if he actually had to govern, or make one of his deals in a zero sum world of politics where the other side just says no. What then of his notoriously short attention span, temper, or non-stop need to tweet his every frustration?

4. **The devil IS in the details.** "Winning so much we will get tired of winning," "Make good deals with China," or even "Make America great again" are slogans that don't actually say anything. We are not stupid; share some details with us, so we can figure out whether you know what you are talking about. For Donald, however, in the few instances when specifics do follow, like perhaps the 1000 mile 35 to 55 foot wall or the deportation of 11 million immigrants, the details never come. Never are we told that to build the wall, even to the lower 35 feet, by actual construction estimates would cost, $25 billion dollars, even if you could get the land to build it (most of the border Trump wants to wall is in the middle of a river and land in many cases could not even be secured for a fence). His magic to make Mexico pay for it? The only suggestion I have heard is to take it out of remittances from folks mailing money back home or one of his "45 percent tariffs". How is that going to work for the Americans sending the money to relatives or all of us paying 45 percent more for Mexican-made merchandise or the American company doing the manufacturing? How about the fact that the wall would do little to stop illegal immigration, more of which is "overstays" of visitors than "over the border" and likely will

generate few, if any, jobs for the folks Trump has whipped up into a xenophobic frenzy. Then let's take the deportation and just focus on the big stuff. How exactly do you round up and deport 11 million people? Is he going to use stadiums and nationalize cruise ship lines? Who will be doing the rounding up, certainly not the police, the army perhaps? The children left behind? How about the fact that American farms, restaurants, not to mention landscaping and construction labor jobs will go unattended? Vital jobs for sure, but are these the jobs that Trump plans to provide for his "real Americans" to make America great again?

5. **Words matter.** Everything is not a "disaster," "stupid," or a "disgrace," Neither is it "tremendous," "huge," "fantastic," or "amazing," Everyone is not a "loser," "low energy," or a "bimbo." Talk of former presidents being liars or his favorite "a disaster" and foreign dictators being great leaders does not advance the discourse. Americans are mostly not prudes, but vulgarity from the dais, penis size allusions, reveling in sexual conquests, menstruation-based criticism and crass insults of every shape and form just doesn't cut it from a President. We have children.

6. **Reading is good, so is studying.** Donald Trump recently told us that he does not read much. We know from the recent revelations by Tony Schwartz his ghost writer on the Art of Deal (yes, I do have my autographed copy from when it first came out autographed with Donald telling me "to keep up the great work"), which Donald says is second only to the Bible as the must-read book, that he certainly has not written a book, at least not that one. Even though for many years I owned a bookstore and would not let my kids watch TV on weekdays to help them become readers, I do not believe you must read to lead. I do believe, however, that those who seek to lead us need to study hard, seek to gain wisdom from others, and try to master very complex ideas and relationships. I think being President is hard. I am glad that after a long day, President Obama retreats to his

private study almost every night for 3 or 4 hours of quiet study...and reading. Any fair interpretation of Trump's many bizarre statements and flip flops—makes it clear he has not the slightest inclination to read or study. In his own words he makes decisions "with very little knowledge other than the knowledge I already had, plus the words 'common sense,' because I have lots of common sense and I have a lot of business ability." It is a special and unique form of arrogance to think you could even consider being literally the leader of the free world without doing the work to deeply understand the job.

7. **The new vocabulary we are adjusting to is not a good one.** Xenophobe (intense dislike or fear of people from foreign countries), misogynist (strong prejudice against women), nativist (preference for established inhabitants as opposed to immigrants); fascist (authoritarian and dictatorial); bigot (intolerance for those with a different opinion); demagogue (inflaming passions based on popular desires not on rational arguments); dystopian (describing a place, typically totalitarian, where everything is unpleasant and squalid), racist (oh, you know what this one is). We have all had to get the dictionary out to understand many of the not household terms that had to find their way into print to describe the unique phenomenon that is Donald Trump. The scary thing is that these strange words are at least close to the mark. What happened to statesmanlike, well-qualified, or even brilliant, as words we can use to describe people we want to elect to high office? Haven't heard any of these associated with the Donald.

8. **We need to be careful with "Tough."** Donald Trump says "in the good old days they would have carried him (a protester at one of his rallies) out on a stretcher." His world reveres this brand of toughness. This toughness is not about the strength it takes to use restraint or to make really hard decisions, it is about "punching that guy in the face" or, at a minimum, saving face, his. I will resist the temptation to belabor the nuclear codes point again, and rather just query do we really want a thin-skinned President who, as he suggested, if a

government leader (Castro) was not on the tarmac to meet his plane, "would turn around Air Force One and come home." Or one who confronted with the fact that whether or not his careless re-tweet of a white supremacist created Jewish star and dollar bill backed attack of Hillary Clinton was anti-Semitic, can't even just give one of those non-apology-apologies "I am sorry if I offended anyone." A "tough-guy" who instead declares major newscasters stupid and sick and makes it all about the media who dare to criticize him, with never a word to David Duke and the ugly element high-fiving him and resending his initial offensive post. Whether or not the post was intended to even more firmly entrenched this segment of support, Trump demonstrates his version of toughness, one that glorifies his opinion and his being right over all else. Nowhere in his world can "tough" be humble, respectful, restrained, or diplomatic.

9. **Success does Matter.** Donald Trump's business success is greatly exaggerated and his skills limited. Donald Trump is a great salesman and a showman/promoter in a league only with PT Barnum. This we can give him. He has also been very good at making his name a brand and selling its use. For a while, he had some pretty high TV ratings by telling out of work celebrities they were fired. However, even in his own playing field, ask any large New York real estate developer, of which—surprise, surprise—he is not one, at least not as large (14th in New York City on the latest list) and you will learn his successes are few. Four business bankruptcies (1991, 1992, 2004 and 2009), the Plaza Hotel, Trump Air, all three casinos, a couple times, the steaks, the water, Trump Centre in NJ that I worked on, the West Side rail yards, where buildings do bear his name as a consolation, certainly, the much hyped $35,000 get rich scheme, Trump University, all failures by any measure except of course to Donald who "has no regrets, whatsoever." Then there is basic business ethics, 3500 lawsuits, the fact that he has a penchant for not paying bills fully or on time, or that he calls himself the "King of Debt", a king made rich by running up debt then renegotiating it. Is this the skill set we want for the President? Even

Trump's fabled net worth, always exaggerated by billions more than others calculate, one has to wonder if his true net worth wouldn't be just as much if he took his considerable inheritance from father Fred and just passively invested it. We'll never know from Donald. Certainly not from those tax returns he won't release.

10. **We could not be the great country we are without the First amendment, but our media may kill us.** The media is not Donald's enemy as he keeps announcing from the stage. It may be the enemy of the rest of us, however. It sure feels like it lately. The air time Donald gets and his ability to, especially with the cable media, to phone in his rants, is nothing short of, to use one of his words, "disgusting." Donald, who lives by polls and ratings, understands it is ratings, not newsworthiness that dictates what is on the airwaves. Donald dominates almost every news cycle, simply by being more outrageous than anyone or anything else. The "false equivalency" created by point-counter-point talking heads then makes over-the-top positions seem legitimate. It is reality TV writ large and it is very out of control.

11. **Temperament, demeanor and character are important.** In many ways, Donald represents the very worst in all of us, or at least many of us. He is all about continuous gratification. He is the petulant child who wants his way. He is a selfish teenager with no big picture yet. He is the spoiled young man of privilege with the "right" race and religion, education, good looks, and family fortune to succeed easily who looks down on others lacking in any of the above who do not. He is a man who thinks it is okay, to call someone fat or ugly or stupid, or to make fun of a handicap. He is the collector of trophy wives and trophy properties, the guy who wins, or so he thinks, because he has the most toys.

12. **The emperor and his clothes.** Donald says he knows more about the military than anyone else. Why? Because he went to an expensive prep school where they wore uniforms and sometimes marched?

How about, "I know more about ISIS than the generals do." Please can some real soldiers evaluate this. Donald says America never wins anymore. Compared to and at what? No doubt we have problems; democracy is messy, witness the present campaign, and the long slow recovery from the 2008 recession has not included the middle class nearly enough, and, yes, trade in a world that is now fully connected and integrated is hard to figure out—but by what measure is America as Donald tells us, a "disaster?" How do you actually say and believe, "This country is a hell hole. We are going down fast." Compared to whom, Mexico, China or his most bizarre new favorite, Russia, he tells us "beat us all the time," "because our leaders are stupid?" Give us a break.

13. **Sophomoric speech tricks don't work—at least not with most of us.** Says Donald, "I am not going to talk about" the libertarian VP candidate's alcoholism. "I refuse to say…I cannot stand to say…that I cannot stand the sound of Clinton screaming into the microphone all the time." You just did, Donald. We get it that with these statements even you know you are on shaky ground, so you are trying to play it both ways. Doesn't work. Nor does your even more insidious, not so clever trick of attributing to others wild accusations that even you are afraid to make, but that you want to advance. How about when discussing the Orlando massacre, "there are a lot of people that think he [that would be, the President] doesn't want to get it. A lot of people think maybe he doesn't want to know about it. I happen to think he just doesn't know what he is doing, but there are many people that think maybe he just doesn't want to get it. He doesn't want to see what's really happening. And that could be." Who are these "people" who have placed the President on the side of the terrorists? Perhaps the same people who with Trump saw the masses in New Jersey celebrating the destruction of the twin towers, or those convinced Hillary Clinton murdered Vince Foster, that Ted Cruz's father was working with Lee Harvey Oswald to kill President Kennedy or his favorites, President Obama was not born in the United States nor did he grad-

uate from Harvard or Colombia. Two possibilities, the likely one, "lot of people," is just Trump code for "I want to now float something so outrageous" even red-faced Donald can't get it out without this qualifier, or perhaps the "lots of people" is a select group, the closed loop of the loyalists who attend his rallies that heard it from him!

14. **A thin skin does not work for a President.** "The politicians have again chosen this Presidential pigmy as their nominee." So said, the long defunct New York Herald about Abraham Lincoln, now nearly everybody's choice for our nation's best President. Consider the statement when George Washington left office, "the time has now arrived for the source of all misfortune of our country... [to be] reduced to a level with his fellow citizens." U S Presidents, all of them, have had their critics, and in our land of wonderful free speech, the critics get to have their say. Thank goodness. That Donald does not do well with criticism is not really open to debate. Ask Megan Kelley ("third-rate talent"), Rosie O'Donnell ("nice little fat Rosie," "total loser") or Elizabeth Warren ("Pocahontas") or, for that matter, virtually any of his recently vanquished adversaries: Cruz, Kasich, Rubio, or Bush, in just the first tier. Even the one most like him, now apparently looking for a post-New Jersey job with him, Chris Christie felt his sting when he suggested Donald was "thin skinned". He just can't let anything go, ever. He obsesses even when he wins. Republicans who broke "the pledge" to support him, they "should not be allowed to run for office again." In Donald's world, disagreeing with him has to have a consequence, a serious one (death too much?) and pursuing this goal is worthy of effort and energy even when it makes no difference. Do we really think our President has time for this? Do we really want a man with such sensibilities and such an authoritarian bent in charge of, say, the FBI or the IRS? Does the concept of "secret police," a favorite of leaders of this type elsewhere, seem too extreme? Probably yes, but if I was Donald I would float it with one of his "people are saying," declarations. There I just used his trick. See how easy it is.

15. **Bully's will always exist somewhere but the White House should not be that somewhere.** What does a bully do? Most of all he or she seeks to intimidate, physically or at least verbally. So far this character trait of Donald's has been exclusively verbal and aimed at business adversaries, and more recently politicians and journalists—and, of course, then ex-ghost writer of his book, and ex-employees or those contractors he cheated (those who do not have anti-disparagement contractual handcuffs) who dare to candidly assess his conduct. What happens when this guy gets the world's strongest army at his disposal, and a bully pulpit that guarantees him notice? Seems like a bad idea to anyone else?

16. **Law and Order.** Before it was an Emmy winning TV show "law and order" was a campaign theme used by Richard Nixon in 1968 to get himself elected in a year when our country had two very public assassinations and destructive demonstrations, even riots, in 110 US cities. Nixon sought to mobilize what he called the "silent majority" around the need for more police. He also tapped into the racial and economic divide between black and white and working class and "elite Eastern liberals," and the evil media that his Vice President, Spiro Agnew called, "nattering nabobs of negativism." Is Donald Trump seeking to bring this back? Of course yes, yet no. Yes, he wants to separate and mobilize angry voters, who feel left behind by an increasingly diverse culture. No, because his dystopian version of lawless, besieged, pitifully weak America is not what Nixon preached, nor for that matter Ronald Reagan. It is unique to him, at least in our country. It is, however, a textbook version of the rallying cry of countless dictators and strongmen. It is a demagogue's basic tool, to gin up a problem then declare he is the "only one who can fix it." As bad as all this rhetoric is, what next? He tells us, "On January 20, 2017, the day I take the oath of office, Americans will finally wake up in a country where the laws of the United States are enforced…crime and violence that today afflicts our nation will soon—I mean very soon—come to an end." How's this work, Donald? Martial law? Does he honestly believe President

Obama, and for that matter all of his 44 predecessors would not have liked to have all laws effective and fully followed? If only wishing could make it so! However, since the states, not the federal government, hold sway over most criminal law, the President acting alone has no Constitutional power to do any such thing. What then? More water boarding and killing families of terrorists logic? "I alone can fix it!"

17. **Incoherent rants, often contradictory, do not make a foreign policy.** Convince Japan and South Korea to seek nuclear arms. Eliminate NATO. Crush ISIS but do it without Muslim allies and no troops on the ground. Sometimes attack Libya, sometimes not. Sometimes attack surgically, but don't let it come out the way it did. Sometimes good we attacked Iraq, sometimes not. Do not nation build, but fix Syria. Stop Iran by making better deals. In fact, come to think of it, that is the solution to almost everything "just make better deals" everywhere. Oh, yes and never apologize for anything. We are America, very, very rich and beholden to no one. Like us or else. Sound like someone we know?

18. **How will anyone effectively be President if we don't at least respect the office?** In the 1960s during an unpopular war we all endured a President adorning himself with a flag pin and declaring anyone who did not agree with him, which included a heck of a lot of young people on campuses all across America, including me, somehow un-American. Although political opposition is as old as our nation, we begin to slide down the slope of dangerous disrespect when disagreement is replaced with vilification. This Republican nominee for the Presidency thinks it is okay to accuse a former President of his own party of intentionally going to war on false pretenses and the current President of being in conspiracy with Muslim terrorists. Any thoughtful American of either party or no party, of any political philosophy must see that this must stop. Truth or at least a semblance of the same has to come back. Outrageous lies just have no place in meaningful discourse, outrageous liars even less so. They cannot

become the backbone of a point-counter-point talking head media circus that is so much more about ratings than truth.

19. **Rich and powerful guys have to play by the rules, too.** Let's not kid ourselves. Trump University was not an academic institution, far from it. It was a get-rich-quick scheme by a guy selling a get-rich-quick scheme. It is not the first or the last of its type. Late night, cheap-advertising-time-television will always feature this fare. Donald's efforts, however, were on so much a grander scale…$35,000… "a University"…really? What this was is an out and out fraud scheme by a man now trying to become the leader of our country and the free world. We all know, or at least have read, that suckers are born every minute. But can't we at least disrespect those who prey on these poor folks, and when they really go too far, sue them? "No," says Donald Trump. The court case brought by a whole class of plaintiffs against his scam, according to him, is only still in Court because the long-time and distinguished federal judge is a "hater" not capable of giving him justice because his parents are from Mexico. In Donald's world, the only individual capable of judging him would not be Mexican or related to anyone from Mexico, likewise folks of the Muslim faith, and oh yea likewise, women. In this world rich, entitled, egotistical, ethically-challenged older white men should then only be judged by rich, entitled, egotistical, ethically-challenged older white men.

20. **We must stand for something.** Donald Trump's version of America does not include folks not like him. Instead, he is all about what Sara Palin labeled "real Americans." The fact that all us others seem to be utterly expendable is deeply troubling. Targeting an entire religion, Islam, with 1.6 billion adherents, 3.3 million being US citizens, for extra scrutiny or worse, is patently inconsistent with traditional American values, if not those of the "real Americans." It is also unconstitutional, and, beyond all this, incredibly counterproductive as it hardens the lines of controversy by wholesale moving of the allies we need to solve terrorist problems into the enemy camp. Similarly,

waterboarding and other forms of torture, not to mention targeting families of an enemy, strategies championed by Donald are not just illegal, they are, to use another one of his words, "stupid." Like most of his other plans, this one does not work either, very likely making situations worse and our enemies more numerous and passionate. One has to wonder what the America of the "real Americans" looks like. A bunch of intolerant, hyper aggressive, folks behind a big wall, isolated (not trading with anyone and thus with a sick economy and very expensive goods) with a lot of enemies. No "Shining City on the Hill "for sure. Hard to see anything but ruin ahead for such a place.

We can do so much better! For me, better comes easily in the form of former Senator and former Secretary of State Hilary Clinton. For those who do not come to that conclusion easily (I get it), this year it will have to be the lesser of two evils. No matter what, don't even think about taking us into the abyss that is Donald Trump.

Not only did my warning not work, but the guy also got sixty-seven million people to vote for him and was elected president. Even worse, from my point of view, four years later, voters who had actually seen him in action gave him seventy-four million votes. Never mind that the opposition got more votes and Trump lost.

As I finish this book, Donald Trump has been elected president for a second time. I was so sure this would not happen, I had declared and I think I believed I would leave the US if it did. I have not, at least not yet. What I have done is go into a quiet time. I have cut back drastically on my consumption of news. I am focusing on people around me and in my world and on good things I can do, including internationally through WMI. Since I, unlike the other side, believe in respecting elections, I have tried to respect the message of losing one.

I still believe that a fascist, deeply selfish approach to the world, and a leader who lies, cheats, is mean-spirited, lazy, genuinely vile and, supremely narcissistic is terrible for America. I thought Americans knew better. For now, I just feel the need to quietly watch. Although I expect bad results from all this, it is against my nature to wish bad on our country, so I also quietly hope some good can come.

When I am confronted with a friend, colleague, or family member in crisis, I often encourage deep breaths and thoughtful contemplation. When it is all too much, I advise "One day at a time." If a day is too much, "One hour at a time." If the crisis is severe, "Just figure out how to get through the next few minutes." Right now, I am following my own advice.

So what explains the attraction of what I have described as such a monumentally unattractive man? Why did millions of followers adore this man? How come seemingly principled conservatives abandon all dignity and principle to support him? Perhaps most shocking, why did evangelical, what-would-Jesus-do Christians treat Donald as their ultimate apostle, not the Antichrist character that all objective evidence points to?

Donald Trump's "magic" is surprisingly clear, if painful to say out loud. Simply put, Donald Trump taps into a darker, more selfish side of human nature. Much of this was masked in a convoluted belief that the United States was somehow a racially pure (European white) Christian nation and should always be. Virtually all the "others" were inherently evil and causing every problem our big, diverse country now faced. Thus, Donald Trump became the beacon of truth for inherent selfishness and longing for a past that never existed, and a large chunk of America found this liberating. I am not a biblical scholar, but I wonder if any of my evangelical brethren might want to spend a little time in the book of Revelation to study the concept of an Antichrist.

Like most arguments, even the MAGA world was not without some truths. Millions of Americans bought into this. These folks, and others, had grown very tired of politicians of all stripes who became less and less authentic even as their positions and their words became more the result of poll testing and calculation. Middle class, rural, less educated, mostly white people had seen their economic prosperity stagnate for more than forty years.

Into all the overdone political correctness and lofty speeches addressed to our better angels, and real issues for many, especially rural Americans, walked a guy who declared being selfish not just okay but the test of being a real American. In a country where some degree of this selfishness was always there, if kept quiet and hidden, this bold public declaration was a breath of fresh air for many.

Unfortunately, it was life breath not just for those who felt left behind on prosperity but for the darkest side of our society. Trump and Trumpism gave first-time recognition and acceptance for white supremacists, those who do not like women in positions of power, anybody anti-LGBTQ, and haters of broader swaths of their fellows (including liberals of any kind, intellectuals, Jews, certainly Muslims, basically everybody not a less-educated white man and those who identify with them). And then there are the evangelical Christians. Shockingly, our evangelical Christian brethren had quietly developed a deep sense of exclusion and derision from a liberal and to them to an overly sophisticated and secular society, such that they bought into all this too.

We have all heard the fairy tale of the much-admired clothes of the, in reality, unclothed emperor. Could that be it? We are certainly on a strange road.

The dictionary definition of a "sociopathic individual" is characterized by a mental health disorder with a disregard for other people: a tendency to lie, break rules, and act impulsively. Seems to fit. Others argue "fascist" was the correct term for this guy. Here the dictionaries tell us fascism is a philosophy, movement, or regime that exalts nations and often a race of individuals and prefers centralized autocratic government headed by a dictatorial leader, severe economic and social regimentation, and forcible suppression of opposition. A lot of Trump here too, although he seems to lack the world dominance goal exemplified by Hitler and Mussolini, the two best-known prototypes.

So what do we do about all this? While I remain no fan of Donald Trump, I get that the problem is much bigger than him. The numbers do not lie. A lot of people buy into this. I believe, like all complex problems, the solution will require many different tactics. First, it is not wrong to aim our society toward our best instincts, our better angels. At the same time, we are a large, diverse group of people under a very big tent.

Here comes another list I created. You know I love lists. Here is some of what I believe we must embrace to take us forward:

1. **Compromise must come back in style.** We do not all get to have it our way.
2. **The other side is not evil** nor un-American just because they see it differently.
3. **We need to find our way back to some sense of objective truth.** "Spinning" and strong opposing opinions are certainly always going to be part of our First Amendment free-speech world, but truth is truth. The media and politicians who tell bold-faced lies must be stopped. Social media and cable programs cannot become a place where wrong facts can be circulated and amplified. Opinions must be tied to their real source. Facts must be factual. As a good first step, an opinion should have value only when its proponent is identified.
4. **Democracy is messy, but it is what America is based on.** Rule by the people. Rule of law. Autocratic leaders need to be exposed and removed. Efforts to do anything but promote free and fair elections must be routed out. Gaming the system cannot be allowed. Gerrymandering must be curtailed.
5. **Tyrannical minorities must not be allowed to control.** In view of our present deeply divided political landscape, the only logical path back to a democracy we can believe in, and be proud of and trust, is with majority rule.
6. **The nominating process that gives inordinate power to the fringe must be reformed.** The fringe on both the left and the right should certainly be allowed to express their views and influence policy, but logic tells us imposing the ideas of a small ideological group on a far bigger group cannot have a happy ending. Not just a

majority, but I would argue a majority in the middle is the only way out at this point.

7. **Our leaders, in particular the president, do not have to always be formal and presidential, but they should always be civil.** The president should speak in a way we can easily defend to a child. Clear lies, taunting rhetoric, name-calling, and the like should be rejected by the voters and never again seen.

8. **The norms of basic honesty must be enforced and made laws.** Politicians should not be allowed to profit from their positions. Never should any government action be connected to personal gain.

9. **We need to aspire to our best ideals but be levelheaded about reality.** Utopian democracy and utopian communism, even a "benevolent" dictatorship, all have good points. We all yearn to be free to make our own decisions, and for others to be so too. But if working together, who can argue with the sharing to each according to their needs from each according to their abilities, or that living in a perfect and just world with a single leader are always bad. As in most things, compromise somewhere between people-led freedom, community-based solutions, and strong leaders is what works. It will come as no surprise that, as a proponent of the primacy of the Golden Rule, concern and emphasis on the common good very much trumps (in this case, pun intended) the inherent selfishness of Trumpism and MAGA. The Rubicon has been reached. Believing there are two paths ahead in the great American experiment, and the correct one must be chosen, is not an exaggeration.

SECTION V

End Game

If you made it this far, you have had your fill of my humorous, at least to me, stories and all my passionate opinions. I am now going to continue where I began in Backstory, on my personal pilgrimage through life. You will now get to learn about my bucket lists and plans beyond age sixty; what happened with the gorgeous blonde I met at nineteen; and meet my kids, not just by anecdote, growing up and find out what they are all about. Finally, I will tell you about my latest project, Camp Carol, and then I'll wrap up this book!

Bucket List

ON THE OCCASION OF TURNING SIXTY, I BECAME VERY FOCUSED on end-game planning. My feeling was that anything I really wanted to do should be planned to happen before Carol and I turned eighty. Life would hopefully go on after this age, but still, this seemed like a good cutoff for high-activity stuff. I made, in effect, a bucket list. You know I like lists, but this one was never strictly formalized or written down; it just rolled around in my head as a new set of end-game goals.

First on this list was a plan to triangulate residences. Instead of one big house in Vermont—I had considered a couple of radical addition plans—I would first downsize in Vermont and then get places in New York City and in the Caribbean. I got right on this, and we bought the St. Thomas condo in June and the New York apartment in September 2012. Camp Carol on the lake was also a part of the plan but not a fully developed idea or to be as big as it has become.

At this point, my first step was to sell our place in the woods with a view, the place where we had raised the kids, Heath Road, and move to a building we owned downtown. The building, the Dunshee Block, was an historic three-story Italianate Main Street building. I had bought it with partners twelve years earlier and then later bought them out. We refurbished and prettied it up over the years, but it was still as it had been when I bought it, two Main Street stores on the first floor and five apartments above. The two apartments on the second floor were big ones, three bedrooms each.

When we sold the Heath Road house, we moved into one of these bigger apartments and immediately gutted the other one to rebuild it to be our new home. A new, bigger, and decidedly fancier kitchen, new bathroom, and one less bedroom, not to mention high-end finishes, a fireplace, and a deck with a hot tub out back were the result. It was nice. What the new downtown digs lacked was a place to stay for the kids when they came home, so when we moved to the new place across the hall, we kept the three-bedroom apartment, already made comfortable with our moved-in furniture and decorated in our style, as the natural overflow for the kids to stay in.

And come they did! Everyone enjoyed their separate but connected place. They did not come all that often though, so eventually we decided to rent this place to Bristol visitors. For this, the apartment got a name, the Pocock Suite, Pocock being the original name for the town of Bristol.

Renting the apartment worked well and was fun, so eventually it grew to become Bristol Suites, our now seven-unit country inn, but this is another story I tell elsewhere. Here, you need to know only that we lived downtown for the next ten years until we declared our apartment "Main Street Suite," and moved it into the inn rental pool. We stayed there when we were in town, but other folks did as well.

The Camp Carol plan was for Carol to run a two-week Vermont "summer camp" for our grandchildren. Ever the big thinker, I expanded the plan to buy a place to have an actual camp. Eventually this became, perhaps, my number one bucket list item. I was overflowing with ideas for what this place could include. To start, though, I would need the right piece of land and lake frontage.

The rest of the bucket list was to travel more, and we have, and for me to retire from the three-day-a-week slog back and forth to New Jersey and the practice of law. The pandemic helped get this last item done. I also wanted to keep helping our kids get their own lives on track, as in help when we could, but stay out of the way.

Next on my list, I wanted to get WMI on track to continue indefinitely and without Wells's—at least without Carol and me. Last, I wanted to write the book you are now reading. All my goals at sixty are now in some form of completion. How cool is that? And I still have seven years to go until I hit eighty.

I had one more goal. I have always known that my love of food and ambivalence to vigorous exercise since my ability to jog was curtailed by my ski accident was a bit of a time bomb. I knew if I did not want to check out before eighty, if not sooner, I would have to make getting myself in better shape a priority. I knew this, but in an intellectual, oh-so-logical way. The emotional buy-in was a whole different story. I can't tell you how often Carol reminds me of this, and I deeply appreciate that she does not do it even more often, as a favor to me. As I said, intellectually, I get this. I really do. It is, therefore, very much in the plan.

My Family, the Girls

In my earlier chapters, I lightheartedly shared the mixed joys of living with a wife, three daughters, and no sons. What I didn't share there, but will now, is I loved every minute of it. My three girls are my pride and joy. While raising my daughters and watching and supporting them as adults has had a few challenges, my relationships with them have been much of the magic that makes my life feel unique and special.

Having children is first of all totally in line with my love of giving back of our blessings. It is in essence the primal act of doing just this. Done well, the parenting required after the miracle of birth has delivered a new human is hard, very hard. Beginning from the endless diapers and spectacular neediness of an infant to the surly rebuttals of a teenager, there is plenty to want to forget. But there are also the seared-in-my-memory moments of meeting a joyful little girl of, say, four years, full of love and with arms open exclaiming "Daddy!" on arriving home after a long day. There are endless other special moments as well.

All our kids were planned. That is why they are five years apart. We thought we wanted each one to have his or her own space and identity. Practically, we thought, never two in college at once. What was not planned was the gender triple. If it was going to be three of a kind, however, girls are absolutely great by me. For a guy who grew up liking to read more than play ball, who had not received passed-down masculine traditions of sports, or even hunting or fishing, being a guy's guy would have been a challenge for me. I might have risen to the challenge, but I never had to find out.

Ciera was our firstborn and arrived in 1977, although this name was not hers until about twenty years later, when it was chosen by her. She was Courtney until she changed it. When she was born, Carol and I still lived in our college town of Lewisburg, Pennsylvania. My life adventure, kicked off by law school in 1978, began soon enough, but at this point we were enveloped in small-town life, still with our downtown store and me running the district offices for a congressman. We were settled and had been married for four years, so it was time.

Ciera, who came a month early, taught me my first lesson of parenting before she came home from the hospital. About to leave to come pick up Carol and the new baby at the hospital, I got a call from Carol. "The baby," she said, then started to cry. Before she could explain, I went for a moment to a spot that only parents know. Already this little girl was mine, she was precious, and if something had happened to her, I would be wounded beyond words. She would be fine it turned out, but as she was a preemie and had choked a little overnight, they wanted to keep her another day.

The second lesson I learned from Ciera that would continue through all my girls, and then my grandkids, was that while I am not really a baby guy, as in I prefer to look at them, not so much to hold them, I love mine. There are few things I can think of more special than having a baby of mine sleep on me.

Father and mother and wonderful baby in a small town was just too easy, I guess. I had to shake us up. I would do this again, years later, when I decided I wanted to move us full time to Vermont, but now, the first time I radically uprooted us, was not too long after Ciera arrived.

Sixteen months after she was born, we found ourselves 250 miles away, living in Shaker Heights, Ohio, a suburb of Cleveland with me a full-time law student and Carol managing a retail store. In the first two years after Ciera was born, I left the congressman, opened and closed an energy business, closed our little store, applied and got accepted to law school, and worked as a construction laborer just for the needed paycheck. I was twenty-five years old and still figuring out life. Carol, always supportive, was along for the ride.

Because I was now a full-time student, I got to take care of Ciera more than I would any of the others. A very special memory was taking her for rides to the park and for Saturday breakfast on the back of my moped. I had illegally attached a bike seat to the vehicle, and we loved to ride. During this period, we developed a silent message of "I love you" being communicated by three hand squeezes passed from daughter to father and back from father to daughter while we rode.

Ciera finished first grade in Shaker Heights and then continued the rest of her school years in Ridgewood, New Jersey. She was always a good student. From an early age, she exhibited a lot of artistic talent. By the time she was eleven, she created paintings we still have hanging up today. Those were shades of the amazing talent that would later turn into costume design and finally all-around design.

Ciera's other passion growing up was horses. From about eleven until she went to Europe as a high schooler, she was all about things equine. She went to a two-week horse camp in New Hampshire for three years. For two summers, we also leased horses at the farm in Vermont. Honestly, much of the camp and stable experience was mucking out and caring for the horses. This privilege I never fully understood. She loved to ride as well. I would go along sometimes but never really developed any skill or similar affection for the sport.

At sixteen, Ciera became the first of our decidedly international daughters. With the Rotary program I had been involved in for some time, she had experienced foreign exchange student "siblings" over the years. Ciera wanted to do this too and headed off to be an exchange student in Belgium for her junior year in high school. She spoke pretty good high-school-taught French, so she felt prepared. When she was sent to the much smaller Flemish-speaking part of the country, that plan was shot to hell.

Ciera persisted and, despite this language barrier and a less-than-friendly first-host family, grew and prospered from her experience. The next two host families, each with a mother from a local village (they were sisters) were fantastic. These families became lifelong friends who she still visits almost every year. She went back to be with them for another semester when she was in college.

When Ciera first lived in the village of Hove with these families, the grandpa of this family, called Opa, and the grandmother, Oma, of this clan had all the cousins come over for lunch one weekday every week. I loved this idea as soon as I heard about it, and in a way, Camp Carol, with its focus on cousins and grandparents, was partially born of this. So too was my affection for the moniker Opa for grandfathers, which is the name I would take on for what I would be called by my grandchildren.

I can't tell Ciera's whole story here as she might want to write a book of her own someday. In short, three years of graduate school at New York University, which she had also attended as an undergraduate, resulted in a fine arts master's in costume design and a fast-paced mini career as a costume designer. She was really good at it. Marriage to a great guy, Dave Jones, in 2015 after a couple years of dating was followed by son Max in June 2016. Max made his appearance a whole month early, dramatic also because of his red hair that remains a singular feature to this day.

With Max, I learned the incredibly deep love I would feel for the next generation as well as my kids. I would also learn that grandkids were the ultimate perfect gig. Love, affection, ability to enjoy and even occasionally spoil a bit, with no responsibility for discipline or all the hard stuff of parenting. I also got to experience the incredible joy of seeing my daughter be a mother, and like her mother, be an extraordinary one.

After Max was born, Ciera did not go back to costume design and instead joined Dave at his business, Sets & Effects, a design and construction company that built everything you can think of for movies, commercials, trade show events, or what have you. Everything is built on a deadline. Nothing was too unusual to take on. Along with miles of walls and backgrounds, they've built a full-fledged haunted house, the Oval Office, a spaceship control room, a submarine, giant sunglasses, giant cakes, and cell phones in frozen blocks of ice. Ciera began as a designer. Now they are true partners in everything, and they have built a great business.

Did I mention Ciera was thirty-nine years old when Max was born? A little old for a first child, so the plan was for him to be an only child. Surprise, in July 2022 at forty-five, Ciera popped out yet another healthy, perfect kid, this time a girl. This little one, Juno, would in every sense complete this lovely, always exciting, fast-moving family. They are all so much fun to be around.

Our daughter Jordyn was born in 1982, the year after I graduated from law school and while I was still working in the large Cleveland law firm. Carol had changed companies and advanced but still managed a retail store, just a much nicer one. Ciera was five years old and in kindergarten, so it was the right time again.

Because I was by then making "lawyer money" when Jordyn was born, Carol could now stay home and end her tough four-year stretch being our primary breadwinner. While at home, though, she watched other kids as well as ours to make extra money. This lady has never, even for a day, been lazy.

Jordyn was pretty much a perfect child. A great temperament, cute as a button, and with her mom's blonde hair. She even, like her mom, had childhood braids. She also had dimples! She was amazing to discipline, even as a toddler, as she would need no more than a disapproving look to shape right up. We all loved her, even her big sister.

Later Jordyn would declare herself an introvert among a family of those decidedly not, and from the beginning, she was quieter. She would almost brood as she quietly considered the world, rather than speak up. I remember a long car ride when Jordyn was about seven years old, when from the back seat we heard crying. She suddenly burst out, "I don't want to die." As it turned out, she had heard me exaggerate, some months earlier, that all of New Jersey would soon be underwater with the pace of global warming. The reality of this had apparently quietly tormented her for months.

The never-ending deference and easy guilt wore off by Jordyn's teenage years. At one point during a rather heated discussion, she told me, "You don't know anything about my life." I, of course, protested, and asked her where all the guilt was that she used to have. She snapped back, "I used it up."

Jordyn was our hippie daughter, especially in her teenage years. Her style of dress, her casual manner, actually felt reminiscent of our sixties experience. Her experimenting with alcohol and marijuana, although never a serious problem, was real enough and a bit more concerning. Also a certain level of discontent and rebellion of the status quo seemed to haunt her.

Two things kept Jordyn motivated and moving forward. The first was a program at school called ART, a theater program through which she left the regular high school each day for the theater program at our regional vocational school. Although acting would come and go as a passion from her, this program grounded and motivated her while she participated.

As an aside on her acting, I will jump ahead a little and relate that when she landed a part with an amateur company presenting in English *The Vagina Monologues* in Brussels, Belgium, during a gap year after high school, she ended her acting career with a flourish. I flew over and surprised her by being in the audience. Even for a guy who loves to make memories, this was a standout.

Jordyn's other high school passion would become a central part of her life in the years ahead. Her interest in Africa led her to a month-long trip in her sophomore year and a full semester in Ghana her senior year. She was hooked and studied African culture and history along with art in college and went back to Ghana to spend another semester during college.

At this time, my interest in helping young people in the developing world was growing and Jordyn's host sister in Kopeya, Ghana, became the logical first candidate for a scholarship, and what is now Wells Mountain Initiative was born.

Although on the board of directors from the beginning, Jordyn was not active in WMI operations in those early years. After college, she interned and then quickly rose in positions to the C-suite within three years at a New York City charity called Do Something. This organization attempted to combine efforts to motivate high-school-age American young people with corporate America's desire for PR, and occasionally, good intentions.

One of Jordyn's assignments while at Do Something was to help select the annual Do Something Award finalists, young people who had done extraordinary things. Think CNN Heroes, but with just young people. The winner one year was Jessica Posner, who together with her Kenyan boyfriend, Kennedy Odede, started a Kibera slum-based charity called Shining Hope for Communities (SHOFCO).

When Jordyn hit the point of burnout at Do Something in 2005 and decided graduate school was the right next step for her career, she went to visit and help at SHOFCO and two other award winners to give them her skills and time, a month each, before her master's program began at Columbia University in New York.

The stop at SHOFCO resulted in part-time work all through the two years of grad school and summers and school vacations in Kenya. When she graduated, this became full time; for about two years, she lived in Nairobi.

By December 2016, the exciting but truly exhausting founder period at this fast-growing nonprofit began to end, and it was time to move on. After six months of consulting with a handful of interesting clients, one of which was to do the strategic plan for WMI, she came on staff. Over the next six months, she wrapped up her consulting business and became the first full-time executive director.

As I write this, Jordyn's next phase is underway. After five years and a year of transition, she left WMI. Most recently, Jordyn lives in the Hudson Valley community of Saugerties and has two Rays in her life:

husband Ray, an engineer, outdoorsman, and good guy; and son Raymond, who is, like all of my grandchildren, over-the-top spectacular. As she moves back into the working world, Jordyn is focusing more on the clinical than administrative side, and is now moving to become a licensed therapist with particular emphasis on children. There is a whole other story coming, and I will leave it for Jordyn to tell.

Carlyn was and is our baby. Even though it was always likely she would be our last child, she absolutely confirmed this by being far and away our most challenging infant. Carlyn, just as adorable and cute as her sisters, nevertheless had temper tantrums. These episodes would spring from being overtired or overstimulated, or from absolutely nothing at all. Once the screaming, stiffened body, and all-around bundle of rage started, it was not curable by anything rational, only utter exhaustion: hers, that is. Our point of exhaustion would usually be long since passed. This only happened maybe a couple hundred times, ending when she was about four years old. Somehow, she survived; we did not kill her.

Carlyn, from her earliest signs of a personality, was the most headstrong of our kids. Destined to be the bossiest and most domineering, rather like me, she always, also like me, often had a plan she was busy executing. She had extra mothering from sisters who were eleven and five by the time she arrived.

Jordyn, who as an adult, is now very close to Carlyn, as she is to Ciera, was a little bit of oil and water with Carlyn growing up. Jordyn knew how to push her buttons and did. Carlyn, the more serious and always more conservative of the two, was utterly shocked by a hippie sister who would spontaneously lift her shirt and show off her boobs to enjoy the always-horrified reaction by Carlyn.

Carlyn, unlike Jordyn, who from her early years developed a very strong social conscience, as a young girl was very much our material girl. Makeup, hair, and fashion were all of utmost importance. Carlyn also always had a posse. She kept friends around and reveled in their mutual joy of all that girly stuff. That reveling later expanded to include boys.

By the time Carlyn was in middle school, our house was usually the base station for all social events. Groups of anywhere from three to five young ladies would sleep over, primp, and get ready for a dance, and then come home to debrief after the event. Sunday morning pancakes for Carlyn and posse was a regular event and among my special memories.

Carlyn became an only child, at least the only child in the house, when Jordyn went off to college. We had worried about how this would affect her because with the other two girls they were more independent and wanted much less parental involvement during their last five years at home. It turned out that Carlyn had been itching to be the only star in the show. She absolutely loved and flourished in the role of pseudo–only child—her and her posse, that is.

Carlyn also had a serious boyfriend all through high school. He was a big part of her life. He was a year ahead of her and a star football player, a quiet guy but popular, so was considered a "catch." He was great for Carlyn as he really cared for her and was wonderful for her self-esteem, but we never saw him as her ultimate guy. This was something we kept to ourselves as she was very definitely not interested in hearing our opinion on this. Although the relationship continued, if occasionally a little battered, him going off to college and then quitting two months later, and her leaving for college the next year, at some point all by herself, she figured out it was time and ended it for good.

Boston was now Carlyn's town. The big turning point for Carlyn came her sophomore year. Two things happened that year. Carlyn joined a sorority, Delta Zeta, and also figured out what she wanted to study and do for the rest of her life: physical therapy. DZ gave our most social of daughters a home and the beginning of a new posse. She made one fast friend, Kelsey, in the line waiting to enter the sorority process. They pledged DZ together and roomed together for the rest of their time at Northeastern.

Carlyn's summer job during the last couple years of high school and the first summer home from college was at Bristol's creemee stand. Creemees is what Vermonters call soft-serve ice cream and our creemee stand had plenty of the same, along with burgers, hot dogs, and other fast food. Carlyn's last two summers there was as the manager. At just nineteen, she ran the place and managed a dozen part-time employees.

Like my experience managing summer movie theaters years earlier, also at nineteen, this job was a major character builder for her. I was so proud of how she did this, in particular her efforts to break a long-standing tradition of servers giving away food to friends. I remember thanking the owner, who was thanking me for Carlyn's good work ethic, for giving her more education than any year in college would, and paying her as well. We both came out great on this deal. Carlyn was perhaps the biggest winner.

Once Carlyn latched on to physical therapy, she was on her plan and never looked back. Northeastern is a co-op school, so they combine work experience, called internships, with school. With three internships and school during each summer, she graduated in six years in 2012 with her doctorate. She went to work at one of the places she had interned, Spaulding Rehabilitation Hospital in Boston, and loved it.

At Spaulding, Carlyn met a guy named Mike Smith who was a college graduate but not a PT. At this point, he was a wheelchair expert and called a PT assistant. His emerging plan was to go to PT school. Post college this would be another full three years to get his doctorate.

Carlyn first met Mike as this cute guy at the lunch table, then arranged to bump into him and eventually, in her words, man-trapped him. I said she was the planner. Her plan, which went off without a hitch, was for Mike to finish school while she kept working, get engaged, then married, then have children. Sure enough, in 2017, a graduation and engagement; in 2018, a wedding; and in 2020 and 2023, two babies, first Etta and then Callum. There is pretty much nothing this great young couple can't do.

Unless I want this memoir to have two volumes, I have to stop somewhere, so I will leave you hanging without telling you about my grandkids. They are five in number, and they are all absolutely fantastic. What else could their Opa say? Their stories are largely unwritten, and I am sure they will be spectacular. As this book has been written first and foremost for them, and for future generations, I need to pause here and tell you, Max, Etta, Juno, Callum, and Raymond, and any future heirs, that I really love you guys. If you learn anything from reading this book, great, no matter what, be your best self.

Gorgeous Blonde Gets Even Better

When we left the Gorgeous Blonde story, I was still nineteen years old and had fallen head over heels in love with mine, who you came to know had a name, Carol. More than fifty years have passed since then, and it has only gotten better. Carol produced for me (I helped a little) three equally gorgeous, and just as smart as her, daughters, mothered them into womanhood, and has taken care of me as a kind of fourth child for all these years. She is no less talented as a grandmother and mother-in-law, all the while still taking care of me.

We have enjoyed a true partnership in so many ways. In parenting for sure—I am the stricter one, she is the always understanding friend—but it all worked. We also owned and ran businesses together: three stores over the years, real estate properties, even a Vermont inn. I am, as always, the big-picture, idea man. Carol needs to make it all work. We are a great team.

On the big stuff, we are very alike. In "Soapbox," you were treated to my political views, best summarized as pragmatic and middle of the road, but with a clear veer to the left, especially on social issues. Carol and I are in sync on most of this, which keeps the peace between us. Our only difference is, despite my almost visceral anti-MAGA views, I am content to leave this matter undiscussed with folks who I otherwise care about, and in the case of family, love. Carol often wants to go right into the lion's den and confront deeply flawed logic wherever she finds it. I usually win this argument; hence we get along with more people than we might otherwise.

If politics is a hot button, so is religion, but here too we match up nicely. We are both old-fashioned, mainstream Christians. We are generally churchgoers but do not feel the need to attend particularly deeply, and thus miss as much as we attend. We both believe more in actions than words and do not like judging others. We are all about giving back, walking the walk, and living by the Golden Rule.

The similarities go on. We both like to read and, in recent years, enjoy hours of big-screen TV binge-watching. We both enjoy travel and have been to more than forty-two countries, and most US cities, in recent years with a lot of cruising. We both love St. Thomas for a chunk of winter and Camp Carol for the rest of the year. We love having our kids and grandchildren around us. We also like hanging out, just the two of us.

So how about the differences? We binge-watch historical stuff, period pieces, westerns, but when I get to choose, I go for rom-coms and even Hallmark formula stuff at Christmas. Carol likes heavier, more complex, often darker movies. I read more nonfiction than fiction; Carol, mostly fiction. She loves her gardening and keeping track of plants, birds, and everything else. I just nod when she tells me about these. Carol loves to play games. She does Wordle every day, playing this game with herself. I hate games. I know it seems un-American. I would really rather talk than play games when relaxing.

I tell Carol she nags me too much. She says, "You do not know what nagging is." She just takes care of me. Both of us are probably right. I tell Carol I love her every day, all the time. In recent years, my line has become a never-ending mantra of "I love you." She responds with the same words. I respond, "I love you more, much more!" She then responds, "I love you better, much better!" On consideration, this is probably right. I get the "more," she gets "better." The discussion closer is the holy grail, "I love you infinity muches." We have established that infinity has no topper—as in, "two times infinity," which I have tried, does nothing. Whoever uses this closer, mostly her, but sometimes me, gets the response, "Show-off." The I love you battle is then over, until we do it again, say twenty minutes later. We never go to sleep without this dialog.

Carol takes care of me in the very literal sense, making almost all the meals, washing our clothes, keeping the house. I pay the bills and the taxes, still work at making us money, and the outside stuff, but in recent years, this outside stuff is more supervising our handyman than working all that hard at it. While I still work hard on actual work stuff, so does she. "Star boarder" is not an unfair description of my status.

Carol graduated from Bucknell at the same time I did, her with a BA in physiology. She started at Bucknell, then later attended John Carroll University in Cleveland for a master's degree in counseling and human services. Although this was her career path, departing on it was delayed in the first couple years in Lewisburg, then in Cleveland, when she worked as a retail store manager to help pay our bills while I was in law school.

It wasn't until about 1984 that Carol began working in her field, first at the Department of Family Guidance and then at our county special services school district. She stayed on course, working as a school social worker when we first moved to Vermont. At that point, her career path careened into my dream purchase of the bookstore. This happened when we figured out that in Vermont she was paid to be a school social worker just a little less than we paid our bookstore manager. Carol went back to retail and loved and was much loved as a bookseller. Elsewhere you learned this dream made no money. No matter, we kept at it for ten years.

Like me, Carol was also all about giving back to the community. Over the years, in Bristol, she headed the local arts association and the PTO, was elected a member of the Selectboard (what Vermonters call our town council), and served on numerous committees and boards.

When we closed the bookstore and started our foundation, she briefly thought about going back into counseling and going back to school for an art therapy certification, but instead, she helped with the foundation. She also took a part-time job as the executive director of our local downtown economic development association. Needless to say, she was great at both.

These days, Carol is the rental manager for our forty-four rental properties with tenants and she also supervises our Vermont inn and Vermont products store. Both can be done at least in part remotely, so we manage to spend lots of time at Camp Carol and in St. Thomas. She still takes very good care of that fourth kid. Since she will soon, like me, be seventy-three years old, we are working on an exit strategy for her too. That is, of course, except caring for that fourth kid. She is stuck with that job for as long as I am around.

Fifty years is a long time. Has it always been perfect? Nope. It took us a long time to get compatible in the physical and affection areas. Our differences in parenting made us a good team but frequently left us quite frustrated with each other.

I grew up with parents who were affectionate but who also would fight. I brought this to the marriage. Carol saw virtually none of either so thought we were headed for divorce the first time I yelled at her. She learned to yell back. I also had to learn that a woman who can be endlessly sweet can also be just as endlessly stubborn. Here all the similarity helps, so we have little to fight about.

Like my nonspecific D, this need for physical affection has a name I use for it. I call it my "hole." Therapists might call it an attachment disorder. The hole has been around since I was a kid, and it seems to know no bottom, as sometimes it is virtually not capable of being filled to the top. It always seems to need more filling. Sex was a part of it for sure, especially in the early years, but my condition was more about physical affection, intimacy, and tenderness, than any act.

I understand all too well this is very much a therapy issue and anybody with a bent toward psychotherapy, whether Freudian persuasion or not, could have real fun with this. Although I have spent decades contemplating and studying this very thing, my go-to solution was not so much to figure it all out, just to press on.

My otherwise spectacular wife has no such hole, nor did she really understand mine until maybe the last ten years of our marriage. Honestly, until she did, the sledding was sometimes kind of rough.

Carol is not just the love of my life; she is my best friend. I have had a handful of other good friends, both male and female, but none whom I confide everything to like Carol. She gets to see the real me, all of me. Not just the confident, outfacing exterior, but sometimes the tired and depressed little boy who just needs to be hugged. Having a partner who has your back to this extent, especially if you think she is knock-down gorgeous and smart as a whip, is as good as it gets.

I love this woman with an intensity and depth that defies words. I thank God every day for blessing me with her.

Making Memories

MEMORIES SUSTAIN US IN OUR LATER YEARS. MY GOAL IS TO have plenty of them. Based on what came up while writing this book, I suspect I will.

Making memories was always a central part of my parenting plan. I wanted to create traditions and events whose memories would stand the test of time, so even without a photograph, they would be easily relived in one's mind, leaving a warm, special feeling. I have worked hard on this. However, especially in the early years of the law firm, unfortunately when the kids were also growing up, I worked long hours and many nights and weekends. I have plenty of law firm memories, for sure, but that is a whole different book. Since I worked so much, I made a conscious effort to take vacations when the schools did and to also be the token father on the school trip. Vacations provided a great event for making memories.

One such school vacation trip that stands out was to Southern California in 1991. The girls were four, nine, and fourteen. A never-forget moment on this trip was a side trip over the border to Tijuana, Mexico. At one point, Carol, a bit paranoid about having a cute little blonde kid get snatched, frantically asked, "Where is Carlyn?" Only to be told by me, "She is in your arms, honey."

Equally memorable was Jordyn's face when we arrived in Palm Springs for the last day of spring break, and she saw naked or mostly naked coeds riding on the backs of motorcycles. I will also never forget an unbelievably challenging four-hour horseback riding adventure through high-desert mountains with Ciera and a guide—and me, always far behind them. And we can't leave out the amazing saddle sores I had for the next few days. Then there was the joyful, amazingly unsophisticated, jump-on-the-beds, scope-out-everything, wide-eyed entry of my family into a high-end Beverly Hills multiroom suite I had won in an auction and that we stayed in for a few days in Los Angeles.

We enjoyed another special western trip a few years later. This time to Idaho and Wyoming. I had been to Idaho often as a member of a Boise bank board. In 1995, Carol and I took the three girls to the famous "river of no return," the Salmon River. We took off on a guided raft trip from Salmon, Idaho, then spent five days going downriver, heading west.

The rapids were exciting and special, likewise always-scenic lunch stops and luxury camping each night. Guides set up the tents, cooked meals, even put in a luxury latrine (popular with girls in the woods). They played guitar and harmonica tunes, and, at one point, were combing hair for my long-haired daughters.

I remember in particular one day when we were all along the river, building rock cairns from the oh-so-smooth river rocks, starting with very large and extending upward with rocks gradually getting smaller. When it worked, the cairns could be three or more feet tall and include as many as eight to ten stones. Another special memory was a natural hot-spring-fed rock tub halfway up one of the banks. The trip also included a visit through the incomparable Yellowstone with ample bison and the unique Old Faithful geyser.

Trips to Europe with all three girls, earlier to Italy with just the older two, a week in Wells Beach, Maine, and another at Southport Island near Boothbay, one to Cape Cod, ones with the whole Wells family to the Outer Banks in North Carolina and Silver Bay on Lake

George, with just Carlyn and me to Disney World, and many back-and-forth and extended stays in Vermont all provide similar memories.

Some of my favorite times were spent at our first house in Vermont, in Orange, and the weekend trips Jordyn and I took, just the two of us, in the mid-nineties when she was in her preteens. I wrote and cut grass, and we both hung out with each other. I remember in one of our attempts to cook for ourselves, we chose fresh pasta and Classico spaghetti sauce at the grocery store to bring home and make. It was great. To this day, these products remain family favorites.

The trip with Carlyn to Disney World was her compensation for not being invited on the Italy trip with her big sisters. She was six years old. We stayed at the resort, just a monorail ride away from the Magic Kingdom, and did little kids' stuff the entire three days, including the character breakfast, and we went on all the rides she chose. She was an avid fan of Splash Mountain, and we went on it twice…or maybe it was three times.

One of my other favorite memories of Carlyn on a three-sister European adventure in 2002 was standing out front of the Moulin Rouge in Paris, about to enter, consoling her as she bemoaned that she was for "the first time ever" missing a high school dance. This was very much our Carlyn, and these memories stand out in my mind to this day.

The Wells family celebrates all the regular holidays that everyone else does: those unique to Christians, Christmas and Easter, although Christmas has by all rights become a secular bonanza of spending, giving and getting; and Thanksgiving, Memorial Day, Fourth of July, and Labor Day. The Fourth of July has become more special since we moved to Bristol in 1996. This little town has fireworks, a parade, a midday party on the town green, and its unique preparade outhouse races. Nobody does it better.

Our more unique holidays, more family traditions at this point, are very much tied to our longtime Vermont homes, and are almost always big memory makers. This all started when we made Vermont our vacation home state in 1987. At the farm we bought in Orange,

Vermont, we started what became our oldest and most enduring tradition: cider weekend. Based around picking then pressing apples into cider, the event is usually held at about the time of Columbus Day each year, the first weekend of October. It is not a coincidence that this weekend comes as close on the calendar as possible to the peak of fall foliage. There are very few places on this earth that surpass the beauty of Vermont when our myriad of tree species burst into their symphony of reds, yellows, oranges, maroons, burgundies, russets, and golds.

To accomplish the cider making I bought a hand-crank grinder and press, which, with one overhaul, has served us all these thirty-plus years. In the beginning, we were very careful about the mix of apples. It turned out the cider was always great no matter what mix of apples we used. Family and friends have joined us every year. Carlyn, who was one year old when we started, has never missed. We moved much of the cider pressing to Basin Harbor in 2019 to include it at her wedding reception.

This event has moved as we did, first held in Orange, then Bristol in front of the bookstore for two years, then Heath Road, then behind 25 Main, and finally Camp Carol. Camp Carol is where it will remain. This final location is perfect because Shoreham, Vermont, where Camp Carol is located, is the home of Champlain Orchards, one of the state's biggest and best orchards—and where we now get our apples. The year one of our nieces was married on Long Beach Island at the New Jersey shore, we took the whole operation out of state. The apples and all the equipment were transported in the back of my pickup truck.

Once the kids grew up, the tradition, if anything, expanded. Friends and family come from all over to join us, and often fill Camp Carol and our Bristol inn. My nephew Phil has come at least six or seven times. Our yield has settled in at about twenty gallons, of which everyone who participates gets to take home a few half-gallon jugs.

A newer tradition is maple syrup making the first Saturday of April. Since 2018, we have gathered sap from our fourteen maple trees at Camp Carol, then boiled it all day over a wood fire, resulting in two gallons of syrup in little eight-ounce bottles. A fire, and lots of drinking beer, makes this effort more fun. Our whole family has been there, but not too many others so far. Nephew Phil, now with wife, Jenn, has also made it north for many of these weekends.

Another tradition of ours was mother-daughter Mohonk weekends. On the occasion of turning fifteen or thereabouts, Carol took each of the daughters off to Mohonk Mountain Resort for a mother-daughter weekend of quality time. A variation and extension of this has been Kripalu Yoga retreats for about the last eight years where mom and daughters leave spouses and kids behind to stretch, meditate, eat healthy, and commiserate together.

Finally, let me tell you about Macy Day. Set anywhere from Black Friday until Christmas, every year I would take the girls to a day of shopping together at Macy's Herald Square in New York City. The ladies would share a big dressing room. I would sit outside and maintain the piles of chosen garments. They had fun rebuilding wardrobes for another year. The day usually ended with the rest of the men joining us all for dinner, most often at Monte's Trattoria, a fantastic little Italian neighborhood restaurant in Greenwich Village. To the best of my memory, we began doing this in about 2007 and sad to say, in 2020, this special time came to an end. You never know; I am game if the four girls ever want a reunion event.

One last memory-making tradition worthy of relating is not an annual event but something Carol and I do. We celebrated fifty years of marriage while I was writing this book. Here is a fun fact. We have sent Christmas cards, holiday cards for our friends who do not share our holiday, that we created ourselves every single year of those fifty years. In the early years, the cards were homemade. Later, they were duplicated photographs pasted onto paper. Finally, when the creation of the photo cards became ridiculously easy, we created family pictures.

What has not been so easy is our tradition of writing a Christmas letter. We have almost always alternated years writing it—one year Carol, the next me. Recently, I pulled all these letters and cards together, digitized them, and put them in a book. Two problems. First, we needed to find them all. The early ones were in a box somewhere, but we haven't found them yet. The second problem is this book came first. One major nostalgia project at a time.

The letters were always about two pages long, very chatty, and we bragged about our kids a lot and created a snapshot of the past year. Lots of folks told us they love getting them. Most recipients say nothing, of course, so who knows. They are fun to write.

Camp Carol

WE'D KICKED THE IDEA AROUND FOR YEARS. AS CAROL CONceived it, there would be a camp for cousins run by their grandparents, us. When she first voiced this idea, there were no cousins because there were no grandkids. I think when she first got the idea there were not even boyfriends, much less husbands. The camp then got a name when it was no more than an idea, "Camp Carol." That was my main contribution early on. One of the kids kept the momentum going for the idea when they bought us an old-style megaphone with the letters CC stenciled on it. Although I think it was from Champlain College, the CC certainly worked for Camp Carol.

Not content to just go with Carol's simple grandkids camp, my idea—I have always been the big thinker—was we needed an actual camp on Lake Champlain to make this work. Consistent with my age sixty bucket list, I looked for the perfect place. It took a while.

We first saw Five Mile Point in Shoreham in 2016, but it took more than a year to cut the deal. It was twenty-two acres of property owned by a widow with an astounding three thousand feet of lake frontage. The land was a peninsula that jutted out into the lake. It was heavily wooded and had no structures except a solitary outhouse on a spot identified as a potential house site.

The seller and her husband, before he died, had sought and received permission to build a three-house subdivision on the property and to add septic systems. We did not want to build three houses. I wanted the site for our family camp. To make a deal, I needed to get the price down, a lot. Eventually, I made a lowball offer and was prepared to wait. With a final small compromise back in her direction, I got my price, and I also got the seller to take back a mortgage for three years. It was the fall of 2017, five years into the bucket list period. I had our camp property.

Work at the site began the following spring. At this writing, eight years later, there is a beautiful lodge, with our little house attached to it, a multibedroom guest house, a live-in tree house, three tiny houses (one for each of the girls), a barn, a pavilion, a pole barn, two miles of cleared trails through the woods, docks, boats, kayaks, and other water toys, ATVs, a snowmobile, and, of course, my boy-toy tractor and Gator. In progress is a mini golf course, for which each family will build a hole. Also in the plan is an addition to the lodge. It is a vacation heaven.

All this did not happen at once. The first spring we worked on the roads and trails. The road was truly a dirt road and had many deep ruts and low spots, not to mention grass often growing in the middle. It took loads of gravel that year and future years to firm up the road. Although the gravel worked its way down and the appearance went back to being a dirt road, consistently applying the gravel and grading ultimately made the road much better.

We graded the trails, adding gravel only in the bad spots along with wood chips.

We should talk about the land itself. It has lots of history. The name, Five Mile Point since colonial times, came from the pointed end of the peninsula, which marks a spot as close to the New York side of Lake Champlain as any. This point is exactly five miles by water from Fort Ticonderoga on the New York side.

Fort Ticonderoga was built in 1755 by the French, then taken over by colonials after they defeated the French. It was the site of a battle lost to the British in 1777. Interestingly, its cannons were remarkably dragged three hundred miles overland to Bunker Hill on the other side of the Charles River from Boston. The revolutionaries didn't get the job done there either as the colonials eventually lost what is now Charlestown to the British, but the fighting was so intense, the British paid attention.

Until last summer, when Camp Carol was the brunt of an oh-so-rare Vermont tornado, there were four three-hundred-to-four-hundred-year-old oak trees lining the lake close to the bank. Carol named them Professor, Ancestor, Shiva, and George. I had cleared around them a bit so you could see their splendor. After the storm, the only one still standing tall is George. We have made the stump of the Professor, which is near the tree house, into a memorial. I do not know what to say about the trees that watched four hundred years of history being felled by nature. It certainly was not my plan.

The entire center of the peninsula, now wooded, has nothing this old. It was cleared fields until sometime probably in the 1940s. When I think of that I am always stunned to remember this land was cleared before the time of chain saws and tractors. How much work it must have taken to clear this field!

From what I can tell, the property remained farmland well into the mid-1900s, when it was allowed to fallow, and new trees began to grow. The internal road, which for the second half is just a trail, runs the length of the property anywhere from one hundred to two hundred feet off the lake, just as it did when it was traversed by the ferry travelers that I will tell you about. The property is now predominantly evergreens, sugar maples, oaks, elms, ash, basswood, poplars, and way more invasive species than we would like, including buckthorn, hawthorn, and honeysuckle.

Nowadays we have no fields to speak of and most of the clearing on the property has been done by us, just enough for the main lodge and other buildings, for some parking near the barn, and the trails. The trails are by design serpentine, which makes them much more interesting. I was also determined not to cut down any large trees to create the trails.

The sugar maples are all identified and each has a little plaque on it with a maple leaf. These we know well because we tap them each spring as the thaw comes in March so we have enough sap, usually about one hundred gallons, to make maple syrup.

My original plan was to have no grass and to leave everything wooded and natural around the buildings. This plan collapsed a bit as areas of grass "sprung up" and got planted near the lodge and many of the little houses. Even some of the natural areas are supplemented by spreading wood chips. In summertime, it takes a solid three hours to cut grass and make everything look pretty. So much for all natural. This maintenance does not take into account Carol's gardens out front of the lodge, which, with a mix of annuals and perennials, reflect hours of her loving affection to produce spectacular results every summer.

Along with fixing roads and trails, in 2018 I added our first building to Camp Carol, my little red barn. I loved this little building, especially its barn-red color. Calling it a barn may be more my pleasure than reality. It has never sheltered a single piece of livestock nor farm equipment, unless you count the lawn mower and weed whacker.

The "barn" is a fourteen-foot-by-twenty-five-foot, two-story, high-pitched roof structure made by the Amish in Pennsylvania, then assembled on-site. My version has a garage door on one end, barn doors on the broad side, and other well-placed windows on both floors. I erected it down the road a little from where I planned to build the lodge and initially used it for all tools and equipment on the lower floor and sleeping quarters upstairs. The water supply came from a gravity system, which fed elevated fifty-five-gallon drums that got their water from a gutter on one of the roof slopes. The toilet was a composting model. Electricity came from a small generator.

The lack of electricity brings me to one of the important parts of Camp Carol. It is off the grid, as in no wires, no connection to electricity, no phone lines, no cable. The reason for this is easy enough. First, I absolutely love the idea of it. Also, and this was a significant factor, running power down my half-mile driveway from the main road was going to be very expensive. By power company rules, it would require a ninety-foot cleared area for the power. Camp Carol's charm was its woods and remote location on the lake. Even the driveway was only one car wide, and in summer, through canopied woods, tree branches hung over the road. I would need to build my own power plant if I didn't want to clear this ninety-foot strip through these woods.

So, I built a power plant. Before I tell you about this, let me give you one significant piece of history about the property. I told you we bought it from a widow. This widow had been married for many years before her husband died. They were both college professors. She taught law, he about environmental issues and forestry. They had owned the land for twenty-two years and camped on it in summers, but never developed it. The husband was the one who did the research that informed us about the old oaks and the colonial times on the property.

The owner before these folks was Central Vermont Power System (CVPS), who had purchased the property in 1966 with the plan to put a power plant on it, by some reports a nuclear facility to match Vermont Yankee nuclear plant. They built Yankee in 1972 on the other side of the state and shuttered it in 2014. CVPS never did this. I am so glad. So are my grandkids and I suspect millions of others too.

CVPS eventually sold the property to the couple who later sold it to us. The history of the property from its first recorded owner, John Reginald, in 1774 until the CVPS purchase in 1966 was entirely as a farm or just woods.

Significantly, the other big piece of history for this property was that Five Mile Point, sticking out into the lake as it does, was the landing point for a ferry that ran from this spot to the New York side of the lake from colonial times until the turn of the twentieth century. Reports have George Washington, as a general, and later Presidents Jefferson and Madison, using this crossing. The little trail through the woods from the point that becomes our driveway for its last half mile from the lodge to Lake Street was the thoroughfare to reach this ferry and thus has a three-hundred-plus-year history.

So, back in this century, there would be no power plant, nuclear or otherwise. My little barn does have its own power station. This one was designed and built by me. It is supported by solar panels first on just the barn, later on a pavilion I built down the road, and finally on both of the south-facing roofs on the main lodge. From my hub in the barn, wires run underground to the lodge, all of the kids' houses, and every other building on the site.

Happily, the sun is all we need most of the year, and thanks to lighter use in the winter months, when Carol and I head south to St Thomas. When we come up short with power at this time of the year, we have backup propane-fired generators.

We also have a geothermal system, so summer cool and winter heat come mostly from the ground. On this I must confess my off-the-grid efforts in the coldest part of winter have their biggest challenge, as we fall short of the power we need to run heat exchange pumps. I also have a propane-fired furnace that can kick in.

As our kitchen stove and clothes dryer also use propane, in my experiment in energy independence it would collapse mightily if it were not for occasional visits by the propane truck. It is a state secret how often they come.

We could not even think about doing Camp Carol as it has developed without Greg Cromis. Greg has worked for us as an all-purpose handyman and caretaker for more than a dozen years. He takes care of all our old but well-maintained Bristol buildings. While we hire builders, electricians, and plumbers for all the big jobs, he can do all of these things, and way more. He fixes motors, all my toys, both on land and sea. He handles any crazy project I think up. On our smaller buildings, these projects are usually Tom and Greg productions. Tom on design and supervision, and Greg on all the real work. Since we started our efforts at Camp Carol, he has divided his time between the camp and Bristol.

Two results of the Tom and Greg team are the guesthouse, two bedrooms, a living room, a bathroom, two loft sleeping areas, and, most recently, a tree house. The tree house, fourteen feet in the air and right on the lake's edge, has not just a deck but a full live-in space with bedroom and bathroom. It is a favorite of all who come to stay at Camp Carol. Both the guesthouse and the tree house are just down the trail from the main lodge and the little house for Carol and me. The girls and their families have their little houses along the lake and the driveway coming into the property.

The main lodge is just that, with a two-story "little house" off to one side for us old people. My original plan was for our tiny house to be separate like those of the girls, but Carol vetoed that idea.

The lodge has all the amenities: three bathrooms, a full kitchen, oversized dining and great rooms, a theater room. Plenty of room for the whole growing family and it is all wood, glass, and stone, my favorites. It's got an open floor plan with amazingly high ceilings, twenty-seven feet at the peak; a deck around the whole place, another must for me; and finally a breathtaking wall of windows looking out on the lake from its first and second floors.

I did not build this building but I was the general contractor and hired and supervised everyone. I confess it was really hard. Harder than fixing up old buildings, which had always been my specialty. I learned, among other things, that I can never hire out as a GC because I came in spectacularly over budget by the time I added everything I wanted and did all my high-tech smart house and off-the-grid stuff. Who cares? This lodge and Camp Carol are our forever home. As I write this, a two-bedroom addition is planned for construction this year.

I say forever with more emphasis than you might think. I know at seventy-three, the time of Tom and Carol is, at least, entering its twilight. Carol may go past one hundred, but I most certainly will not. With a buy-in from my kids (I think they understand it), I have put Camp Carol in a perpetual family trust. This trust owns the property and by the time of my death, will have enough securities to provide income to keep the place running forever.

The trust gives family members the right to build on tiny house sites and to use the entire property and all its improvements and toys. This right passes to all lineal descendants who can inherit a little house from their parents or build their own if they want (there are fifteen more sites). My plan is that this family compound is for the Wells family forever. No one or even a group of descendants can sell or even rent out their house. The plan is for the vacation gathering place to be here forever, with everything maintained and replaced as needed. If someone does not want to use the property or even to keep a little house, they can give it up, but that is all they can do.

I tell estate planning clients that when you leave something to your kids or grandkids, you should not overly "rule from the grave." Trusts do this. This trust, perpetual in nature, does this in spades. It also provides that should all the lineal descendants want to let Camp Carol go, whatever it and the securities in the trust are then worth will go to WMI or another charity. When I really believe something, in this case the importance of family and a place to be together, I can be so damn bossy.

I admit it. I get real joy thinking about a time, maybe a couple hundred years from now, a bunch of generations down the road, and some grandchild with many greats in front of this title asks, "Who is the Carol the camp is named after?" Then they will be told about the special story of the wonderful woman who cared so much for her family and her husband who created a camp to honor her. This makes me really happy.

Right now, the whole family visits a bunch of times every year. Cider weekend in October and Maple Syrup Saturday in April are entrenched traditions. With the fourth and fifth grandchildren now having recently arrived, the actual grandchildren camp should be in full swing in the next couple years. Max, the oldest of our grands, has spent two or more weeks for seven of his eight years. Etta and Max have both been here the last two years. Being "potty trained" is the only entry ticket, so it won't be long until all five cousins, Max, Etta, Juno, Callum, and Raymond, will be with us. I often wonder, sometimes out loud in earshot of Carol, does it get any better than this?

Born out of the idea of quality time with our grandchildren, Camp Carol has become something bigger. It's a place for the generations of our family now and in the future to commune with nature and each other. If my plan works, no matter how the world changes, and it will change a lot, this family retreat will be a special place of solace and warmth.

What Makes Me Happy

ONE LAST LIST AS I WRAP UP THIS BOOK.

- Mac and cheese
- A good Cuban cigar
- A glass of Johnnie Walker Black on the rocks with a twist of lemon
- A sunset over water
- Living near water
- A comfortable room—wood, stone, glass, leather, books, soft lighting, a fireplace
- My daughters
- My grandkids
- Watching my kids be parents
- Carol, my best friend and my love
- Physical contact, hugs, kisses, a head on my shoulder; when appropriate, skin on skin
- Sailing along without power in a light wind on a sunny but not hot day
- Being a child of a God with endless grace
- Fall leaves
- Chocolate chip cookies and chocolate chip ice cream

- Pancakes and syrup
- Having my back scratched
- Having my head scratched
- Giving back, and people who do this
- The Golden Rule and folks who walk this walk
- The WMI Scholars
- Sunny days in the seventies followed by wear-a-sweater cool nights
- The first real snowfall each year
- Electric cars
- Solar power
- Good conversation
- A fire in the fireplace
- A soft leather couch or chair
- Naps on a couch
- Hanging out with Carol
- Camp Carol
- Politics, but not so much politicians
- Honesty, integrity
- Travel
- Being an American
- Being part of my big family: my mom and dad; all my siblings and all their spouses, kids, and progeny; being the oldest of six kids; being one of more than eighty-one of us
- The quirkiness of my sister, Kerry; the preschool my sister Holly founded and ran for thirty-seven years; my brother Peter's all-around good-guy nature; my brother Jeff's joy-boy endless optimism; and my sister Julie's super mom abilities
- Reading
- Writing
- Tracing my ancestry and learning about all my Wells grandfathers (eleven of them) back to the Thomas Wells who emigrated from Colchester, England, to Ipswich, Massachusetts, in 1635
- Love

Tapping maple trees at Camp Carol, 2021

I "do" Santa Claus every year. This was in front of our downtown Bristol, Vermont store and inn in 2022. I no longer need a pillow to fill out the costume!

My extended Wells family at Long Beach Island, New Jersey, 2019

Wells family gathering at Camp Carol for cider weekend, 2019

Family picture at Jordyn's wedding, Starksboro, Vermont, 2024 (Rae Ann Photo)

Family picture at Camp Carol, 2020 (Amy Donahue Photo)

Me and Carol, 2014

Family with all the "grands" at Camp Carol, Christmas, 2023

Yup, I am an old man now!

Epilogue

I HAVE COME TO THE END OF THIS STRANGE COLLECTION OF writings I call a book, my memoir. I know it is a reflection of me more than anything else: complicated, opinionated, driven, blessedly accomplished, sometimes sentimental, often a bit preachy. I have had fun writing it all down, less so trying to organize it into something coherent. I suspect in this last task, I have not done so well. If you are reading this last of my words, you can answer this better than I can.

I have owned and sailed a half dozen sailboats in my life. My first was a pram; think rowboat with a sail. Actually, the Brant Beach Yacht Club owned this one. Then came a Sailfish; now think oversized surfboard with a sail. Next came a sixteen-foot O'Day daysailer, open cockpit, tiller, two sails, with a mast that came down easily and a trailer. This one was called *Preface*, and I sailed it in Ohio and New Jersey.

The next boat was a twenty-two-footer I found for sale in a side yard in Ridgewood, New Jersey, while I was jogging one morning, fixed up over seven or eight years and practically never sailed. This was *Chapter I*.

Serious boating came with *Chapter II*, which most folks thought was Chapter Eleven and caused them to want to know about the bankruptcy I endured resulting in a boat. This one was a twenty-eight-foot O'Day, and Carol and I sailed it all over Lake Champlain for three years right after the turn of the millennium. This and all future boats had two sails, a mainsail and a jib.

Chapter III came next, and it was my all-time favorite. It was a thirty-six-foot Hunter with two sails and a spinnaker. It had an interior like an RV, including an efficient galley and, for the first time, a queen-sized bed I could share with my first mate. We cruised this boat to every conceivable destination on Lake Champlain, later Long Island and even Block Island in Rhode Island, then the Chesapeake and down the Intercoastal.

Chapter III's unfortunate demise came offshore on its crossing to the Virgin Islands in 2013 and was a tragedy for us. The mast came down and the engine failed. We had to abandon it. Eventually, months later, still drifting, I think the Coast Guard sank the boat. I still miss *Chapter III*.

Epilogue was our last sailboat, the biggest and best of all the boats but not necessarily my cherished favorite. I bought this boat used and then spent three years modifying and refurbishing it. It had a deluxe master cabin with its own en suite head and shower. It had two more staterooms for visitors, both with en suites. *Epilogue* was fifty feet long and sailed well.

Epilogue's end came rather dramatically too, but not on the high seas. Hurricane Maria in September 2017 raised it from its strapped down offseason home ostensibly safely tucked away in a Virgin Gorda shipyard and dropped her 32,000-pound mass as a twisted remnant of smashed fiberglass with a broken-in-half fifty-five-foot mast about thirty-five feet away on top of another boat, and with a third boat on top of it. I hope my end is less dramatic.

I told you all this because it occurs to me that perhaps my sailboats are a metaphor for my life.

The first two boats, the pram and the sailfish, are like my Backstory, my beginning.

The third boat, *Preface*, was my first venture out on my own, much like my decision to live by the Golden Rule and give back.

Chapter I and *II* are Just Living: glorious yet routine, what I learned along the way.

Chapter III, the favorite of all my sailboats, is like On the Soapbox. Here, I am in my glory singing out to the world, but with ideas and opinions.

Epilogue is the closing chapter, the endgame, backstory told, life lived, lessons learned and shared, and opinions voiced, with me reveling in all that has passed and enjoying every day.

How the final pages are written is yet to be seen. I am still running down the highway, but now, with my clothes on, always.

Acknowledgments

As I have shared, this book was written over the years in spurts of activity and scribbled stories. To write it has been a plan in the making for many years. I set out to seriously turn my scribblings into a memoir and wrote the bulk of this manuscript starting in January 2023. The process, which began with a very rough draft, then grew a lot and finally slimmed down; it was more fun than I thought it would be. It was very much guided by my editors at Scribe Media and Houndstooth Press. Sincere thanks to Emmy Koziak, Holly Gorman, Candace Sinclair, Caroline Hough, and Greg Likins for their efforts in improving my scribblings. Thanks also to Carol, who despite warnings that you should never let a spouse help on a memoir, took a valuable critical pass through an early rough draft, did some final proof-reading, and is my support in all I do. I changed just a couple names to protect the innocent. Whether I named you, or hid your name and just talked about you, thanks to all who have been a part of my well-lived life and for your part in my story.

About the Author

THOMAS M. WELLS is the oldest of six children and grew up in Paramus, New Jersey. After a period practicing law in Ohio, Tom founded the Wells, Jaworski & Liebman northern New Jersey law firm and practiced law for more than forty years before retiring and becoming "of counsel." He continues to run a real estate holding and management company together with his wife, Carol, to manage Wells Mountain Investments and a substantial number of trusts and to serve on several public and charitable boards.

In 2005, Tom founded Wells Mountain Initiative (WMI), a 501(c)(3) charity working to build a network of global grassroots leaders to foster social change and funding undergraduate studies of more than eight hundred scholars from fifty-five high-need countries. For his work with WMI, Tom received a Distinguished Citizen Award from Bucknell University in 2015 and an honorary doctorate in humane letters from Middlebury College in 2023.

An alumnus of Case Western Reserve University Law School and Bucknell University, as Tom shares in this memoir, despite a focused career, he has held forty jobs beginning with a paper route at eleven years old and created and owned eight, mostly very successful, businesses.

As a mentor, Tom loves to preach the importance of "giving back" and the WMI call to action: Dream, Plan, Do!

Tom and Carol are the parents of three daughters and grandparents of five grandchildren. They make their home along Lake Champlain in Shoreham, Vermont, and in St. Thomas, US Virgin Islands.

www.ingramcontent.com/pod-product-compliance
Lightning Source LLC
Chambersburg PA
CBHW060512080526
44586CB00012B/463